J. T. Hansen is Professor, Department of English, University of Puget Sound, Tacoma.

A. Susan Owen is Assistant Professor, Department of Communication and Theatre Arts, University of Puget Sound, Tacoma.

The late **Michael Patrick Madden** was Adjunct Professor, Department of Communication and Theatre Arts, University of Puget Sound, Tacoma.

PARALLELS

COMMUNICATION AND SOCIAL ORDER

An Aldine de Gruyter Series of Texts and Monographs

SERIES EDITOR

David R. Maines, Wayne State University

Advisory Editors

Bruce E. Gronbeck • Peter K. Manning • William K. Rawlins

David L. Altheide and Robert Snow, **Media Worlds in the Postjournalism Era**

Joseph Bensman and Robert Lilienfeld, **Craft and Consciousness: Occupational Technique and the Development of World Images** (*Second Edition*)

Valerie Malhotra Bentz, **Becoming Mature: Childhood Ghosts and Spirits in Adult Life**

Herbert Blumer, **Industrialization as an Agent of Social Change: A Critical Analysis** (*Edited with an Introduction by David R. Maines and Thomas J. Morrione*)

Dennis Brissett and Charles Edgley (*editors*), **Life as Theater: A Dramaturgical Sourcebook** (*Second Edition*)

Richard Harvey Brown (*editor*), **Writing the Social Text: Poetics and Politics in Social Science Discourse**

Norman K. Denzin, **Hollywood Shot by Shot: Alcoholism in American Cinema**

Irwin Deutscher, Fred P. Pestello, and Frances G. Pestello, **Sentiments and Acts**

Bruce E. Gronbeck, **Sociocultural Dimensions of Rhetoric and Communication**

J. T. Hansen, A. Susan Owen, and Michael Patrick Madden, (*editors*), **Parallels: The Soldiers' Knowledge and the Oral History of Contemporary Warfare**

Emmanuel Lazega, **The Micropolitics of Knowledge: Communication and Interaction in Work Groups**

David R. Maines (*editor*), **Social Organization and Social Process: Essays in Honor of Anselm Strauss**

David R. Maines, **Time and Social Process: Gender, Life Course, and Social Organization**

Peter K. Manning, **Organizational Communication**

Stjepan G. Meštrović, **Durkheim and Postmodernist Culture**

R. S. Perinbanayagam, **Discursive Acts**

William K. Rawlins, **Friendship Matters: Communication, Dialectics, and the Life Course**

Vladimir Shlapentokh and Dmitry Shlapentokh, **Ideological Trends in Soviet Movies**

Jim Thomas, **Communicating Prison Culture: The Deconstruction of Social Existence**

Jacqueline P. Wiseman, **The Other Half: Wives of Alcoholics and Their Social-Psychological Situation**

PARALLELS

The Soldiers' Knowledge and the Oral History

of Contemporary Warfare

J. T. Hansen
A. Susan Owen
Michael Patrick Madden

Aldine de Gruyter
New York

About the Authors

J. T. Hansen is Professor, Department of English, University of Puget Sound, Tacoma.

A. Susan Owen is Assistant Professor, Department of Communication and Theatre Arts, University of Puget Sound, Tacoma.

The late **Michael Patrick Madden** was Adjunct Professor, Department of Communication and Theatre Arts, University of Puget Sound, Tacoma.

Copyright © 1992 Walter de Gruyter, Inc., New York
All rights reserved. No part of this publication may be reproduced or transmitted in any form or by any means, electronic or mechanical, including photocopy, recording, or any information storage and retrieval system, without prior permission in writing from the publisher.

ALDINE DE GRUYTER
A Division of Walter de Gruyter, Inc.
200 Saw Mill River Road
Hawthorne, New York 10532

Library of Congress Cataloging-in-Publication Data

Hansen, J. T., 1934-
    Parallels : the soldiers' knowledge and the oral history of contemporary warfare / J.T. Hansen, A. Susan Owen, and Michael Patrick Madden.
       p. cm. — (Communication and social order)
    Includes bibliographical references.
    ISBN 0-202-30391-8 (alk. paper). — ISBN 0-202-30392-6 (pbk. : alk. paper)
    1. War. 2. Combat. 3. Military history, Modern—20th century. 4. Vietnamese Conflict, 1961–1975—Personal narratives, American. 5. Vietnamese Conflict, 1961–1975—Campaigns. 6. Afghanistan-History–Soviet occupation, 1979–1989. 7. War and society. I. Owen, A. Susan, 1953-   II. Madden, Michael Patrick, 1948-1989 III. Title. IV. Series.
U21.2.H353 1992
355'.0092'2—dc20   91-28403

Printed in the United States of America on acid-free paper

10 9 8 7 6 5 4 3 2 1

FOR
DAN HANSEN
JIM, JOHN, AND BILL OWEN
SHARON, JOHN, AND MATT HANSEN
GENE DEWEESE

The mind that has conceived a plan of living must never lose sight of the chaos against which that pattern was conceived. That goes for societies as well as individuals.

Ralph Ellison, *Invisible Man*

Table of Contents

Acknowledgments	xi
1. Introduction	1
2. Dave Nelson	13
3. Backgrounds	35
4. Horror, Abjection, and the Experience of Contemporary Warfare	63
5. The Brotherhood	129
6. Aftermath	155
7. Steve Tice: Healing	211
8. The Soldiers' Knowledge: A Summing Up	231
Select Bibliography	249

Acknowledgments

Parallels represents the kind of community effort we envisioned from the beginning of this project. It is, therefore, "our book." The veterans educated us, made their oral histories available, and trusted the academy not to misuse their experiences. Students attended Vets' Night forums, recorded and transcribed many of the oral histories, helped with editing, and provided steady encouragement. The Post-Traumatic Stress Treatment Program at the American Lake Veterans' Hospital made this opportunity available and assisted us in finding veterans with a variety of backgrounds and experiences. We therefore consider the following persons as coauthors of this book. We regret that we have been unable to locate the names of many others who were involved.

Veterans: Steve Bates, Andy Slatt, Don Patterson, Jeff Russell, Dave Holden, Roy Robbings, Mike Carey, John de Long, John Hodge, Fred Stark, Bill Walker, Jack Coyle, Tom Shaver, Mark Lomax, Rich Baker, Herb Olsen, Kurt Easterbrook, Hill Hansen, Mike Brinks, Richard Koffmoel, Pat Gilligan, Pete Reuben, Bob Long Crane, Pat Kennedy, Leonard Dunn, Pat Wingo, Mike Martin, Joe Siedlecki, Fred Grin, Paul Johnson, Tim Conter, Hammond Dane, Ted Meisberger, Ralph Paduano, Ron Sims, Brendon Carroll, Barry Hallopeter, Bob Willis, Ron Otstott, Jerry Boss, Roger Hart, Ervin Tilton, Mike Hamilton, Jim Lester, Harold James, Pete Matanane, Richard Eli, Steve Inman, Billy Cannon, Joe Figueroa, Billy Tucker, Beau Delaney, Tim Burton, John Gibson, Harold Sauer, Wendall Hall, Tom Joseph, Mike Gilbert, Richard Gove, Gary Germain, Robert Collard, Warren Work, W. C. Riley, Guy Madison, Carl Berna, Willie Riley, Robert Burris, Michael Kiss, John Crane, Michael Barber, Earl Burnell, Richard Cavazos, John Fritsch, Ralph

Fugate, Jesus Gonzalez, Uwe Koenig, Tony Lambeth, Richard Putman, Steve Ravert, Melvin Warner, Frank Waters, Joseph Sgroe, Larry Smith, Roger Hart, Jerry Svien, Ernie Tuengel, Robert Morgan, Warren Work, Jim Adams, Don McKay, Cliff Williams, Steve Erickson, Pete Zachrison, Dennis Seber, Robert Schirman, Mark Schultz, Ben Hammack, Archie Reading, Dave Trout, Thomas V. Nelson, Dale Clifford, George de los Santos, Gordon Dempsey, Michael Foley, Lloyd Gibson, Mike Kurhajetz, Don Leighty, Steve McDonnell, Richard Villalovos, Al Hicks, Tim Mahoney, Larry Heinemann, three additional Soviet Afghantsis, and the nineteen whose oral histories are included here.

Students: Ann Keefer and Shelby Swanson (editorial assistants), R. J. Hilgers, Teri Platt, Julia Jones, Rob Rosenahl (transcribers), Sean Cross, Tom Olsen, Mollie McDonald, Warren Clemans, David Berg, Laurie Zettler, Loren Willson, Katie de Gutes, Mike Kurz, David Chaney, Matt Goldstein, Paul LaBarre, Rebecca Neilson, Heather Sontag, Kelly Wheeler, Mike Zeils, Krista Messmore, Howie Green, Matt Aujla, Megan O'Neill, Jason Carl, Karen Halberg, Julie Hornick, Kris Munger, Angela Overbaugh, Kim Pecheos, Leah Travis, Mike Arnold, Tim Carey, Mark Corcoran, Stephanie Day, Mike Dega, Hoobie Greenwald, Shelly Hagen, Karen Lofland, Kelly Metcalfe, Linda Naumer, Tim Olsen, Dave Organ, Diane Pintard, Jerry Stultz, Maria Colby, John Hanson, Sharel Lund, Amelia Young, Brian Carpenter, Jaimee Christman, Matt Hansen, Erin Sabo, Rebecca Summers, Matt Thacker, Doug Vaughn, Dave Vitcovich, Julie Tinkham-Ray, Lynee Bradley, Lara Cajko, Karina Copen, Rod Emmons, Wake Gregg, Pete Haliniak, Inga Hansen, Molly Hornbeck, Liz MacKinnon, Krista McArthur, Corrie Mertl, Julie O'Donnell, Seema Prasad, Xandra Trostel, Jason Werts, Jennifer Baker, Marshall Baldocchi, Karen Baruck, Lief Edmondson, Matt Holm, Ruth Ison-Worbs, Jeremy Los, Kendall McDevitt, Ron Meier, Mike Morse, Robin Nermo, Sharon Plante, Bill Potter, Barb Rohling, Kirstin Senander, Jennifer Snow, Brooke Stroup, Adina Turchin, Martina Walters, Cynthia Whitmore.

PTST Staff: Ray Scurfield, Gene DeWeese, Steve Tice, Art Owens, Bob Coalson, Jim Carioso, Teri Wingate, Lori Daniels, Ann Gregory, Al Trujillo, Gary Bartholomew, Beryl Hammonds, Bill Vandenbush, Kathy Olsen, Dale Smith, Dale Miller, Alyce Neal, John Hofstetter, Willie Robertson, Maria McEntee, Jerry Sneed, Bob Lusk, Jim Burke, Jim Hardesty, Charlie Kuhn, Don Hoffman, Tom Olsen, Elke Zeerocha, James Robinson, Russ Anderson, Rico Swaine, Carrie Johnston, Bill Hook, Jim Kelly, and Maggie Wyman.

Aldine de Gruyter: Bruce Gronbeck (Advisory Editor), Richard Koffler (Executive Editor).

Logistics: Pat Madden, John Hansen.

Illustrations: Michael Kelley, Art of the Vietnam Experience, CO"D" 1/502nd Inf, Republic of Vietnam 11-69-9-70.

CHAPTER 1

Introduction

War stories present two problems to authors striving for The Truth. First of all, if you live long enough to tell them, and have enough of an audience to practice telling them *to* through the years, war stories become just that— stories. Just as time distances the storyteller from the events themselves, so do the repeated tellings. Gradually the stories are embellished in places, honed down in others until they are perfect tales, even if they bear little resemblance to what actually happened. Yet the storyteller is completely unaware of how far he may have strayed from the facts. Those countless tellings have made the stories The Truth.

The second problem . . . is they have their genesis in the fog of war. In battle, your perception is often only as wide as your battle sights. Five participants in the same action, fighting side by side, will often tell entirely different stories of what happened, even within hours of the fight. The story each man tells might be virtually unrecognizable to the others. But that does not make it any less true.

David H. Hackworth, *About Face*

The history lesson is that for veterans of all wars there is a conspiracy of silence on the consequences of war for veterans. It is a combination of the reluctance of institutions, clinicians, and the public to talk about it and the natural reticence of veterans because of the response from their environment.

Ray Scurfield, Director, Post–Traumatic Stress Treatment Program, American Lake Veterans' Hospital

The people of the United States are currently revising their social definition of war. A social definition of war is a loosely formulated, tacit, consensual agreement by a nation's citizenry about the policies, people, and events that they believe characterize, or ought to characterize, military conflict. With the demise of the Cold War, it is increasingly unlikely that a long and bloody land war will happen again; yet we collectively still believe that war is like, or ought to be like, the European and Pacific Island campaigns of World War II. Even Operation Desert Storm has, as many commentators have pointed out, been couched in the language of World War II, with its Hitler villain and its military leader using Field Marshall Montgomery's African tank campaign strategies for quick victory. In the public mind, wars are military conflicts between clearly defined combatant forces having radically different political objectives. Citizens become soldiers in order to defend their countries and to defeat enemies aggressively seeking to force a wrong, if not evil, outcome upon their nation. They fight for specific political and military objectives, confident that their cause is just. After peace is secured, they return to civilian life and pick up where they left off before they answered their country's call to arms.

Contemporary wars do not fulfill these expectations. For military powers such as the United States and the Soviet Union, recent wars have not been fought to defend the homeland, lack a political cause that citizen and soldier alike believe in, and despite military success do not achieve the originally intended political objectives. Militarily, land is not taken and held, and there are seldom well-established battle lines. Failure to integrate political and military strategies results in an ambiguous postwar situation in which military victory or defeat is rendered moot by the persistence of political conflict. From the veterans' perspectives, society fails to honor its good faith commitment to integrate them back into civilian life, and it does not respect the knowledge that they have had to gather under the terrifying conditions of mortal combat.

The soldiers' private knowledge of these wars represents a series of highly personalized enlightenments as they cross symbolic lines and boundaries throughout their lives. Warfare does not begin with declarations of war and end with the signing of peace treaties. In order to make sense of their lives, many veterans have had to go back to their childhood and adolescent years to discover why they went off to war so naively in the first place. Their naivete—plus the dislocations of leaving home, going through training, and arrival in a Third World combat zone—has left them vulnerable to the profound psychological trauma that naturally results from maiming and killing other human beings. These traumatic experiences have exposed the shallowness of their knowledge of war and the degree to which their beliefs could be de-

Introduction

stroyed. By joining into tactically efficient Brotherhood communities, they have survived. To this day, they honor their brothers and sisters in arms, sometimes at the expense of their own well-being. Return from these wars has been complicated by social marginalization, partly caused by the "conspiracy of silence" Dr. Scurfield has identified. Attitudes toward them are also influenced by continuing disagreements over the merits of wars that some citizens consider immoral or unnecessarily lost. As the years pass, veterans realize that the experience of war is open-ended. Wars do not end: they have aftermaths, which are in some cases excruciatingly painful.

PARALLELS

Regardless of the theater of war or their nations' political objectives, these veterans' experiences are eerily parallel. In preparing this book, we have been struck by the extent to which parallels span ethnic, gender, and national boundaries. The Brotherhood communities that were formed in combat institutionalized these likenesses. For many years after their wars, these veterans believed that the only person who could understand them would be a veteran of the same side at the same time in the same war. However, when Steve Tice visited the Soviet Union and Bob Swanson returned to Vietnam, the most dramatic revelation was that there is an "international brotherhood of warriors," which is based precisely on the parallels among the experiences of American, Soviet, Vietnamese, and Afghan veterans.

Post–traumatic stress disorder (PTSD) therapies are based upon the parallels inherent in contemporary warfare. Leon Borzov, a noted Russian therapist, visited the American Lake Veterans' Hospital PTST program recently. When we interviewed him and asked what he learned that impressed him most, he said, "I am struck by the exact identity—the exact parallel—between the experiences of Soviet and American veterans." For these reasons, we use the term *parallels* to identify roughly equivalent similarities and differences in personal experiences. As James William Gibson points out in *The Perfect War*, "No single 'logical structure of propositions' informs [the soldiers'] memoirs" (p. 466). Their experiences are parallel rather than equivalent or reducible to a single set of logical categories. They are coextensive, existing in similar circumstances, yet also unique because of the peculiarly claustrophobic and technologically intensified nature of contemporary wars.

THE SOLDIERS'* KNOWLEDGE

While this book is not a political tract, seeking to justify or to attack political and military policies, we emphatically believe that a nation which sends its armies to war has an obligation to know what its young men and women are going to encounter when the shooting starts. Along with military analysts such as Colonel Hackworth, Captain Andrew F. Krepinevich, Gibson, and Paul Fussell, we believe that the firsthand memories of soldiers add a reliable, critical perspective to the process of revising our social definition of war. Utilizing the soldiers' knowledge is essential at times of rapid and profound change, especially as our leaders configure the "New World Order" that is to follow victory over Iraq.

There is, however, an even more powerful argument for the authority with which these veterans speak. Even a cursory reading of their stories reveals devastating criticisms of various "official" views of warfare. Formal analyses by military officers, historians, political leaders, and academicians have been privileged in American public debate. Their conclusions are considered the most authoritative contribution to national understanding. Based on the testimony of veterans, however, privileged authorities present at best a partial understanding. An important part of the soldiers' knowledge involves knowing they have been isolated and, however benignly, ignored. Further, rhetorical critic Philip Wander shows that the public has been taught to think that abstract, cognitive analyses of war are more objective, more penetrating, and more reliable than the soldiers' firsthand testimony. Many of the veterans in this book have spent fifteen to twenty years trying to come to terms with fundamental changes war has made in their lives. With the passage of time, they have developed a guarded distrust of society and a refined cynicism toward social institutions and national political leadership. In the terms of contemporary discourse, veterans are thereby marginalized, sometimes leading unproductive lives, and unable to make their voices heard. The missing perspective in our current understanding of war is its impact upon the combat soldiers.

A climate now exists to make the process of revising our social definition of war more precise, better informed, more inclusive, and more analytical. We have endeavored to meet these goals—and to avoid the shoals identified by Colonel Hackworth—by collecting oral histories from an extremely varied group of combat veterans and organizing the book according to the parallels inherent in their stories. Our intention is to empower the soldiers' knowledge by making it available to the public in published and therefore authoritative form.

*In the interest of conciseness, we refer to all the men and women, military and civilian, who saw action in the combat zones of these wars.

Introduction 5

The soldiers' knowledge in these narratives has a number of claims to authority. These veterans fought in Vietnam, Afghanistan, and Panama, and many of them nearly died. More than that, we have been most persuaded by the stark, yet sometimes remarkably subtle clarity of their stories. The verbal precision of their speech is reinforced by the care, dignity, respect, moral anguish, urgency, decency, and ironic humor that is palpable in their stories.

Excerpts from two oral histories illustrate the content of the soldiers' knowledge:

> Vietnam *was* different. You were charged up like a battery. It was one of the most difficult things I ever encountered in my life. The Vietnamese were beautiful, peaceful, quiet people. We'd go in with our Zippo lighters and burn everything. You become numb to that. We'd go on an operation, and we wouldn't see anything. Some way, they *knew* we were coming. That kind of enemy doesn't have any identity. You lose respect for humans, then you come back to this country, and people are treating you like shit. I tried to gain back all the bullshit I had before. In Vietnam, I lost my sanity, I lost my humanness, I lost my trust . . . I lost my faith.
> (Henry Talmadge, U.S. veteran of World War II, Korea, and Vietnam)

> I was personally convinced that I was doing the right thing by serving in Afghanistan. We even had a feeling of pride that we were fighting down there. We believed we were part of an International Peace Brigade. Even before I got to Afghanistan, there seemed to me to be something—a strange sort of power of necessity in war—something awful that you can't do anything about. Toward the middle of my tour, I was sucked into it. Man is such a strange animal that under strange conditions, you can't tell what he will do. I thought I would spend the rest of my life in those kinds of circumstances. Only upon returning did I become conscious of what war really is. War can never be noble.
> (Yuri Kirichenko, Soviet veteran of Afghanistan)

Soldiers go to war with pride in doing the right thing by helping to protect a Third World democracy. The closer they get to the combat zone, the more they become aware of the inexorable power of necessity in war. Veterans of previous wars soon realize that contemporary wars are different. The stranger aspects of human nature manifest themselves uncontrollably in wars of attrition. Although the native population seems exotic and attractive, it is impossible to distinguish friendly civilians from the enemy. The most difficult tactical problem is finding the enemy in order to engage them. Enemy intelligence appears unerring, further heightening the soldiers' frustration. They are gradually sucked into the destruction and killing. To survive psychologically, they numb their emotions, and eventually they lose respect for the enemy's humanity. They return home changed and are estranged from normal peacetime society, especially by their fellow citizens' negative attitudes toward them. In retrospect, they realize they have lost their humanity, trust, and faith. Many of them believe—the Soviets perhaps even more than the Americans—that making their knowledge available to the public may prove to be their most lasting contribution to world peace.

THE SOCIAL DEFINITION OF WAR

Our social definition of war—what we think war is or ought to be like—is distilled from many sources within our society. Political and military leaders promote their military agendas, warfare is featured prominently in the history students learn in our schools, patriotic occasions include military displays, war documentaries pervade cable television, the services and military suppliers advertise in national media, and so forth. For many veterans—and many others in the United States and the Soviet Union as well—our current understanding of how wars are actually fought is most influentially expressed through popular myths about war and the warrior. Most of us have been inspired by the myth: heroic Americans and Russians perceive threats to their country, voluntarily answer their nation's call to arms, quickly learn soldiering, fight bravely, liberate populations and territories, come home having undergone a major rite of passage, and return to civilian life.

World War II myths are without doubt the greatest casualty of contemporary warfare. The Vietnam writers who attended the 1985 Asia Society conference, "The Vietnam Experience in American Literature," concluded that "John Wayne never played too well in Vietnam" (Lomperis p. 28). Yet it is important to note that the veterans in this collection are most conscious of the influence of World War II war movies in establishing the expectations of what they would encounter. As many commentators have demonstrated, media dramatizations of war have been changing from John Wayne's World War II movies (as well as *The Green Berets*) on through early Vietnam movies such as *The Deer Hunter* and *Apocalypse Now* and to the more recent *Platoon*, *86 Charlie Mopic*, and *Born on the Fourth of July*. With its emphasis on the unromantic brutality of war and the voices of individual soldiers, Ken Burns's widely viewed television series "The Civil War" has accelerated that process.

This book is filled with graphic reconstructions of the actual nature of war in Vietnam, Afghanistan, and Panama: Chuck Simms up to his hips in rotting bodies; Boris Volkov understanding why a man left behind on a mission committed suicide; Phil Pearson describing the terrorizing effects of daily rocket attacks; Nikki Nicol remembering the emotional charge she got from treating masses of wounded; Darren Gates carrying a wounded comrade to an aid station, only to discover that he was himself badly wounded; Emmett Finn momentarily losing his grip on sanity as he verified the dead after his unit was overrun.

Paul Fussell analyzes public responses to the two world wars from exactly this sociocultural perspective. War movies, newsreels, and television news rarely show dismembered bodies or intrude on the anguish experienced by men and women in war. The public, he argues, is grossly misinformed, and at great cost to its soldiers and its culture. In the first-person narratives of war lies a corrective that must be used to develop an "understanding to re-interpret and re-define the national reality and to arrive at something like public maturity" (p. 268). The soldiers' experience of war in the twentieth century, he concludes, has been wasted. He comments several times on the far greater difficulty of reconciling the Vietnam experience and the public understanding of war. Our present social definition of war is no longer tenable, and it is simply an act of good faith with men and women in military service to redefine war, more accurately and certainly more sensitively, in the public forum.

THE AMERICAN LAKE POST-TRAUMATIC STRESS TREATMENT PROGRAM

Much of this material was made available to us through a unique and interesting process. In the spring of 1989 the interdisciplinary Vietnam Studies Program at the University of Puget Sound began a series of exchanges with the Post-Traumatic Stress Treatment (PTST) Program at the American Lake Veterans' Hospital near Tacoma, Washington. Our students believe that the war in Vietnam and its aftermath have been slighted in their educations, and the veterans find it therapeutic to communicate with an age group from which they have felt permanently estranged. Many students have relatives who served in Vietnam, Grenada, Panama, and the Persian Gulf. Participation is purely voluntary on both sides. Veterans come to our campus for "Vets' Nights," and our students go out to the hospital to record their oral histories. In order to participate in these events, students must have evidenced interest in the Vietnam War, and many have read extensively in the literature. The Soviets were part of a Russian group that visited the program at American Lake. Students collected the majority of the stories in this collection; we collected the balance, some from veterans not associated with the PTST Program in order to ensure greater diversity.

The American Lake PTST Program is itself unique and interesting. It is an inpatient, eleven-week program in a secure environment with a staff that is dedicated to establishing trust relationships. Fourteen-member peer groups enter and graduate together. Therapy consists of reviewing their lives and learning the causes, effects, and treatment of PTSD. Small-group therapy techniques predominate. Reliving traumatic events with others who have experienced similar trauma has several advantages. The veterans learn that they are not uniquely crazy and that PTSD begins with an entirely human response to events gone out of control. Innovative exposure therapies rebond veterans into Brotherhood communities quite similar to those in Vietnam. Dream therapies assist them to resolve the "issues" in their nightmares. Vets' Night forums give them the opportunity to interact with the college students they have so long dreaded. Their graduation ceremonies are among the most moving, forward-looking events in our experience.

THE RELIABILITY OF THE SOLDIERS' KNOWLEDGE

As Colonel Hackworth suggests, the truth of a first-person narrative is not so much a documentary history as it is the steady accumulation of remembered facts, additions and subtractions, traumatized distortions, and maybe even innocent lies, of veterans reflecting upon their lives. In the "How to Tell a True War Story" chapter of *The Things They Carried*, Tim O'Brien says "Absolute occurrence is irrelevant" to a true war story (p. 89). Factual accuracy decreases with the passage of time. It follows that the details of a war story tell as much about a veteran's state of mind at the times it is told as it does about the exact facts of a given war.

We used several standards of judgment in selecting and ordering the entries in this book. They are the most vividly defined, most intensely examined evidence of the soldiers' knowledge of contemporary warfare available to us. Since PTSD treatment involves prolonged reliving of the experiences of war and its aftermath, most of these veterans' memories have been tested for significance, plausibility, coherence, and accuracy under very demanding circumstances. For that reason, we have carefully selected those veterans who are most respected by their peers. We had heard of Mike Mitchell, Steve Tice, Henry Talmadge, Dave Nelson, Bob Swanson, and others long before we met them. Nelson used his chapter in relapse therapy, and another veteran of the 101st Airborne had his daughter read Dave's story so that she would understand her father better.

We also chose the nineteen oral histories in this volume because of the

Introduction

scope and diversity they represent. As a hedge against merely reproducing the results of the American Lake program, we include four veterans who have utilized Vets' Centers, two who have not sought war-related therapy, and three Soviets with PTSD diagnoses. We further emphasize diversity by coverage of military conflicts from World War II and Korea through Vietnam, Afghanistan, and Panama. We include histories from American whites, African-Americans, American Indians, and Hispanics as well as three "Afghantsis." We have included only one woman because there is no need to duplicate Keith Walker's superb women's oral history, *A Piece of My Heart*. Fortunately, Nikki Nicol is also included in Walker's book, so she forms a direct link to a fuller examination of gender likenesses and differences.

THE ORGANIZATION OF THIS BOOK

We have a very explicit contract with the veterans. It is their task to describe, vividly and candidly, the impact of war upon their lives. It is our task to enable nonveterans to understand these stories by publishing them and by providing a cognitive framework for them. They have accepted this contract, quite aware of its promise and its limitations. Our thesis is that the soldiers' knowledge of war is inchoate—it is embedded in war stories and is therefore tacit, incipient, and anecdotal. That is so partly because the soldiers who actually fight wars are not schooled in the forms of analysis that would make their knowledge available to the citizenry in language and formulations that are directly applicable to electoral and policymaking debate.

We have organized this book to mitigate as many of these problems as possible. Chapters 2 and 7 frame the intervening chapters by presenting Dave Nelson's and Steve Tice's oral histories in their entirety. We begin with Nelson's story because it shows so dramatically how even an exceptionally well-prepared soldier's conception of war is obliterated under the onslaught of events. We end with Tice because he is so well qualified to address issues such as healing the physical and psychological wounds of war and the role of the warrior in contemporary society.

Chapters 3 through 6 break seventeen oral histories down into the components that we believe most clearly reveal the parallels. Since the experience of war begins long before armed conflict begins, Chapter 3 discusses the backgrounds of the otherwise diverse group of individuals we have included. Chapter 4 covers the horror, abjection, and experience of contemporary warfare. Chapter 5 investigates the most significant social institution in their experience, the Brotherhood. We have discovered with weariness and sadness that the experience of war for veterans does not end with the signing of peace treaties. Chapter 6 examines the aftermath, which is in many ways more traumatic, and is certainly more prolonged, than the period actually spent in combat. Finally, in Chapter 7, The Soldiers' Knowledge: A Summing Up, we describe the general outlines of their knowledge and suggest some of its more important theoretical implications.

We have broken the oral histories into three components in order to emphasize the fragmented, ambiguous, ephemeral qualities of the experience of contemporary warfare. As John Clark Pratt said at the Asia Society conference of Vietnam writers, the fragment is by far the most basic characteristic of contemporary warfare, hence writing about contemporary wars. If the reader is to get an authentic understanding of combat in contemporary wars, the act of reading should parallel the experience. As the soldiers had to make sense of the fragments, so must the reader. Vietnam narratives thus present the reader with fragments and oblige the reader to figure them out (Lomperis, pp. 81–91). This demand is a test of the good faith of the reader. Veterans understand, even if society seems to have forgotten, that their going to war is a form of social contract. A society that sends its young to battle owes it to them to respect and understand what happens to them. To minimize the fragmentation in these middle chapters, the oral histories are in the same order in each chapter.

NOTES ON THE TEXTS

The recording sessions with the veterans ranged from the shortest, forty-five minutes with Boris Volkov, to the longest, six hours with Henry Talmadge. On average, we used about three-quarters of the material we recorded. We have rearranged about half of it in order to clarify or to highlight certain points. The quality of the tape recordings varies considerably, primarily because of military air traffic over the American Lake Veterans' Hospital and the University of Puget Sound. We have been unable to have some of the veterans read their oral histories for accuracy. As a result, some details such as unit numbers and landing zones may be slightly inaccurate. Subject to that proviso, we assume responsibility for any errors that remain in the text.

In order to capture the veterans' individual voices, we have changed little of their language and few of their sentences. We have retained the characteristic vocabularies, syntax, and cadences of their speech. We have indicated changes in their tone of voice by the use of punctuation. Commas signify a slight drop in voice tone, with very little pause, to indicate compound sentences, series, appositives, and so forth. Dashes indicate an upward shift of voice tone for interjections, sudden shifts of topic, parenthetical information, and so forth. Ellipses (. . .) indicate pauses, some lasting several seconds, when narrators appear to be working through their feelings or experiencing flashbacks. We use extended ellipses (. . . .) to indicate those rare but anguished moments when they simply could not continue without taking a break from the recording.

Leon Borzov, Boris Volkov, Yuri Kirichenko, and Darren Gates are pseudonyms. Vladislav Tamarov speaks English fluently enough for our purposes, but translators were required for Borzov, Volkov, and Kirichenko. Gates made it very clear that he would say nothing about Operation Just Cause in Panama that might compromise national security or violate secrecy regulations or that he had not said when he has been asked to speak at local schools. Publishing only one oral history of the military conflict in Panama is chancy, but after considerable reflection and at the urging of veterans who have read the manuscript, we decided to include it. As the reader will see, while Panama was very different from Vietnam and Afghanistan, many of the significant parallels in the soldiers' knowledge of contemporary warfare stubbornly resist change.

CHAPTER 2

Dave Nelson

> When we marched into the rice paddies on that damp March afternoon, we carried, along with our packs and rifles, the implicit convictions that the Viet Cong would be quickly beaten and that we were doing something altogether noble and good. We kept the packs and rifles; the convictions, we lost.
>
> Philip Caputo, *A Rumor of War*

If anyone should have fought superbly in Vietnam and returned home whole, it was surely Dave Nelson. His father, a World War II hero and first sergeant at the Jungle Training School in Panama, "raised me and my brother to be warriors." This training inculcated in him a deep commitment to what Colonel Hackworth would call the "old army" concept of the warrior, yet he has for years felt torn apart as his beliefs have been destroyed. His narrative documents this process dramatically, from absorbing his father's lore, to the eager volunteer who loved John Wayne and Audie Murphy movies, to his first tour as a sniper, to the debilitating traumas of his second tour, and on through periods when he has lived in the woods, found ways to live "on the edge," or been in PTSD therapy after the war.

Dave uses the word *concept* to identify a group of abstractions ranging from having a definite purpose, to the exacting requirements of professional military life, to the "puppy shit" norms of civilian life. In order to feel integrated and purposive, he wants to understand the concept inherent in anything he thinks or does. He details his conception of the warrior as he describes pivotal moments in his life. The warrior believes that serving his country is honorable. He wants to be the best, so he perfects his skills and hones his instincts until he reacts—correctly and instantaneously—to any threat. He respects his enemy as an equal. He kills quickly, cleanly, and efficiently, and he does not allow another man's suffering to increase. He acts on a deeply held, reciprocal obligation to provide his brothers in arms with whatever they need. He respects himself and is respected by others for his competence, his bravery under fire, his intimacy with death, and his self-discipline.

Nelson is therefore not a typical soldier, from whom he consciously distinguishes himself. He entered the service knowing what to expect and believing in it, whereas they came with civilian concepts that they had to give up in order to master soldiering. He shares with Jim Goldstine (West Point, 1961) and Henry Talmadge (marine drill instructor and gunnery sergeant) quite different values and behaviors from their more typical, citizen soldier comrades. All three retain memories that reaffirm the old army and maintain a rather distanced reserve from others. They tell war stories vividly and succinctly, without what they would consider false modesty, in almost perfect narrative sequence, with emphasis on the consequences of decisions made in the heat of battle. Although their post–traumatic stress does not appear to differ in degree from other veterans', they do not feel the same kind of guilt or anguish as their citizen soldier counterparts. Killing civilians and "going over to the dark side" are nauseating violations of their concepts, rather than the radical psychological and spiritual dislocations experienced by their more typical brothers and sisters in arms.

The concept of the warrior sustained and motivated Dave through his first tour, in large part because he deliberately sought out a combat zone where it worked. He found it intolerable to be a REMF (Rear Echelon MotherFucker), to kill civilians, or to wait like a sitting duck for the enemy to strike. He was widely recognized for his proficiency as a sniper. He returned to this country satisfied that he had fulfilled his obligations honorably. The second tour was much more problematic, primarily because he was responsible for others. As a result, his abiding sense of his obligations to his men backfired on him, and the consequences were so traumatic that he lost control of himself and "went over to the dark side . . . in order to maintain my sanity." Since early in his second tour, he has lived what Philip Beidler in *American Literature and Vietnam* identifies as "an equally nightmarish mixup of fact *and* phantasmagoria" (p. 7).

That process is straightforward and direct evidence of the destruction of his concepts, but there are subtler forces at work. Dave is also torn between the professional military values of his father and those formed by his Chilean mother's terrifying experience in Germany during World

War II. The problem is that he is much less self-consciously aware of his mother's influence—those values are much more submerged. Killing a civilian is bad enough to a warrior, but to Dave it is multiplied because he knows only too well the devastating impact of war upon his mother.

Nelson's narrative is also a manual on how to fight wars such as Vietnam. Small-unit tactics can be very effective. Fear and death sharpen the instincts and give the true warrior a psychological edge. (For example: Don't eat C-rations because the enemy can smell those who do. Jungle animals warn each other of predators, and men can be detected because only man does things in straight lines.) His life since the second tour has in many respects been a prolonged and agonizing process of trying to reconcile value conflicts occasioned by the brutal clash between what his father and society taught him to expect in war and what he actually encountered, including the honor he found in the Brotherhood.

DAVE NELSON

My father was a career soldier, Airborne to Ranger. He was highly decorated from World War II. He made every major combat jump in Word War II. He had letters of commendation from guys like Eisenhower, Montgomery, and Churchill. He was in the invasion of Normandy. He was in the airdrop when they dropped the Airborne onto the German headquarters at Ste. Mere Eglise and was blown away there. He was coming down on top of one of those steep roofs, so he hit his harness release. As he dropped to the ground, he was hit by machine-gun fire. He woke up in a British hospital. They told him they had to graft him, and one-third of his intestines were sheep intestines. He lost some other stuff. Basically, he was a career soldier. He was a first-generation immigrant from Sweden. The only relatives in America were his mother and father, my grandparents. He served in the military all the way up until '64. He was very well-respected in the military. He stayed in the military until '64 and got a medical discharge because he was getting cancer in his intestines. He died in September of '67 from the wounds he got in World War II.

My mother was born in Chile. Just before World War II, she went to visit relatives in Germany. One of her cousins had married a German magistrate. She went to visit them for a week and then was supposed to go back to South America. Three days after she got there, Hitler sealed off Germany. She was trapped in Germany during World War II. She was a dark-skinned Latin in Germany. The only reason she didn't go to a concentration camp was the fact that her cousin was married to this guy. She was brutalized through the whole war. During the bombing raids, the Germans would throw her out of the bomb shelter. She would survive the bombing raids out in the buildings—that's why she had PTSD. As a kid, during this one period when my father was in Korea, my mother would wake up in the night screaming. She would come in to me and my brother's room and just sit there and cry—so I was raised by two people who had PTSD.

My father was the first sergeant in charge of the Expert Jungle Trainer's School facilities in Panama. I lived there when I was twelve and thirteen years old. I used to hang around in the barracks with the GIs and took care of their mascots—a boa constrictor and an alligator. I used to go out on maneuvers with them in the jungle. I used to spend a lot of time in the jungle by myself practicing survival on my own. To make money, I used to go out in the jungle and catch boa constrictors and iguanas and sell them to the Panamanians. It was great fun. I made my first parachute jump at thirteen. I was really into the military concept. I was into parades and the pride and the honor and the glory that these guys shared.

I can remember hearing war stories ever since I was a little kid. My father and his buddies would sit around the kitchen table getting drunk and telling each other war stories. My brother and I would sneak out into the hallway and listen to him talk about World War II. I thought it was an honorable thing. Everybody did. There was a lot of pride and camaraderie. I got to ride in tanks and shoot guns. I got to ride on helicopters and planes. My father exposed me to everything about being a soldier and taught me the concept of being a warrior. He taught me how to shoot when I was six. I got my first deer when I was eight. He taught me how to survive on my own. I could live alone in the woods at ten. I learned how to survive in all kinds of climates because we lived in Fairbanks, Alaska, where the temperature gets to like sixty below zero for three months. I loved the hell out of that just as much as Panama. We lived in Alaska, Panama, the Philippines, Washington, and California.

I used to spend a lot of time by myself because in the military you were either the new kid in town or the next one leaving. Things in Panama were really rugged back then. Panamanians were really hating the Americans, and we had incidents—like I had knives pulled on me in the bathroom. This was when I was in the sixth grade. The school was located two miles out in the jungle. It was an integrated school, Panamanians and Americans. We had to take an hour of Spanish every day. There were always fights. They had major riots there the year after I left. These American guys took the Panamanian flag and threw it in the mud and put the American flag on the pole and marched around the school. Growing up in the military was a very aggressive thing because you didn't belong in the social area where you were. It was always us and them. If you went off base, you had to put up with the hassles and fights. It taught you how to scrap and take care of yourself really young.

In January of 1967 my father took my brother and me aside and said he was going to be dead before the year was up and that we had to figure out what we were going to do. I was seventeen. I decided that my father had his war, so I was going to have my war. Besides, I suppose it made my father feel good that I joined the military with the assumption that I was going to make a career out of it like he had. I joined in late spring of '67. My father died in September of '67. I guess it was one of the last few things I could do for him. The only family I had in the United States was my brother and my mother and father, so it was like it was time to move on—so I joined the military.

I went into the military with the concept of the warrior. Other soldiers were different from me. My dad's advice was a code for acting for the core group. The warriors' code is not a sport. It has significance, honor, and consequences. The others were middle-class and rural kids, and they had to learn a new concept. It was a concept I grew up with, so the war impacted me differently than it did them.

I went through a short-course Basic Training and to Infantry Training. I went to Airborne Training. My dad was dead, and I wanted to get through it as fast as possible—I didn't even take leaves. I went to Europe after Thanksgiving. I went to Communications Training. I was stationed in a NATO Communications Center. They were continually sending people to Vietnam. It was like you go to Europe, spend a few months there, and they transferred you on what they called levies. Working in a NATO ComCenter, they gave me top secret clearance. I was handling highly classified material. It was great at first. I just turned eighteen. Europe at eighteen was Disneyland, especially back in the sixties, but I got tired of it.

That wasn't why I joined the army. I joined the army to go to war and to become proficient at being a soldier. June of '68 was the third time I volunteered to go to Vietnam. They refused to let me go. They said it had taken them too much time and trouble to get those classified clearances, that I was in a highly critical job, and that I would have to grin and bear it. I told them to shove it and reenlisted to go to Vietnam. I said, "You're not going to deprive me of my war." I was raised on Audie Murphy, John Wayne—the military. It was the thing to do. My father raised my brother and me to be warriors. Everything I had grown up with was based upon being a warrior, so that is what I was going to do.

I reenlisted to go to Vietnam in October of '68 and came home on leave. I left for Vietnam on the fifth of January 1969. On the plane everybody was apprehensive—nervous and quiet. Even at that time, I was looking forward to it. When we landed and they popped the door, we were hit with this 120-degree heat with about 100 percent humidity and no cloud in the sky. There was this awful odor of burning shit and diesel. It was the predominant odor wherever you were in Vietnam. There was a really bad stench, but I couldn't wait—I was looking forward to it. They took us on a bus from the airfield to a replacement depot, and I was just eating it up. I thought it was great. When I got to the replacement depot, they assigned me to a transportation company, which really bummed me out. They sent me up to Chu Lai, which was a base camp. They asked me if I knew radio procedures and how to operate a radio. I was proficient in communications and electronics, so they sent me to this transportation company at Duc Pho.

When I first got to the camp, nobody was there. I walked into the operations tent and asked what was going on. There was a sergeant there. He asked me who I was and then said, "Your jeep's out there. Go take a look at it." I walked out to this jeep. There was blood on it, and bullet holes were in it. The crew who had been on it had been wiped out. I just sat around. There was nobody there. Towards sunset this whole convoy comes roaring in. There were a couple of trucks that just went shooting straight over to the hospital because they had wounded on them. There were people running around crazy. Everybody was ignoring me—I was the FNG [Fucking New Guy].

I met the two guys I would be working with—Sonny and Junky. Sonny was from Ventura Beach, California—a big surfer kid—and Junky was a junky from New York City. He was the M-79 grenade launcher. They put me standing up in the back of the jeep wearing what I guess was an old helicopter pilot helmet hooked to a radio—so that we could communicate with each other during air strikes and ambushes and still fire the machine guns. The jeep was just a basic army jeep. It had a half-inch steel plating in the bottom with a layer of sandbags and a cast iron pole going up to mount the machine guns. There was a passenger in the right front who carried a thumper—an M-79 grenade launcher—and a gunner-radioman and the driver.

I ran three convoys, and on my third convoy I made my first kill. They had gone out and informed these people in the villages that if they got too close to the road while a convoy was coming through, they were going to be killed. I was riding shotgun on a truck that day. I was looking off to the left. The driver yelled, "Hey, shithead, get him!" I saw somebody walking toward the trucks on the right. I shot him . . . that was my concept—to be ready and to kill quickly and cleanly. It was a kid, and . . . it was a kind of a weird feeling, but it was my first kill, and I really didn't get the whole concept of what I had just done until the convoy got back in. I went out and just got totally blitzed out of my mind, which was basically what these guys did every night. Every night they would come back in and get totally fucked up out of their brains. After I made my first kill, they decided they would put me on the jeep to work the jeep gun.

The reason I volunteered for the infantry was because of one major ambush. We hit this pass with forty-seven trucks, four gun jeeps, and one gun truck . . . only one gun jeep and ten trucks made it out. My jeep wasn't one of them. We came through the pass, which had a series of switchbacks so you couldn't get going very fast—like you were going through a ravine. We hit the ravine . . . and they had two .51 calibre machine guns set up to fire on us. When they first opened up, there must have been twenty or thirty RPGs, which were rocket propelled grenades, in the air at the same time. They blew the first gun jeep and the trucks to scatter them all over the road to stop the rest of the convoy.

I was standing on the right side of the jeep firing off to the right, and we were going pretty fast. An RPG would come at you about as fast as a really hard thrown hardball—so you could see it coming. I was standing on the back of the jeep, and the RPG hit the left front down by the tire. The jeep went up in the air . . . and Sonny's head, left shoulder, and left arm were gone just like that . . . I remember looking at him as I started flying through the air. It snapped my neck when the cord running to the radio ran out. Junky used to tie himself into his seat so he could use both hands to reload shells while the jeep was in motion . . . he never got a chance to get out.

I was flying through the air, hit the ground, slid into the ditch. The jeep came flying in on top of me . . . there wasn't much left of Junky . . . his whole upper torso was gone. I lost it . . . I just lost it. I was trapped under the jeep, all this shit was going on, and I couldn't get out. I was bleeding through my mouth. I was trapped under the jeep for a good twenty minutes while explosions were going on around me. I couldn't holler to anyone . . . and I really freaked out. They almost missed me. They got me out, and I was flown back in to Duc Pho, where they had an aid station. I came out of that with just cracked ribs and some bad lungs.

The only other significant thing during this time was the first time I was in close combat. We got overrun one night. They got through us. They came through the wire near the bunker I was in. Bunkers are L-shaped so explosions can't blast straight into them. When they penetrated the wire, one man in the bunker was to go out to the back door. I went running around the corner and ran straight into a sapper. We both hit the ground . . . and I remember just freaking out. I had to back up to shoot him. It was weird . . . everything in his head was gone. His face was there, but the eye sockets were empty. I emptied his whole head out, and it all happened in an instant.

The sappers were *really* weird. They would come through wearing these little diapers and Ho Chi Minh sandals—and they would have explosives tied to their chest and back. Their sole purpose was to go in somewhere, to dive into a helicopter or something, and blow themselves up. I remember shooting this one guy in the legs, and he was so loaded he could still move them. We'd search the bodies, and we'd find opium on them. Some of them would inject opium into their major joints . . . so that if their arm was blown off, they could still keep going. It was basically suicide. That was the whole concept behind it.

That was my first real exposure to the real sickness of human death. We weren't able to get out of the perimeter in the morning and do a sweep, because we were still taking fire until late into the day. There were huge rats, and you could sit there watching the rats eat the dead bodies. The bodies would start to smell and move. They'd burp and fart. Eventually their stomachs would distend and split open. It was a horrible stench. It was almost as bad as burning bodies. It was one of the smells you couldn't get used to. Diesel and burning shit was, "Oh, well . . . ," but the human body really stinks bad. It's grosser than anything I've ever smelled.

At that point I remember thinking, "This isn't the war I wanted to fight." They talked about all this conflict between grunts and REMFs, Rear Echelon little MotherFuckers, and the grunts who were in the field. Being in the rear—which I was most of the time except when I was out on the road—was a paranoia feeling. You had nothing to strike back at. We'd get mortars and rockets coming in every night, and there was nothing we could do about it. You didn't know when they were going to hit. You didn't know who they were going to hit. That could drive you nuts. I had to get out there where I could put my hands on that sucker.

That was my concept—that was the way I had been raised. My father had raised both my brother and me to be aggressive and very combative. He took pride in showing up to the other guys how big and badass his sons were. It was a trip. You don't have normal social structures when you grow up around army posts, so it's kind of like a pecking order. I never really understood it any other way. When I was just about starting kindergarten, I got in a fight, and this guy beat me up. I ran home crying. My father threw me out of the house and told me I couldn't come back until I beat that guy up. That was his attitude. Everything in the social interaction of living in the military was combative. I wasn't going to ride around those roads any more like a sitting duck—especially not after that last ambush. I couldn't handle it, plus being in the rear, so I volunteered for the infantry, and they sent me to the First Infantry Division.

We operated a lot in the Ia Drang Valley. Base camp was at Zeon.

When I first arrived there, I ran into a guy I had known from high school named Bob Ward. Bob Ward was a sniper. He was in getting his scopes realigned when I ran into him. He was the one who told me that if you really wanted to be in a position where you would be responsible for your own actions and nobody else's, and nobody can get you killed, then that's what you want to be. Bob Ward has since been murdered. There was Guy Davis and Bill Lloyd—who have since committed suicide. Gary Mobile and John Brown—who were killed in-country. That really causes me a lot of survivor guilt. All these guys had good families and things going for them. I just had me. I couldn't understand the meaning or the purpose behind these guys' getting wasted like that and my still being around.

In the meantime I was assigned to First Battalion, Eighteenth Infantry. They called themselves the Swamp Rats. An incident that really made me a sniper occurred while we were working on a sweep at the edge of some rice paddies. I was walking point [i.e., walking at the front of the unit]. I had been in the unit not even two weeks . . . there were not supposed to be any civilians there. They had a helicopter fly over and tell all the civilians to return to the village and stay in the village. This was a pacification program going on, and a lot of the villages were being displaced and destroyed, and the people were being moved into camps. As I walked along the trail, I saw someone come out of the bushes . . . this girl came out of the bushes . . . I just reacted . . . and I shot her three times straight across the chest . . . she couldn't have been twenty. I remember looking at her, and . . . she wasn't dead yet. I was looking at her . . . and she was looking at me with such a profound hate. She died while I was looking at her . . . I never had anybody in my life look at me that bad.

Because of my concept of the warrior and what I felt about war and what my parents had experienced, I could not allow or tolerate to see things like that. As a kid, during this one period when my father was in Korea, my mother would wake up in the night screaming . . . she would come into me and my brother's room . . . and just sit there and rock us and cry. Knowing that, I could not tolerate the abuse of civilians—especially not children and women. It was a very personal thing with me . . . it went against everything I had been taught. That made my decision to be a sniper. Killing clean shows respect for the enemy, but to kill civilians or to lose control of yourself and your concepts in life in combat is wrong . . . that is respect for your enemy . . . that's the concept behind the warrior. Kill cleanly, kill quickly, kill efficiently, without malice or brutality.

They assigned me TDY.[Temporary Duty] to headquarters to a recon sniper platoon. I was issued my choice of a special weapon. I selected an M-14. I went to the munitions specialist at Long Binh. I would lay prone and hold a rifle and just pick it up and snap a shot. He balanced it perfectly for me. I had a daylight scope and a starlight scope. I spent three and one-half days continually firing that weapon all day long. After that they assigned me to work with this other sniper. We worked either on two-man teams or sometimes by ourselves. We did a lot of diversified things. We were at a firebase that was taking probes at night. They couldn't control it, so they brought us in. Gregg put me on a tower on the high point of the perimeter, and after dark he went out through the wire. I would sit there and try to spot where they were coming through, and I would talk to him over the radio and position him, and then he'd kill.

That was really strange at first. It's one thing to be in a firefight, and everybody's shooting and scrambling—but to look down the scope and watch this guy . . . it was a really weird sense of power. People believe God chooses who lives and dies . . . at nineteen I thought that was bullshit. I chose who lived and died because I looked through the scope and pulled the trigger . . . but you don't abuse that power. I was really good at it and really proficient at jungle warfare because of the training I went through when I was twelve and thirteen years old. The jungle was second nature to me. I loved it. The jungle was a beautiful place.

They started working me out into the more remote areas with this guy Gregg. Gregg was a weirdo. He used to like to take ears. He had been there for three years. He was just lost into being brutal. He loved it—and for him it was good fun. My father raised me with the concept that you respected your enemy. If you fought as a warrior, you fought cleanly—you were the best you could be. I started working my first operations along in the Hobo Woods in the north end of the Michelin Plantation. I would go out with a pack of about sixty pounds—basically ammunition, spare batteries for radios, hand grenades, and things like that.

We took very little food. If you know what you're doing you really get into it, you can do it. We used to eat their food. I'd find caches of rice. I used to live off small birds and snakes. If you're out there a period of time, you develop an odor which is undetectable. You can see someone drawing on a cigarette for about a mile. Plus—human beings stink. You can smell another human being. You could smell Americans because of the garbage they ate—especially C-rations.

I really got into the trip that I was doing. I was going to be the best sniper there ever was. It was the kind of war I came to fight. I did some pretty weird things, but they all had a purpose. I had seventy-two kills. Some guys made a game of it so they could cope with it, but I wasn't about to cover it up or hide. To kill another human being—a civilian or women and children—is wrong, but to be in a war and kill another warrior is different. I took pride in it. I still do. We used to hunt other snipers. That's how good I got at it. We would be sending in platoons in the areas, and they would get harassed by snipers. So they would withdraw them and send in smaller units to document where the snipers were, and then they would insert us. They'd insert us using a Loach [light helicopter].

A lot of times we were out there where we didn't even have direct radio communication. We had to use the Bird Dogs. They had these light airplanes flying twenty-four hours per day to communicate with outer units. That was my only line of communication with the rear. I had set escape and evasion routes I could radio in so they would know where to pick us up if we were in trouble. When we were hunting other snipers, I would come into an area—and sometimes it would take me an hour, and sometimes a week. I would move in sections until I found that critter. A person has to come out to use the bathroom and to eat. They used to sit in these little holes in the ground. We would isolate the area where the guy was, and I would track him. These people were not Viet Cong. They were not the Popular Forces. These guys were hard-core NVA [North Vietnamese Army] soldiers who were as well-trained as we were. We fought each other as warriors. It's kind of like playing tag—only if you didn't win, you died.

I guess I did have to leave the main war zone in order to fight my war. I developed a lot of instinctive things that I took pleasure out of . . . the pleasure of accomplishment. Sometimes when I'd shoot a person, it would take me four or five hours to get to him because I didn't know who else was around, so I'd have to work my way in slowly. When I got a really good sight of him, I'd look to see if I got a clean hit, if he had time to booby-trap himself before he died, or if he wasn't quite dead. You couldn't just walk right up on this guy. If I got a good clean hit, it made me feel good, because the concept is you don't allow another man to suffer. A clean hit was an accomplishment. My best range was eleven hundred meters. I could drop a man in one round. At night with the Starlight Scope—when it would be so black you could take your hand up to your face and never see it—I could drop a guy at five hundred meters. I took pride in that. That was what a warrior was. I enjoyed being a warrior. I still think of myself as a warrior.

When they were building up to the invasion of Cambodia, there were a lot of units infiltrating into South Vietnam. They would insert us and tell us to engage and detain until they could get an air strike in. I remember setting myself up in a tree where I had an excellent field of fire across a ridge line and through a valley where there were a lot of trails. I tied myself to the tree, and then I tied my weapon to me so that if I were shot, I wouldn't lose my weapon, and I could keep fighting until I was dead. That was the whole concept behind this . . . and I accepted it. Once you've accepted your own death, you can become really proficient at killing because it is no longer important if you die. If it isn't important to you, if it doesn't mean anything to you if you die, then everything else becomes a lot easier. I'm not saying I wasn't scared. I was scared shitless on many occasions. If it came down to it, I was going to die in that tree . . . it's scary.

Accepting the fact of death is what a warrior does. He fights, he kills, he dies, and to die is an honorable thing. Dying is not bad. Once you accept death, it lowers a lot of your panic. Even on my second tour I was scared shitless. Sometimes I spent days in the jungle where we didn't make contact with anybody, but I always had that fear in me. That fear is what gave me the edge. It tuned my awareness. When you're in Vietnam, you're allowed to leave on R&R [rest and recreation]. I never left the country. I never left the jungle, because I didn't want to lose that edge. If I lost that edge in what I was doing, I would be dead. Fear fine-tuned that edge. That's when the adrenaline was out there. That's when the senses were out there. That's when you were aware of everything.

That's what the warriors' code is all about. That awareness is what saved your life. You became aware of the sounds, the movements, the shapes. There are no straight lines in nature. Man is the only thing that makes a straight line. You could watch the birds in the jungle and tell where animals were moving or where predators were. The monkeys and the birds would flutter off. It might not be the enemy, but you know there's a predator moving out there. The magnitude of things I learned about tracking, about awareness of nature and what's around you. I still use that today, and I love it. It's all involved in being out there.

I came back off my first tour in January of 1970. I got stationed at Fort Lewis, assigned to an artillery battery as a communications specialist, which lasted about a week. Then I got pulled to TDY duty as a military policeman at Fort Lewis. This was during the period when they were having demonstrations at the gates. The Indians were trying to take over Fort Lawton and Cascadia Home. They wanted combat veterans in the MPs [military police]. We were getting shot at by the Indians at night at the back gates of the post. I don't really believe they were trying to hit us to kill us, but they were still shooting at us. It got to be about June, and I started volunteering to go back to Vietnam. They really weren't too agreeable to it because they wanted to keep people with combat experience at Fort Lewis as MPs.

In July of '70 I was at the front gate of Fort Lewis, and a car came pulling off the freeway and fired three shots at the guard shack. Three rounds hit the guard shack. I came out the front door of the guard shack. All the MPs carried five rounds and a .45 pistol. I emptied all five rounds into the car as it was pulling back onto the freeway. They were going to give me a general court-martial and then put me away for shooting back at a civilian before one of us was shot. I was given the option of going back to Vietnam, which I readily took.

During that period of time I spent most of it using drugs and drinking alcohol because it was a very confused period of time. I didn't fit in with anybody. I didn't belong to anybody. I couldn't communicate at all, even with the other military people. The only people I could associate with were other Vietnam vets, but at best we didn't talk about anything. We just could tolerate being around each other. I did not feel I wanted to be part of this world or live in this community, and when I went back to Nam on my second tour, it was with the intent of dying. I wasn't into committing suicide or doing anything stupid, but was just figuring the odds. If you stay at war, you're eventually going to die. I don't care how good you are. The percentages catch up to you.

When I went back to Vietnam on my second tour, it was a good feeling. It was an exhilarating feeling. It was the best I had felt since I had left Vietnam. I felt I was back into my world where I belonged, and the only place where I could function and feel that I was doing something purposeful. It was the only place I had any identity. Being able to fight by the warriors' code gives you an identity. I volunteered for the infantry. I volunteered for the 101st Airborne, and I volunteered for units working around the A Shau Valley. I was assigned to the 2nd Battalion, 327th Infantry. I was a platoon sergeant, and I was a combat veteran. There was a lot of contact going on at that time. They had been through the whole period of trying to get into the A Shau Valley. I worked essentially off of some forward fire support bases. Ripcord and Tomahawk were the two I worked mainly off of. Occasionally we would go to Eagle's Nest.

I was in situations where we were overrun twice at LZs [landing zones]. One time was a time when I almost lost it. We had thirty-six men in my platoon. There were fifteen artillery guys there, and we got hit. There were only six of us who survived. I remember in the morning trying to collect bodies . . . fit the pieces together . . . and I remember looking at this one guy that I was getting ready to put in a body bag, and I fucked up and had given him two left legs. I remember that because that's what they meant when they said in basic, "Your other left, stupid!" It was really weird.

They had to pull me back out then. I don't remember too much about that period of time other than that I was in really bad shock. I had lost all but six of my men . . . and I had these people telling me that I had done a good job, that it was acceptable losses, and all this good stuff . . . and I just couldn't rationalize that. I really became withdrawn and cold. I felt an extreme sense of responsibility to people I had working with me . . . I felt any decision that I made that caused somebody's death was my fault. I couldn't rationalize around it . . . that was my feeling.

My feelings on the Brotherhood of what we had over there together and the sacrifices we were willing to make for each other—you take eighteen-, nineteen-, twenty-year-old kids, and you're sitting around talking about if I get shot and I lost my leg, kill me or give me a shot of morphine, and let me die—I strongly believed in that, and I strongly accepted that. You did anything you could to keep a man alive—that was the concept—but you *never* allowed his suffering to increase. That is what was a true act of love for another human being . . . to provide them with what they needed. I had an incident where I was at another LZ. We were on afternoon stand-down. We had a helicopter come in that was shot down. Immediately the call went out, "Bird down! Bird down!" We all scrambled. Seven of us went out the wire. We started taking AK [AK-47, the standard rifle used by Viet Cong and NVA] fire, small-arms fire, immediately. I had two guys get downed, so we re-tracked and pulled back inside the wire, set up some M-60s [machine guns] for cover fire, and went right back out the wire.

We got to the helicopter. The door gunner on the left side was hanging out . . . his head was almost severed. There wasn't much blood . . . so he had been dead when they tried to take his head. I dropped to the ground . . . rolled underneath the chopper, stopped . . . and had blood splashed in my face from the other door gunner. He had been hanging there . . . and he had been alive when they cut his throat, and there was blood all over the place. I remember it . . . falling in my face. . . . I'm going to have to stop a second.

We heard the gooks in the brush, and we could tell they weren't far. The pilot was missing out of the chopper, so we immediately went after them. We came through this small area, and we were gaining on them and putting out a field of fire. Myself and two other guys came through the brush . . . and we found the pilot . . . he was hanging in a tree, and he had been disemboweled. His intestines were hanging out to the ground, and he was hanging about two feet in the air. You can't possibly save a man who has been disemboweled . . . and . . . I knew he was suffering—dying. I remember looking at him. He was young . . . he was crying. He was crazy . . . he looked me dead in the eye . . . and I looked at him. I knew what I had to do . . . and I knew if I thought about it, I would never do it. I walked around behind him . . . and I put a bullet in his head. I remember doing it so it wouldn't mutilate his face.

A warrior does not increase another man's suffering, and a warrior gives a man who is suffering what he needs. I knew if I had hesitated or if I had thought or if I had done anything except what I did, I would never have done it. I was brought up that way. Everybody else just got quiet and backed away from me. They didn't understand . . . they looked at me like I was weird . . . because they didn't understand the concept of it. I personally took him out of the tree and carried him back up to the LZ.

When I did that . . . a lot of me died. I lost a lot of me, but that to me was basically what the real meaning of the Brotherhood was . . . and the love we had for each other, and the extremes we would go to for each other. I sacrificed a lot of my morals and values to provide him what he needed. Since then I've talked to a few people who have told me that he would have never lived anyway, and if anything his suffering would have been prolonged. To me . . . that was like killing my brother . . . but it was something that I owed him and he deserved . . . that's the concept behind it. He deserved to die like a man and not like an animal. Even to this day . . . I've not yet been able to really forgive myself for doing that . . . I've talked to other people who have had similar situations, and they feel probably as bad as I do, if not worse. That man haunts me every day of my life . . . he's been with me for a long time . . . he's going to be with me the rest of my life.

No amount of treatment or counseling or anything is ever going to help that. Part of that, part of being overrun, part of being just sick and tired of being around people is what put me out in the woods after I got back. I used to spend all my time out in the woods with these guys . . . these were the people I used to talk to . . . I used to apologize a lot to them. I know that the people in counseling have been trying to use this as a way of pulling me out of it, because they are telling me, "Well, shit, live some for these guys. If you can't get rid of them, then live part of your life for them." But I lost so much of my life because of them that it's really hard. I go off into a period where I don't feel I deserve to know any other living beings because of what I've caused to happen to the ones I've been with in war. I spent months and months in the woods with these guys. I used to talk to them. I guess my thinking of them and talking to them and keeping them around in a sense was my attempt to share what I had with them . . . but the only thing I had was the woods. I couldn't feel, I still don't feel, I deserve things like marriage, happiness, to be comfortable . . . because every day I am trying to put something together for them. I think about them every day.

A period of time after that incident with the pilot I went over to what some of us term the "dark side" . . . I lost faith in the warriors' code . . . I lost that concept . . . I began to operate out of hate and a drive for vengeance. That's what I felt forced to do in order to cope . . . to use violence as a way to express my anger and frustration. When I lost faith in the warriors' code, I went out of control . . . to kill civilians or to go out of control is wrong . . . but venting my anger helped me stay sane. It helped me hang on to me in the sense that I was totally lost myself . . . I was pretty close to suicidal at that time. But then part of that is what has kept me alive through the years . . . I try to live for him and the other men I lost over there. The ignorance of people and the inability of people to understand is part of what drove me out in the woods. It's like people in the world became puppy shit. The only people I felt comfortable with were the people who were dead.

During the period before I started talking to other vets and thought I was uniquely insane, part of the reason I went out in the woods was because I couldn't tolerate the world. Out there it broke down to its simplest form. The country—nature—it was the only beauty I saw in the world. It was just like before I went to Vietnam when I was a kid in the jungle. The jungles were always beautiful to me, and they still are. Being alone in the woods was the only place I felt comfortable and where I could relax. I'd stay up for days and just wander the woods, setting up probably at most, at any one time, four campsites. Usually one of them was in towards a more civilized area, where logging roads were, and the other three were way out into the brush where the only trails I used were game trails—or I cut my own. Out there it also made what I had experienced and what I had gone through seem a little bit more trivial . . . a little less meaningful when you looked at the whole scheme of the world and nature and the beauty of it that the ugliness and terror and other things that would wake me up screaming in the night couldn't hold a candle to. I tried to share a little of what I was seeing with the people who walked with me all the time—and they still do.

One of the points why I really hate this government—I had seven months left in the service. After I got out of the service in '71, I also found out that my great and gratuitous government kept me fucked up on Thorazine before I left the service—so they could keep me under control. That's why my last period of time in the service is kind of blurry, along with the month or so after I got out, because I was withdrawing from the drug. They were slipping me Thorazine for three and a half months before I was discharged from the military because I was diagnosed as having erratic, impulsive control problems . . . anger . . . aggression. I didn't find this out until I was at American Lake on this second inpatient thing. I really hate those bastards.

When I got home, I was going through some hard times. The war tore me up because I tried to apply the professional concept to Vietnam . . . Vietnam dealt the death blow to the concept of the warrior. In Vietnam—their concept of war goes back for centuries . . . in their concept, booby-trapping little kids is part of war. Plus, we were destroying the basic structure of Vietnamese life, which goes from the village to the hamlet to the region to the national government. We relocated them into strategic hamlets and destroyed their whole basic concept of life. They were sent to the ARVN army [Army of the Republic of Vietnam, i.e., South Vietnam], away from their village, and it was easy to see they were going to be disillusioned.

When I first got out of the military, I came back here to Tacoma. My mother died during my second tour. The only family I had left was my brother in Tacoma. My first night back, I walked up to my brother's house and knocked on the door. His wife opened the door and looked at me—grabbed my bag—and said, "He's up there at that house." Shut the door in my face. I walked up to this house where my brother was. They were having a party. I knocked on the door. This girl opened the door, looked at me, and slammed the door in my face. I finally got let in. Within half an hour, I was standing by myself. Everybody looked at me weird. They didn't want to be near me. I lasted about two years in the "world." I was never a criminal. I never really did anything with the intent to hurt anybody. I was just crazy, and I was doing anything I could to survive.

I ran into a girl I was going out with before the military about three days afterwards. This was my first attempt at any sort of relationship. One evening we were alone and getting physical. She said, "Did you kill any women and children?" I looked at her and said, "Only enough to eat." And I got up and walked off. I never even talked with another woman for at least eight months. I've never been married. I have no children. I've never had a relationship. In the past twenty years, I've lived with three women, the last one about six years ago. That lasted about seven and a half months. One of my favorite phrases is "puppy shit." If it wasn't important, I didn't talk . . . so I didn't communicate. I look at people, and I don't know anything about that kind of life.

When I came back from Nam, I started working as a bouncer at the Night Moves Tavern. Before the military, I was never in trouble with the law. I wasn't using drugs, but I was flying to California with a briefcase full of money and coming back with a briefcase full of drugs and carrying a Granny High Power [hand gun] in the small of my back. Once I was stopped at SeaTac, [Seattle Tacoma International Airport], and I put a briefcase full of drugs on the counter and leaned on it while I was talking to the police—just for the rush of it. Basically, I ran drugs, did collections, and worked as a bouncer. I carried a gun all the time. I was looking for adrenaline. This town was crazy back then. One night at the Night Moves, the police tried to bust me. They chased me for seven miles from the Night Moves on foot. I was having a good time—almost like being back in Nam. I had been to the bathroom with this guy. He gave me two ounces of cocaine to take from the Night Moves to deliver. There was a narcotics agent in the bathroom. I walked to the door, and this guy grabbed me, and I turned around and nailed him.

At that period of my life, I seriously thought I was insane. I really thought I was insane. I never talked to other veterans about Vietnam. Nobody wanted to be around me for no particular reason. It was like life changed. I didn't fit. I didn't belong. I didn't belong with people I grew up with. I didn't belong with people who were my age. They had no concept of what life was about. You didn't really know what life was about until you know what death is. People don't think about dying. Dying is what happens over there. Dying isn't personal or real. Trying to communicate was impossible . . . so I ended up doing things I was doing, standing in the background with a pistol.

I really lost track of anything to do with emotions. I knew fear, I knew terror, I knew rage. I didn't know compassion. I did not know tenderness. I didn't know love. I didn't know how to work these things. They weren't part of me. They're still not quite right. I lost my ability to communicate to myself about my inner emotions. I completely lost track of all of these things. I tried going to work each day and getting myself something nice, but who cares? What did it mean? It didn't mean puppy shit. It was like there was nothing in the world that mattered. I didn't matter. Everybody who I had known who had meant anything to me was dead. The people who were left alive were different—or I was different. Everything I bought for where I was living was with the concept that I could walk out that door and leave it all behind. Nothing mattered. I could go anywhere I wanted to and do anything I wanted to because nothing mattered. It was later on that I really got inhibited by crowds.

That one wild night in Tacoma . . . I ended up going to court for unlawful possession of a controlled substance, conspiracy to sell and attempt to deliver, two counts of second-degree assault on police officers, reckless endangerment, and resisting arrest. I got out of the military in December of '71 and in December '74 I went to prison. It was like I was trying to get killed, but I couldn't. It was really frustrating. Now I realize that I had accepted my own death and now was just waiting for it to happen, but—dammit—it wouldn't happen. When I went to court, they played off my military record. When I went in front of the parole board for my sentencing, they told me I was too big, too mean, and too vicious because of my military record and could not be considered a safe person to be around.

At first I went to Monroe [prison]. I did get some good things out of prison. That was where I found out I wasn't insane, because I talked to other veterans. I ended up being the administrative assistant to the drug and alcohol program at Monroe. That was the first time I ever talked to another Vietnam veteran. That's where I first got started working groups. That's where I first became aware of the fact that there were other veterans who were just as screwed up as I was. When I first went in there, there were eighteen veterans there. Sixteen of them were combat veterans, and all of them were Vietnam veterans. All of them were there for first-time offenses—just being crazy and wild in the streets.

I was in two prison riots at Monroe. I did three and a half years in prison for a crime that most people would do fifteen to seventeen months for because I was a combat veteran. It really racked my jaws. I put my shit on the line in two tours in Nam, and they're telling me that that made me a weird animal—that it made me something that didn't belong in society. It reinforced my feelings of not belonging. Nobody cares . . . and actually why should they care? I didn't care. I didn't give a shit. I wanted to die. I was tired of living. There was nothing that meant anything. I tried school. I tried working, but it was just blank. I thought about kids and a mortgage. I was so fucked up in the head that I would in no way try to raise a kid. Nobody understood. They'd say, "Tell me what's the matter." You'd tell them a little bit, and they'd run. The few times I tried to open up and let somebody know me, they always ran. They couldn't handle it. Who wants to get into bed with a guy who wakes up in the middle of the night screaming? Who wants to be around a guy who, when things get stressful, closes up and can't communicate? It got to where I wasn't part of the human species anymore.

Even after prison, I went out into the woods. If I hadn't gone out in the woods, I would have ended up in prison. I was seeing a psychiatrist irregularly at that time. It was part of what I had to do to get released. I'd come in, see a psychiatrist, and go right back out. The only place I could find peace and comfort was out there, because there weren't any questions, there wasn't any bullshit, there weren't any lies, and people weren't always trying to hustle you for this, that, or the other thing. Being alone was the only comfortable way for me to be, and a lot of times it still is. I went out into the woods with my dead brothers . . . my ghosts . . . my nightmares. It was all right. There were no people around, so you didn't have to worry about people walking off and leaving you. All the things that I wasn't capable of doing, like being affectionate and caring, were not necessary any more. I got to the point where I didn't think I belonged anywhere . . . but out there it was good. It wasn't great . . . but it was peaceful. I didn't have to worry about trying to figure out if I was accepted or not. I wasn't being hurt any more. I wasn't being rejected any more. I wasn't being ostracized. I was just out there being.

I don't know if I'll ever shake that. I never had anything to fear out in the woods. There were bears and animals, but those were nothing to fear. They were just out there living. I spent probably a total of over three years in the woods, but a year and a half was the longest time straight. I still go out. I still disappear for a week or a month at a time. Nature is beautiful . . . people suck. If I hadn't gone out there, I never would have survived. That was one of my problems, too. I kept thinking, "God, I wish I could kill myself." Just put a gun in my mouth and pull the trigger. I've sat looking down the barrel of a gun with the hammer cocked and the safety off, just kind of caressing the trigger, but I just fought too hard to live to do that. Besides, you can't commit suicide unless you lose your sense of humor.

There were times out in the woods when I would go to some really nice places, and I'd sit. I'd have a beautiful view, and I'd think, "Shit—I think this would be a good place to die." I'd sit there and play with that gun. I'd look at it. It was really a trip. My interaction with nature was a trip. I used to track bears and play around and do crazy things, and it was just great. I had no interaction with people. The bottom line is that when you're standing and screaming naked before the world . . . all you are is who you are as a person. Out there makes you realize it. I put myself back in the position where I didn't have to rely on anyone, and nobody had to rely on me. I didn't have to worry about hurting anyone, and nobody could hurt me.

When I was out there, I used to nurture eagles that got shot. I lived with them and kept them alive until they could fly. That was great. Birds of prey are my trip. Every time I come back here, these dirty suckers fuck my head up again—the VA and stuff. I still need to get out and away. I can stand being here for only so long. I'm one step ahead of Gabe in the fact that I have a dog—Jocko. I've managed to have one living creature not reject me. He's a good kid. He's my traveling buddy. I'm tired of everybody I know dying. That was one of the things about Nam . . . it seemed like everybody I got close to died. Just getting a dog . . . and realizing that eventually no relationship ends the way you want it anyway . . . but to accept the fact that he's going to die before I am—that's a trip. I've already got the place picked out where I'm going to bury him, up by Cathedral Rock.

Since the war, I've had a lot of responsible, high-tech jobs, and I've held a lot of jobs that were just jobs. I can't stabilize in anything. I can't set any long-term goals or purposes yet. I'm working on that, and I think I'm getting a handle on it twenty years later. I was a bank computer specialist in northwestern Washington with NCR Corporation, and I just got up one morning, looked at myself in the mirror, went in, and

Dave Nelson

turned in all my tools—and didn't come out of the woods for six months. I couldn't stand it anymore.

Part of what I am doing right now is what I tried to do twenty years ago, but they tell me I have a chance now. I started slowly to feel that maybe I deserved something out of this life, and maybe I could put something together if it isn't too late. I spent a lot of time trying to avoid hassles and people. I had an incident two days ago where a guy told me over the phone that he was going to kill me. I was at his door in fifteen minutes. Stuff like that is stupid, and I really feel bad when I do it . . . and it makes me feel even more that I don't belong . . . because I don't react the way "normal" people do.

I don't accept stress the way other people do. I can't accept love and affection. I don't know how to accept those things. They scare me. I don't know about them. The love I knew was like the love I had for that pilot. The rest of the world scares me . . . and for years I scared the rest of the world. I lost my last job because everybody was afraid of me. I was going through a period of extreme stress. I never had an argument with anybody. I never had a physical confrontation with anybody—just my presence and the way I carried myself started scaring people, along with the fact that they knew I was a Vietnam vet.

I really feel good about this oral history project. It's one of the things that has helped me through this period I am going through right now. The students have given me other people to think about besides the dead people. It gives me a little bit more, and maybe with a little bit more next year or next week, eventually I'll have enough to get somewhere. It's been an experience for me, too, in the fact that I've never been eighteen to twenty years old. I've never known people of that age. To talk to people in that age group and to feel their sincerity—sometimes I think they're a lot smarter than a lot of the older people. Maybe if one of those young ladies sticks around and has a family . . . and their kids get a chance where they might have to go to war . . . if they can relate what they've learned to their children and keep them from going . . . even if I'm not around any more . . . I'll have done one good thing. If I can keep one person from dying on some bullshit trip, then that's enough, I guess. It doesn't take much.

CHAPTER 3

Backgrounds

He wasn't stupid. He wasn't misinformed. He just didn't know if the war was right or wrong. And who did? Who really knew? So he went to war for reasons beyond knowledge. Because he believed in law, and law told him to go. Because it was a democracy, after all, and because LBJ and the others had a rightful claim to their offices. He went to the war because it was expected. Because not to go was to risk censure, and to bring embarrassment on his father and his town. Because, not knowing, he saw no reason to distrust those with more experience. Because he loved his country and, more than that, because he trusted it.

Tim O'Brien, *Going After Cacciato*

Volunteer and draftee alike, the soldiers who fight in contemporary wars are disturbingly naive, innocent, trusting, untested, and unsophisticated. The greater part of their naivete flows simply from their extreme youth. At eighteen to twenty-one, they are too young to analyze or comprehend the carnage of war or to conceive of their own deaths. Although they are high school graduates, few had the time or inclination to go to college. They come from middle- and laboring-class backgrounds, many from families with traditions of wartime military service as citizen soldiers. Most join on some sort of impulse. Phil Pearson was awestruck by a paratrooper courting a foxy lady in Chicago, Don Hedges just wanted to get away from home, and Nikki Nicol was inspired while watching "The Huntley-Brinkley Report." Many join out of a sense of duty and some join to escape marginal socioeconomic conditions. Soviet soldiers went to Afghanistan believing they would be part of an International Peace Brigade. But as O'Brien says, they all join naively and because they trust their governments. Gabe Garcia, raised to be a Catholic missionary, is by no means alone in the bitterness and rage he feels over the government's apparently deliberate manipulation of his innocence.

With the exceptions of Jim Goldstine and Henry Talmadge, these veterans consider themselves citizen soldiers. They believe they are common, patriotic civilians who answered their country's call to duty, and they expected to return successfully to civilian life. That is the terrible fallacy lurking inside our social definition of war. We assume that war is an exception to our peacetime norms, a separate and discrete period of time in which citizen soldiers serve their country, and we believe the war will end for them with the cessation of hostilities and their return to civilian life.

These veterans returned from Vietnam, Afghanistan, and Panama substantially and forever changed. Gabe says, "I got cheated out of a life." Mike Mitchell says that Vietnam stole a year out of his life that he will never get back. The clash between their civilian values and the values war imposed upon them results in depression, survivor guilt, prolonged grieving, moral anguish, and behavior that seems to an outsider to border on the sociopathic. After he had read the manuscript of *Parallels*, Jim Goldstine said,

> We all got there by our own paths, but it appears to me the central thing we have in common was that we were brought up with a set of values and put in a situation which blew the devil out of those values. It's all about choices. Don't teach young men it's wrong to kill and then expect them to kill in war and not be affected. If you want them to fight your wars, teach them it's *right* to kill.

It appears that the military training does not succeed in replacing their civilian values, which are instead submerged beneath an overlay of military values. They leave for the combat zone believing that they are physically and mentally prepared for war. In the conditions of real combat, none of their expectations will hold. The carnage will break through the overlay of military values with devastating consequences. Their own private visions of war, derived mostly from the popular culture's expression of their country's social definition of war, will prove hopelessly inadequate to the tasks of justifying their sacrifices and explaining what they encounter. The deaths of other human beings will outrage their civilian values, their private definitions of war and the warrior will actually endanger them, and they will be thrown back on their own resources for survival.

MIKE MITCHELL

My father died when I was young, so I was basically surrounded by women early in my life. I didn't play sports because I didn't care for systems. When I graduated from Stadium High in 1966, I got my induction notice. The war was starting to be noticed in the media, and there were the beginnings of the antiwar movement. I didn't figure I'd go to Vietnam, but I knew I was going to be in the army. You just roll the dice and take your chances. I told them I was doing drugs at my physical. A lot of guys lied and told them they were gay, but I wasn't able to tell such a lie. I was inducted six months later and did both my basic training and AIT [Advanced Infantry Training] at Fort Lewis. Once you're inducted, you lose all your outside friends and become a number. Basic is designed to break down your individuality. They break you and mold you, but I was pleased to be out of school. I listened to Sergeant Pepper and learned to love my gun. During AIT I tried to figure out how to get out without going AWOL, but there was no way out. I was a real screw-off and hated the army for two years. I didn't pay any attention to the classes—probably slept through most of them—but I graduated. Out of our graduating company, only three went to Vietnam.

I was sent to Germany. The dice came up seven. I got a fourteen-day leave and was sent to Schweinfurt for eighteen months. Our barracks were a college campus before World War II. It was pretty nice. We got passes and got drunk and met a lot of women, but I realized I was still in basic—spit-shined shoes, everything by the clock, and answering to people with an IQ lower than a rock. I was in hell, and all I wanted to do was get out. I'd wake up screaming at night. I got a weekend pass and got in so much trouble they had to bring me back under guard. I was a very unruly soldier, but right then I began to realize what I had got myself into. The sergeant told me I would never get any rank and put me out guarding tanks. I was out there one night at 3:00 A.M. when I realized I was guarding World War II equipment, so I went back to the barracks and went to sleep. Of course, I was arrested—I was up for a court-martial and given no duties. *Everything was depressing.*

Then we had a formation for our company, but we'd never had formations at that particular time of day. It was an infantry company with tanks. I was trained in mortars. The first sergeant hated my guts. He walked up to me and asked me how fast I could dismantle an M-60 machine gun. I made some smartass reply, and everybody laughed because I *was* a smartass. Then the sergeant said, "Gentlemen, the Fourth Infantry Division from Fort Lewis has just been wiped out in Vietnam, so don't laugh. You are all going to Vietnam. In ten days, you will leave for the States. You will have a fourteen-day leave, and then you will leave for Vietnam." Going to Vietnam was just another roll of the dice. All I could think of was that I was getting out of Germany—which was pure hell.

I spent two weeks at home with my family. My mother is a saint. She prays for me every day. The night she drove me to Fort Lewis, she bought me a six pack of beer and a carton of cigarettes. On the way out, I began to become a little aware of what my mother had done for me. I had always been a smartass, but I realized what might happen to me and how much it would hurt her. To this day, she is still concerned. I went over to see her before I came over here. She still prays for me every day.

CHERYL "NIKKI" NICOL

You have to remember this thing took place twenty-three years ago. Memory blends with what I think I remember until I'm not absolutely confident about facts. I do know I decided to join while I was watching "The Huntley-Brinkley Report" on TV. They showed a report on a field hospital, which said the army needed nurses and anesthetists. I really hated my job. My father was a career marine, and I wished I had been around him more, too. Somehow I ended up in Delaware. I was tired of my job, so I joined up. I was older than most of the others. I was twenty-seven when I got to Vietnam.

DONALD NEPTUNE

I volunteered. I was born in Texas and raised in Benton County, Washington. I came from a large family; actually, I was the last in a large family. My brother had went into the service—he was quite a bit older than me. He went into the service in '61 and got out in '64. I remember when he was in the service. He was kinda my idol. I really looked up to him a lot. He was always real good to me, and I had decided I would go into the service before I got out of high school. About a year later—I didn't go into the service right immediately after high school—it was the following March, after the summer and Christmas and the New Year.

I came to Fort Lewis and did my basic training up here, and I went in as a medical corpsman. And I felt as though I was a good soldier. I felt as though I was learning a lot about myself, although I did at times feel I was being brainwashed. And I continued on to San Antonio, Texas, to Fort Sam Houston, and took my medical corpsman courses down there in AIT, which is called Advanced Infantry Training. Out of a class of I think of around four hundred, all but two of us went to Vietnam, and I remember guys passing out early that morning—about four in the morning, when we got our orders to go to Vietnam. And it was quite . . . uh . . . I knew that I was going, but just the . . . that feeling swept over me that I might not come back if I did go.

BORIS VOLKOV

My father died in a tragic accident when I was two years old, and my mother raised me by herself. My grandfather was the only man in my family who had a military background. He was in the second World War and finished the war in Poland. He told me a lot of stories about the second World War. The stories didn't inspire me to be a warrior . . . but when you are a young man, you want to prove yourself. I had no choice about going into the military, and naturally you want to look for the most dangerous thing to do. I was in the Soviet Special Forces.

For my political ideas at the time, I have to go back to my experiences and what my views were about what was going on in the world at that time. I was very young. I didn't know much about what was going on, and I didn't understand much of it. I was led to believe that we were doing something for the—so that the motherland . . . the government led me to believe that we were helping their country by going into Afghanistan. We were helping the Afghan people, and if we didn't help them, then the American forces would be there. The overview of the knowledge of the Afghan customs and how they lived and everything else was very shallow. I knew they were a deeply religious people— also, their government recognizes the Soviet government.

We didn't get much specialized training to begin with. We were just trained in the armament we were going to be using in Afghanistan. Were we specially trained to go into that area? We were not. There wasn't too much time spent on it. We would usually have breakfast in the morning, then we went out and ran and shot—just the general army training. I was made aware that I would be shot at and what have you. It wasn't anything specialized. It's easier to say what we were not trained in until we got there, because we were not trained in guerrilla warfare. We were not trained in helicopters—how to use them and utilize them well. We were not trained in using all the automatic weapons available to us. The training I got in the Soviet Union was mostly drilling, and nobody ever marched in Afghanistan.

RON MITSCHER

A little background to get me to Vietnam: I graduated from high school when I was seventeen. I lived in Detroit. I knew I wasn't going to college, and my escape from the auto class of Detroit was to go into the military. In 1964, at seventeen, I went into the U.S. Navy. I spent three years in the United States Navy, and about that time, in 1965, the war really got started in Southeast Asia. I volunteered about three times to go to Vietnam, but I was never taken. In 1967, I got out of the Navy and went back to Detroit. I got a job with Chrysler, and I was working afternoons. In 1967 there were race riots in Detroit. Areas were burned, but fortunately not the neighborhood I grew up in. It was a mixed neighborhood. It was a confusing time for me. I had been in the Navy, and I felt like I had been dropped off from Mars into a situation I did not understand. I was from a working-class family. We didn't have any more or less than the Blacks did, and they didn't have any more or less than we did. So basically my social life was per se nil. Most of the kids I had grown up with were working days, and I could see this thing in Southeast Asia as probably being a major event in our times.

In March of 1968, I joined the United States Army. That way, I knew sooner or later I would end up in Vietnam. I went to Fort Knox for training as a tanker. I had no problem with the training. I was later assigned to Fort Worth, Texas, and then to the Second Armored Division. The Second Armored Division was a new unit to work on light tanks. These light tanks were used on airborne operations. I was sent back to Fort Knox. Normally what we were using in Vietnam was a heavier type tank—which had more mobility and was a newer weapon.

I went back to Fort Worth. We were practicing for riot control. A lot of people at that time were trying to disrupt the Democratic Convention in Chicago. They had federal troops from all over the country, but our part was from Fort Worth. We actually mounted a battalion of troops, if I remember right. I looked at this, and I said, "Hey, man, there is a war on in Southeast Asia. I am not going to fight my own people." So I volunteered again for Vietnam. The army was very understanding at that time. Anybody who volunteered almost always got his wish. I was sent to Vietnam in March 1969.

PHILEMON PEARSON

Freeport, Illinois—I was born in Freeport, Illinois. My dad was a minister. He was a good Joe, a real good person. He died when I was in Korea in 1969, after my second tour. They were holy rollers—very, very strict. There was no movies, parties, sports, checker playing, cards, TVs, Christmas trees—none of that. That was the way of heathens, and we did not do that. When I was growing up, I couldn't hardly breathe. The grand kids got away with murder, believe it. I finally went on through high school. I was the youngest one of the family, the baby of the family. The closest brother to me was about three years older—a little more than that.

In treatment, I found out that I was the "Lost Child" in the family. My conversation with them was useless. Nobody really responded . . . the Lost Child. That's what they teach you in those things about family. So, I was the lost child. That's one reason why Uncle Sam was my father, just like Uncle Boeing is now my uncle. When I was growing up, I didn't have the attention that was required for a little person. From what I understand, the loving was there, I'm sure it was, but Mom was so strict that she disciplined with the ironing cord like you wouldn't believe. It was kind of hard for me to believe who she loved, and on what day it was. When I did no-no's, I got chastised. All of us did. I was the last one—the rest were gone. I got fed up with it. I moved to Chicago with my brother. That's my second dad . . . I like to call him "Pops."

And one day I saw a paratrooper. He was coming out of the hotel with the foxiest lady in Chicago—no doubt about that. He had on spit-shined boots, and he wore one braid instead of wings. He didn't have a stripe nowhere . . . That started me thinking about the Army right off the bat. I kept fooling around and fooling around. I tested for the Air Force, but I didn't really have my heart into that. I didn't want the Air Force. The Navy—I didn't want to be on the water. I went down and talked to the Army recruiter—more than once. I decided I didn't want three years, either. He says, "Why don't you volunteer for your own draft?" I asked him, "What's that?" He said, "Volunteer to be drafted. It's only two years."

I learned when I got into the Army that you don't volunteer for anything. I volunteered for the draft, and I pulled my two years. I went to Korea. I decided I wanted another hitch because my civilian friends—we wasn't on the same frequency any longer. The things they talked about was childish and foolish, in fact. So, I went back to the Army. Finally, I made sergeant in 1965. They let me go through the Twenty-fifth Division.

I made sergeant, and then they didn't need me as a sergeant. They needed me as a corporal, a spec. 4. That started again that first tour of Vietnam in 1965 with Sixth Gun Battalion of the Fourteenth Artillery. We left from Fort Sill, Oklahoma. We weren't briefed on where we were going or anything. In fact, we was instructed to take all of our clothing, so we were guessing where we were going. We all loaded aboard the train, guessing where we would go. The train pulled out, and we was instructed to pull the shades down on the windows. The train made one stop somewhere out West. By then, we had armed guards on each door, which was the troops themselves. We were not allowed to look out the window or talk to anybody or communicate in any way with the outside.

Later on, I found out we were headed for Oakland, California, but the train stopped, and they broke us into sections—three cars here, two cars there. They pulled us in by a small locomotive, and later on I found out that people were demonstrating against the troops, and the idea of going to Vietnam—and they were lying in front of the tracks, so we were trying to sneak in unnoticed, acting like they were hooking up boxcars, or whatever. When we were permitted to look out the window, we were approximately twenty feet from the ship. It was right next to us . . . I swear. There were approximately twenty-five telephone booths there side by side, and we was not allowed to use them. That hurt.

So we all got aboard the *Breckenridge*. I was in communications, a radio-teletype, high-speed Morse code operator. We had a little gray box called the KW-7, which was cryptographic. They were classified, and I ended up guarding some of the classified equipment aboard the ship. Of course, you had to have the clearance to guard the box.

So we was on the ship for a total of twenty-three days, and after we got there, we had to sit eight days in the strait because the Republic of Korea Army was off-loading in front of us, so we had to wait.

CHUCK SIMMS

I was born on an Indian reservation near Albuquerque. My dad was Scotch-Irish, and my mother was Indian, and we lived on the reservation with my grandparents. However, we were not Navaho or Pueblo or the other tribes that lived around there. It was sort of an intertribal area. I started going to school off the reservation—in a county school, I guess you'd call it. It was my first real encounter with white kids. I had been involved with the Indians only until about the first grade. I walked to school, and I enjoyed it. I enjoyed walking home and chasing the bunnies and playing with the horny toads. We lived in an adobe house, and we had a well and outhouse outside. We were dirt poor. I have pretty good memories of my childhood there.

I was in the army from 1960 until I was discharged in 1964. I was mostly a voluntary policeman in the army. I also served as a security guard and a fireman in the fire department at the Presidio. I changed over from active to reserve because I got extended during the Cuban missile crisis. I had a critical *MOS: Military Policeman.* On top of that, I was from Albuquerque, and everyone around there speaks a little Spanish. The Cuban thing was going on at the time, and they told me they needed me for a while longer.

At the Presidio I had a friend get killed, even before I went to Vietnam. It really upset me quite a bit. I had a friend who was killed in a drowning. I was part of the search party who found him about nine days later. He was fishing with another MP on his day off. A big wave swept them both off a rock into the ocean near Golden Gate Bridge. One of the guys made it out. He was called Big John. The other guy, my friend, floated on around. It took nine days to get down the coast and back up to the Golden Gate Bridge. I was on an LCM, which has a front which lets down so vehicles can drive in or out. We went down to look for the body in case it came back through with the tide, and sure enough one day we found it. We let down the front and scooped him up, and there was my friend with his eyelids, lips, and ears eaten off by the crabs. It was really gross. I wanted to escort his body home to his family, but they would not let me do it because I wasn't the same race. He was white with blond hair. I felt pretty bad about that.

DONALD HEDGES

My mother—well—both my parents drank until I was about eleven years old. Then my dad quit. We moved from California, the Bay area, to Oregon on a ranch near Cottage Grove. That was quite a culture shock, because we had a pretty decent place down in California, and in Oregon we lived in a shack. I had an older sister, a younger sister, and just before I graduated from high school, a younger brother, too. When I went in the Marines, he was six years old. He always looked up to me, and still does. My dad wanted to become a farmer and wanted to be away from California, but my mom, she liked the social life down there.

I think that's when her drinking became a real problem, with anger and resentment mixed in with it. I remember her being real abusive towards me—mostly it was her foul mouth . . . she felt in her later years that I represented my dad, so she took the anger for him out on me. . . and she was physically abusive, too, but I don't think she ever really hurt me. It was just a real uncomfortable situation. It wasn't like I was getting beaten severely. One thing she did that really stands out in my mind that she did to me—once when I was in trouble, she had my dog taken away from me. That's how far she would go.

Cottage Grove had one of the highest rates of juvenile delinquency in the United States, but I had a real successful high school. I was on the track team and did real well—track is very important around Eugene, Oregon. I ran against Steve Prefontaine, and Dyrol Burleson was from Cottage Grove. I was in student government also, so school was really fun for me. I did above average in grades—not valedictorian or anything—but I did okay. My senior year, I had slim hopes of an athletic scholarship, but it never came around.

I didn't really have any goals after school. I didn't know anything about the war in Vietnam except that it was going on. I remember as far back as the fourth grade seeing a film on the war on Laos, so that's all I really knew about Southeast Asia. I knew that was an option, but I really didn't dread it . . . I never thought much about it. But in March of '67, a high jumper on the track team came around and said, "Hey, the Marine Corps recruiter is here. Do you want to go talk to him?" I said, "Sure." So I signed up for four years. I think what I was trying to do was just get away from home. I didn't really have the image of the Marine Corps. I heard they had the best training, but I wasn't aware of the mystique of the Corps. My dad was in the Navy, and he told me if you like to eat, join the Marine Corps. I figured if I did go to Vietnam, I wanted to have the best chance of survival possible. So without any thought, I signed on the bottom line. It was a good lesson, because I don't do things without thinking any more.

I had delayed entry, so I didn't have to go active until July 3, 1967. There were five other guys from my class who joined also, and we were all going to go together on the buddy system. We were all in the same boot camp, which didn't mean nothing . . . and I mean nothing. It was just a big shock. I thought it was going to be just a big summer camp, doing a lot of push-ups and being an athlete—that part of it never did really bother me. But the things they do to you mentally and psychologically and emotionally . . . at the airport, there was this DI [Drill Instructor] cussing and screaming at us in front of real people, and I was thinking, "Doesn't this guy have any manners at all?" When we got on the bus, it got worse. When we got to San Diego itself, he was yelling and screaming at some guy behind me, and I just smiled. I don't know how he could even see me, but the next thing I knew, I got this tremendous slap alongside the head. I didn't smile much more, I can tell you.

I got so tired of being called a "motherfucker" . . . I mean, my mother always cussed a lot, but I kept hearing this word over and over and over again. We were up all night, and all the next day being called motherfuckers the whole time. I remember thinking, "Jesus! What have I gotten myself into?" And, of course, that was just the beginning. The physical and psychological abuse is just amazing. I got beaten severely a couple of times. The Marine Corps choke hold cuts all your air off. I accidentally bumped the DI's Smokey the Bear hat with a broom. I didn't even realize I had done it until I felt myself being dragged backwards by the handle of the broom. He choked me until I was about to pass out, and then he hit me real hard. He did that four, five, six times and then said, "You be more careful with those brooms next time." This is the same DI—he was a maniac. He stuck pins in us. I was lucky because he only stuck me in the hands. We had one private, Private Hill, and he would take pins and stick them in his chest and say, "Does that hurt, Private Hill?" And Private Hill would say, "No sir!" and he stuck the pin all the way into his chest and asked again. He was just a sadistic motherfucker, is what he was.

I barely qualified with the rifle, but it's a good thing I did qualify. We really had a good platoon. I really hate to be critical of the Corps. I'd hate to see them lighten up, because I really think the way they treat you in boot camp is important to your survival later on. That's what makes the Corps what it is—or what it was, anyway.

For the most part, the psychological training was adequate, but the techniques they taught us were worthless. For instance, water—they told us you could get water out of the bamboo tree. What they didn't tell us was that only maybe one in fifty bamboo trees might have water in it, and that they're in sections. You could waste yourself cutting down bamboo trees. They didn't tell us about the banana trees that are about 79 percent water. Some kid from Boston figured this out. We were in the A Shau Valley in '69 without water . . . really suffering . . . and he comes by chewing on this piece of banana tree. Now here's some kid from Boston that discovers this, and the Marine Corps can't teach us that. They taught us to make a boot out of a rabbit, but I didn't see any rabbits in Vietnam. Just all of this happy horseshit that was useless to us. A lot of the tactics we learned can't be used in the mountains. I think that's one of the things I really resent the most, the kind of things we were trained for.

From staging, we went to Okinawa and spent a couple of days there. The most impressive thing there I remember was the guys coming home. You could tell the new guys from the vets real easily. They were just different. They were dirty, and they just had an attitude.

VLADISLAV TAMAROV

I use my own name because I want people to know Vlad says these things. I also give names of some people I want American people to know. To use another name is okay for other people, but for me—I think this must be.

Two of my grandfathers were military people. They took part in World War II. They are different wars, World War II or Vietnam and Afghanistan—very different in Afghanistan. Afghanistan was when your people were in their home living like usual—at peace—but somewhere else there's a war. In Soviet Union, people didn't know how real was this war because of information in our newspapers and television programs—like soldiers who planted trees and built schools and stuff. I tried to go away from army, not to serve. I started in an institute, special kind of high college with biological college and sport department. I was long-distance runner was why I went to this institute, and I finish one year. This year was like fine cognac, but then I need to go.

Okay—about my parents. What was scary for them during Afghanistan was because I came to the time when I had to go into the military. There are no volunteers in Soviet army. You must go. We have a law you must serve when you're eighteen years old. My parents are scared. Our newspapers don't tell anything, but my parents feel this war. My parents didn't believe stuff in newspapers, but still they taught me about how good we live and how badly people in foreign countries live. This May, they were in the United States, and when they come back, my mother, the one who teached me this, she say, "You know, son, I decide not important if this socialism, that capitalism. More important the people live by it." That's what my mother told me.

My grandfathers in their war, World War II—a lot of grandfathers served and died there in World War II, but my family had no people that were professional military people, so when I enter service, I wonder, "Why enter this?" Because I must, only. On airplane to I think you say "boot camp," I found out I will go to Afghanistan. When I flew to boot camp, you wrote first this application. They ask "yes" or "no" about service in Afghanistan. Everyone wrote "yes," since if you write "no," you will have lot of problems, and after that they will send you, anyway.

The worst thing about boot camp is the "You will . . ." order. "You will" make trench, from dinner until dawn, then "you will" fill it back up. Of course, it makes me very angry, but they have to do this if they want to take the feeling of freedom from us, you know? Forget about freedom. Let's just—we can call this the place where we rolled cubes and carried balls. These were a hundred pounds, and the cube we were rolling, and the balls we carried two hundred feet, put down, and carry back. Not an obstacle course even. Sergeant say, "You will carry this and roll that from here to there. You will carry ball. You will roll cube." This is how stupid this was. They make us do everything the most difficult way. I should have stayed in this boot camp six months, but I was only there three months. They need to send us because somebody was return from Afghanistan—or somebody killed.

It is interesting. I saw somebody from my old camp, and they told us of this time when they came to Afghanistan, they just shoot all the sergeants because they understood these sergeants make every kind of move to stay in boot camp and not go out to Afghanistan. Why can't these sergeants fight? We fight the Afghans, and they fight us . . . but

Backgrounds

these sergeants have power, and they say, "You will fight." They did not fight, you see. We are not happy this way . . . we still do not know about Afghanistan fighting. So I have to go to Afghanistan, anyway.

JIM GOLDSTINE

I am a graduate of the Military Academy, class of '61. I had served in a variety of assignments as a field artillery man up until my return from Germany in 1965. I was battery commander of an AIT battery at Fort Sill for about nine months and did everything I could, including volunteer, to get to Vietnam. I wound up receiving a call one morning from the head of the artillery branch asking me if I would take an assignment in Special Forces in order to go to Vietnam, and I said, "If that's all you've got, then that's what I'll do."

I guess I must be a total idealist . . . or romantic is probably a better term. I probably could have ridden with Don Quixote. But I've always had this sense of public service as being something important, and I got hooked early on—about junior high school—to thinking about going to one of the military academies. In September of my senior year I wrote a letter to Charley Hallek, who was my congressman—senator?—at the time and I asked for an appointment. I got a letter back saying, "Go to the Lafayette Post Office and take these tests on such and such a date." I did. Then I got another letter in January that said to go to Fort Sheridan and take the real exams to get in, so I did. Then I got this letter about the middle of May that said, "We're concerned about your acne. Go to the Dispensary at Fort Sheridan to do a reevaluation." So I did that, too. Then about the last week in May, I got a letter that said to report July 2, 1957.

Throughout all of this, none of it was hard. The whole thing was somebody told me to do something, and I did it. There wasn't any sense of it being hard or easy. You just did what you did. I have to tell you what the big recognition was: It was the last time in my life that I let something be easy. After that, if it was going to be worthwhile, it was going to be *hard*—you know?

EMMETT FINN

I think the fact is important that I grew up in a town of about 5,500 people, in which everybody in my hometown knew me. This was Frostburg, Maryland. My family was—I have two older brothers. We were a real athletic family. Irish Catholic. I was an altar boy until I was a junior in high school. We were heavily into church involvement, and I went to church camp every summer—athletics and sports almost from the first grade on in this Catholic Youth Organization. That whole thing of growing up in a small community like that created a really strong bond. My parents . . . they were real old when I went to Vietnam. They were in their forties when I was born and in their sixties when I went to Vietnam. I grew up in the late forties, fifties, and sixties—and GI Joe and neighbors who were World War II veterans—and John Wayne movies. I was pretty primed to go to war and kill a commie for Jesus. I thought we were totally right. I've been forced to take an inventory of my life, to minimize the power of regret and, in doing that, I'd have to say there isn't anything I'd change.

I wasn't raised to go to war. I wasn't raised that way. I wasn't Angela Finn's little boy when I came back from Vietnam. God, but Mom wanted me to be a priest. I even thought about doing it, since I was the last one—the last boy in an Irish Catholic family. Somebody's got to be a priest in the family so the whole family goes to heaven—you know. I thought about it. Thank God I didn't . . . although I would have made a good priest.

HENRY MINCEY

I guess the reason I went into the service was, first of all, the fact that it was a way out. I was a kid from a family that had no way, no physical means, of sending me to college. I really didn't want to go to college. I wanted to get out of poverty—that's basically it, just to get away from poverty. I was born in Alabama. I knew very little about Alabama until it got to be a little later, and I was in my teens. We went to St. Louis and then Detroit, then back down through the South. That's the reason I said, "Well, I'm going to take the first thing and smoke it." I went to volunteer for the Air Force. I had the flu that day, and I couldn't even do simple stuff. They said, "Well, come back in thirty days and try it again."

I was just dead bent on getting away from everything I had grown up in. I graduated from high school, and all the guys that were graduating before me, they'd come back in their uniforms and stuff. The Air Force was what caught my eye, you know. I knew I didn't want to be a ground soldier . . . I knew that, so when I flunked the Air Force exam, I came back, it must have been two or three weeks, trying to figure out what the devil I'm going to do. I got to get away from here.

I called the Navy up and said, "I want to join the Navy." "Come on down." So I went down and took the initial battery of tests. They said I did pretty good. I went to Little Rock and took some more tests. They said, "When do you want to leave?" I said, "As soon as I can." I couldn't wait to get out of there. I went back up to Little Rock for my physical and almost didn't get in because I had what they called flat feet. I guess I had this pitiful look on my face—I guess it wasn't against his better judgment just to say, okay. I was sweating it the whole time because this was my way out, you know? I mean, I was really sweating.

We went down to lunch, and one of the weirdest things in the world happened. You go to this restaurant with these little chits to eat with. Not thinking, we were chatting and so forth. There were three black guys and the rest were white. The waitress told all the black guys that we got to go in the kitchen to be fed. This is 1964, you know. I had heard of stuff like that, but I said, "What? Are you serious?" She said we got to go back to the kitchen. A lot of the white guys who were with us said, "This is bullshit—we're getting ready to go into the service, defend our country, and we got to go through all this crap?" These guys are Arkansas people, too. I was kind of getting militant and loud, and finally one of the cooks came out and said, "Hey! I know how you feel—but keep yourself out of trouble, you know. Go in the service, don't get arrested. Fact is, I'll give you anything you want to eat."

That stayed in my craw—the service started off with a rude awakening. Bad as that was, as appalling as I thought that was, I said, "I'm willing to do anything just to get out of this situation. Even though you're going to put the uniform on, you're maybe going to give up your life, they still want you to act like some kind of animal." I looked at it that these jerks were just ignorant and backwards. Anyway, I went to boot camp, and I decided I was going to do my best. It was tough, but the discipline didn't bother me. I had a father that was a real disciplinarian, so that didn't even bother me. What they was doing was like a joke almost. They were just playing mind games, and that I could deal with—that didn't bother me.

The only thing that bothered me was I couldn't get a grasp on what it was all about—what was the real reason I was here? That was the thing that was confusing. The thing that really tripped me out the most was—behind that—that very night, the company commander verified that we could go into some action-like war. Boot camp may be cut short so we could get troops out there. Then the thing that tripped me out worse was I saw these kids cutting their own wrists, to keep from going to war. Most of them were volunteers. I was saying, "Damn, dummy, you joined. You joined, you do what you have to do, you know?" I got through that, but I thought it was strange that people would go through that extreme to avoid something they voluntarily did. None of them died. Later on, I realized they didn't want to die—just trying to find a way out.

I went home on leave on the way from boot camp to Texas and saw some people. I went by the recruiter to say, "Hey! Look! I got it made."

He congratulated me and said, "Great! I see you made aviation. I told you you had good test scores. That's a hard rate to get into. Where you going?" I told him I was going down to Texas. After I got off leave and checked into the base, things started happening just like that. We get this NCO [noncommissioned officer] thinks he's smart . . . thinks he knows what's going on. He realized that you're in the service with hoodlums, badasses—they're there because they had to do something or go to jail . . . or their family put them out. I kind of felt, "I'm here because I want to be, and I want to do the best job I can." I got into aircraft maintenance. Right off the bat, I should have known what I was into. I was the only black there. I guess the civilian rate would be body man—body work—skinning aircraft.

I had a real good supervisor . . . I'll never forget him. He was an Italian guy. I guess he's about my age now, about forty. We would talk, and he would show me tricks on how to work with a ratchet and so forth. I never knew how rivets got put into the aircraft—he showed me how all that was done. I really got off on that. I really wanted to learn, and he was impressed by that, but I guess—unfortunately—this was the rate that very few Blacks ever been prevalent in. Then they got this little eighteen-year-old kid, bubbling with enthusiasm, wanting to learn everything he can learn. I can see this as a way out because I figure I can get myself a job after I get out.

So I'm thinking all these things, all the right things, and all this BS—this racism—starts popping out. I'd think, "Why? *If* I'm coming in lazy, not wanting to do anything, acting crazy, I'd understand, but I can't figure out why I have to go through all this shit. It's just what you have to do, so you learn to deal with it, my man." Then I said, "Deal with what? These folks don't even know what they're doing. They don't even know why they dislike me. What if I was transparent—how would you deal with me then?" I saw I wasn't getting anywhere, and the militance started building up—this hatred. I was never what you'd call a fighter, but I found myself getting into a lot of fights. I realized what I was doing to myself, but that gave them a reason to put me out of that division. I got sent to mess duty, and I thought I was going to get sent back to my unit. It didn't happen. I got sent to this God-awful place out near the base—no-man's-land, called the Crash Crew. Firefighter—man, I was a firefighter, and I'm terrified of fire, but believe it or not, I got good at it. It was kind of the disciplinary unit. This is where all the disciplinary problems got sent. Nobody else wanted them.

It was real interesting, but I got bored—anybody could do this. I'm still thinking of aircraft mechanics, so I need to learn aircraft, so I ask for a transfer to another unit. They transferred me, alright—sent me to an outlying field. It was an old base that was closed down, but they used it for emergency landings. I ended up going out there, which was good. It kept me out of trouble—it really did. I got real tight with the guys. When my two years was coming up, I got sick. Once you get sick, they have to move you out, so they immediately replace you with another man. I spent the afternoon in the sick bay thinking I'm going back to the old crew.

I find out I'm reassigned to the old crash crew . . . I'm pissed—I'm ready to fight now. I'm ready to do bodily harm. The division commander at the time, this guy must have been . . . he made George Wallace look like Martin Luther King's son. He and I didn't get along. He used to ride me, just ride me, but he was real slick about it. He never did anything overt that I could just latch onto knowing exactly what he was doing—but I knew he was jacking with me. The first time I had a chance to get liberty, I took off that weekend and just got wasted. I didn't show up until Monday. He put me on restriction. I said, "If I'm going on restriction, I might as well go to the brig. I'm going to get around you so-and-sos, anyway." That pissed him off. He pulled out a .45, put it on me, told me I was under arrest, called one of the petty officers, and had them pick me up in a jeep. They locked me up for thirty days—no biggy.

A lot of my friends were marines, and they ran the brig. We ran the streets together. I mean, they talked to me. They didn't show no favoritism, but they weren't hard on me, either. The majority of them was black, you know, so we got along pretty good. I got out and went to my unit—I just said, "Hey, man, there's no use fighting it. Do what you have to do, and get out of here. You only have a few months left." I got my orders. They said I was going to the Philippines, to a naval air station. Well, because you got disciplinary problems, then your orders are automatically stopped. I got a new set of orders that said I was going to the USS *Bennington*. I'm dumb—I don't know exactly what the ship is. I've been in the navy for two years, and I've even never seen one! I asked this one chief, and he said, "It's a fighting carrier. It's an antisubmarine carrier. All the aircraft on that carrier is assigned to hunt down submarines and attack them." "That's all? Okay." He ran all this stuff by me. He said I won't get seasick because it's too big, which was great.

I got my orders, went home, went to San Francisco, where I was going to fly to the Philippines. I'm thinking I'm going to Vietnam. Everybody at home was raising a big stink—"Oh, God! He's going to Vietnam!" They're scared, crying—all that stuff. But to me, I just knew I wasn't going to get a dangerous assignment. What can they do to us on the carrier? Everything you see on TV is in the jungle, so I'm not sweating it, you know? I get to the Philippines, and my ship is already on station, so they have to fly me out. They put me on a tanker that's going part of the way out, and I'm about to die of seasickness at this point. Some sailors had some cough syrup, and I drank that. I don't know what made it worse—being drunk off that syrup or sick from being at sea. The next day, I woke up, and I was still alive, saying, "Oh, shit." A helicopter picked two of us off that tanker and was going to fly us to the carrier—it's stormy, too. I could see the flight deck as we was approaching. I thought, "Damn, this son of a bitch is huge. Is this thing floating?"

YURI KIRICHENKO

I was born and raised in a town about two hundred kilometers southwest of Moscow. My father was very young during World War II, but he drove convoy trucks toward the end of the war. Our family was not intensely patriotic, but we attended all of the ceremonies for World War II veterans. They saved us from Hitler during World War II, and we always went to those ceremonies. In Russia, everyone has a "patriotic obligation," so during my early years, I just assumed I would go into the army for my obligation to my country. Then I would get a job and work and have a family.

The Soviet people were not told much about the war. We were told that our soldiers were going to Afghanistan as part of an International Peace Brigade. We were told that the International Peace Brigade was there helping the Afghans to fight against rebels . . . and also building schools and bridges and canals. We were told the Americans might intervene unless Soviet forces joined the International Peace Brigade in Afghanistan. That sounded plausible, and I went along, and I was inducted and went through basic training. We didn't know until some soldiers came back what was really going on in Afghanistan, and it took a long time to understand—for all of our people. We know now that Brezhnev and a general were in a room, and the general advised Brezhnev not to send Soviet troops into Afghanistan, but Brezhnev made the decision to send in our troops. At that time, we didn't even understand—as soldiers—what the soldiers we met, who had been in Afghanistan were telling us. It got worse as the war continued, but even when I went, I couldn't understand.

I was motivated to be a warrior by attending the World War II memorials and hearing about how the army saved the people. It is true that there were twenty million Soviet people killed during World War II. The Germans invaded us and nearly took Leningrad and could have taken Moscow . . . and then there was Napoleon and other invaders. I understand a little about your traditions of patriotism, but all Soviet citizens know we were invaded, and we know twenty million people died. I know there is no glory in war when people die, but in the circumstances of when I was young and went to serve, I had no reason to question.

We rotated in as units, mostly men from the same geographical location, so when we got back, we followed tradition and founded local veterans' associations. Today we are trying to bring all of these organizations together in something like your Vietnam Veterans' Association. We need to concentrate on what's happening with the veterans, who even in the Soviet Union are not treated intelligently or with certain awareness of the effects of this war on the veterans.

HENRY TALMADGE

My dad was illiterate. When I was in the seventh grade, I was just getting into sports, and the coach said I had to have a jockstrap. I told my dad and explained what it was. He said, "Can you read?" "Yes." "Can you write?" "Yes." "Can you do numbers?" "Yes." He said, "Your education is over. You come with me." At the time we were up in Wyoming, by the Shoshone Reservation between Riverton and Lander. He was an Apache, and the Indians around there were Arapahoes and Shoshones. The two shall never marry—they just argue with each other all the time. My father's name is Tolmich, but they spelled mine as Talmadge. Our great grandfather was a Hungarian. He was in the New Mexico territory, and he was a scout for Kit Carson. My great grandmother saved his young ass. They ran away from the tribe—he died of wounds later.

My father had a '32 Chevy, and he made a box out of the back—took out the rumble seat—and we'd put our stuff there when we moved. He sheared sheep on reservations—mostly in Wyoming—sometimes in Montana and South Dakota. He could shear one hundred yearlings a day, and ewes maybe seventy-five because they were so wrinkled. You had to be careful not to cut off their tits down there in all that wool. They would give me a penny a fleece for every one I tied. They had these big sacks to put them in. I would go inside and pack them really tight. I made five dollars a day for doing that. The old man was always after the dollar. Any money you ever made, he kept it, and he would give you what he wanted to give you. Whenever you needed a new pair of shoes, maybe. He was very skimpy.

With thirteen kids in our family, the depression on full blast, and food scarce, we had discipline as a child. We weren't picky at eating. Anything that was put on that table was consumed. I think the discipline of being able to not have anything to eat for a day or two really helped me out in a lot of ways, and after eating commodities, C-rations don't taste half-bad. I weighed about 170 pounds when I left for Vietnam and weighed 135 when I got back. You can't be picky about what clothing you wear, either. If your mother washed your underwear, you didn't wear any that day. The whole thing—how Mom had to wash our clothes by hand—we had to do the same thing in the service. Being poor does have its advantages, because in war the rest of them were kind of helpless. They'd wear socks until they were falling off their feet before they'd wash them.

We'd take off from one ranch to another, just like a flight of birds. Normally we'd find a young Indian couple, and she would do the cooking for us. If not that, sometimes we would hit up the rancher's wife. We'd get there and work until we were almost through, then the rancher would go into town. At that time, the Indian wasn't allowed to buy alcoholic beverages. The rancher would go into town and bring back wine, whiskey, and beer. He'd pay my dad, then he'd take off with his wife and family. He'd leave a steer back in the corral for us. We'd get our meat ready, then we'd party for two or three days. Then we'd pack up and pull off the road down a ways, and then we'd walk back and police the area—clean it all up so it was like nobody was there. We marked where our toilet was, then we'd leave. Next year we'd come again and set up in a different place. We'd go from one end of Wyoming to the other. It paid cold cash, not checks.

At that time Uncle Sam had the Civilian Conservation Corps. My brother went in. They would pay you thirty dollars a month. They'd give you a uniform and a cot—almost like the army. I went in under a false name. I was there almost three months building reservoirs and spreading prairie grass over the fields. They had an outpost way out in the middle of nowhere, and they needed someone to take care of it. I volunteered to go. There was no electricity—nothing. My closest neighbor was five miles away. The other was seven. They were cattle ranchers. I had a radio, and every night at six I had to call and tell them everything was squared away.

Then the second world war broke out. An officer came in and said the Japanese had bombed Pearl Harbor, so they were disbanding the CCC camps, and all you red-blooded Americans will come to the call of your country. I was fourteen at the time. I didn't have hardly any hair on my armpits, none on my chest, very little in my pubic area. My penis was probably three inches long hard. I had to stand by all these big, burly bastards. They had testicles like goddam bulls. The recruiters said, "What the hell are you doing here?" I said, "I'm ready to go." They said, "They're killing people." I said, "I know. I want to go." They said, "Go home to your mother." That pissed me off, but they gave me my forty-eight dollars I had coming.

My brother wanted to get the hell out of there, so he joined the Marine Corps and left. That left me all by myself. I wanted to go, so I just begged the old man, and finally, when I was sixteen, my dad signed for me. My dad was in World War I. He had enlisted, but when they were going to ship him out, World War I stopped, so he didn't see any combat time. He was pretty gung ho. He used to wear an American Legion hat. Being an Indian, I don't know where he got this gung ho Americanism fight for your country bullshit. He was a pretty smart guy. He used to work in the coal mines with Armenians, Italians, and Mexicans. Although he was illiterate, he could speak just about all the languages. He could speak Spanish beautifully.

I turned sixteen in February and left in March. I was in the South Pacific in '43, '44, '45, and part of '46. I was in the Navy aboard an antiaircraft cruiser, the USS *Reno*. We had hit all the islands—the Marshalls, the Marianas, Iwo Jima. We were responsible for a lot of Japanese planes which were shot down. We had one kamikaze which came down on us. The ship saw a lot of action. The USS *Princeton* got hit one morning, about two thousand yards away from us. We and the *Canberra*, a cruiser, went in there and tried to put out the fire. One of our mounts was hit with debris, and when we pulled out, the *Princeton* blew up. Most of the people on the *Canberra* who were topside got wasted. We were lucky. We came back in again, and the wreck was just sizzling. We let it have it with a torpedo. When it hit, it was just like the atomic bomb. It was just one big ball of fire . . . and there were a lot of trapped bodies of people inside.

Shortly after that, about eleven-thirty one night, I went down and woke up the relief crew. We had eight hours on, eight hours to sleep, and eight hours to do your other tasks. At midnight, it was just a calm ocean—a beautiful moonlit night. It was clear, just like ice. All of a sudden—POW! A Japanese submarine torpedoed us just aft of the quarterdeck. Right away, everyone starts panicking. The hit knocked me down and busted a couple of ribs as it spun me around a 20-millimeter mount. I got a life jacket and went all the way forward to the bow.

We had eight hundred people aboard the ship, and the next morning when we took roll call, there were only two hundred of us left. We kept it afloat until we got to the Admiralty Islands. We put it in dry dock . . . and then we had to go down and bust the hatch open and get all the bodies out. I never smelled anything so offensive. I've seen animals that got bloated and were out in the sun, and they stink . . . but humans who have been bloated and in water, and the water has got to them. . . it wouldn't have been so bad if they were whole bodies, but there was an arm here, a torso there . . . they were very decomposed and soft as hell. You had to be careful, or they would fall apart, just like chicken off a bone. The crew has reunions all the time, but I haven't mustered the guts to go yet.

After the war was over, I didn't want to come home. I didn't know why. I didn't know what I wanted. I got out and went to New York and New Jersey, Virginia—down to Florida. I screwed off for two months. Then I joined the Marine Corps. I was in for two years. They had me in North Carolina. Then I decided to come home. I hung around for a while, but things were never the same. I went back to Fort Hall down in the Shoshone Reservation. It was not the same. Nothing had actually changed, but to me, it seemed like it had. It seemed that I had skipped some beats . . . that I no longer belonged there, like I was misplaced. I couldn't even participate in some of the ceremonies, because I didn't feel comfortable doing that. Then I left for Colorado. I couldn't seem to adapt. I was doing construction work. I was working. I was employed. I have been employed all my life until recently.

From there I went to California in '49. Everything was almost the same as it was a hundred years ago. I took up bricklaying. I worked all over Hollywood. Then the Korean War started. I packed my shit and told my boss I was leaving. I had a convertible, a '46 Ford, and a dog. My folks were up in Washington, in Yakima, so I came up and left my car there and hitched a ride to Seattle. I went to the recruiter and said, "Hey! Where's this place at —Korea? That's where I want to go. I need a place for the night, and I want to be on that bus in the morning."

When we got to Korea, we went up to relieve the Turks. We had to do it at night. It was really different from Vietnam. They had what they called a "Main Line of Resistance." There were trenches and bunkers all over. The trenches were pretty deep. They were dug deep to begin with, but there was erosion, and then the trench line got deeper and deeper. In some of them, you had to climb up above your head to get in a fighting position. The bunkers were full of water. They had listening posts out in front of the MLR about two hundred yards. That was bad because you'd go out in the middle of the night—you wouldn't know where the hell you were. You start looking at the bushes, and they seem to start moving towards you. You look at a stump, and first see a tree, and then arms and a head. Your imagination goes crazy because you don't know where you're at. You go out all night and all day, and then the next evening they'll send somebody else out there. The next morning, you make a visual reconnaissance to see what the hell is out there. Your job wasn't to kill, but to see what's going on. From the listening posts, we'd have outposts, and from there, you ran patrols. It was no-man's-land. Sometimes we'd go on patrol and set up ambushes and never get a bite, and sometimes all hell would break loose. It was exciting.

One time we had had a small skirmish, and we were going back, and I was bringing up the rear. A flare went up, and we hit the deck. You can't look at a flare, or it will screw up your night vision. Then there are no flares, so everybody gets up and starts going again. There was white tape along the trench line so you could walk better at night. The trench line turned, but I didn't see the white tape, so I kept going, right over head first onto the concertina wire. It is very sharp. I was upside down, in mud, and in pain. I could hear the Chinese and North Koreans talking and moving, and here I am in the concertina wire. I was like a rabbit in a trap. The guys missed me down the road. As they came back, they said, pretty loudly, "He must be around here someplace." I was worried the Chinese and North Koreans would hear them, so I was whispering back at them as loudly as I dared, because I was afraid they'd miss me because they couldn't hear me. "Psst! Psst! I'm down here! Psst! Quiet! They'll hear you." They had a hell of a time getting me out of there.

A lot of the guys were scared shitless. If we'd get mortar or artillery fire, they'd be in their bunkers scared shitless. They'd be crying. They'd be worthless . . . no good for nothing. In Vietnam, I knew a staff sergeant who I knew way back. In the past he had been in pretty slack duty. During the first barrage of incoming we got, he just wanted the fuck out of there. He was *non*functional. He was out of it. All of a sudden shit started coming in. He jumped in my hole, and I jumped on top of him. He was Catholic, and he was praying. All I could do was laugh.

I made sergeant just before I left, and I spent a lot of time with Indians from India. It was a rich experience for me, being an American Indian around Indian Indians. They were plain good fighters. I never saw night vision like they had. I'd get my booze from the Indians. They liked tea with their booze. They used to come and visit me, and I used to give them coffee. They didn't drink much of it. I'd go down there, and they would give me tea, and it would just blow me up with gas—but I liked the brandy. So I told them one day, "Meaning no disrespect, if you could put some brandy in a container for me, I'll drink that." He said, "I'm glad you said that, old chap, because that coffee of yours tastes like shit. We like tea."

After World War II it was like celebration time, and there was a welcome home. They gave you jobs and all this stuff. It was like, "We appreciated you folks." The spirit was there. People greeted you. It took quite a while for them to tone down. What the government gave the veterans for services rendered, they in turn made big bucks and put it back in the coffer for Uncle Sam. Then the Korean War came along. It was like it wasn't really a war. It was a police action. But hell—people were dying just like they were in World War II. They thought we shouldn't be doing it, that we should just let an aggressor kick the hell out of another country. When I got back from there, it wasn't that people shunned you, but you didn't quite get the reception from World War II. They kind of forget about that really fast. The VA didn't pay much attention to the veteran of Korea.

Shortly after I got back, I got married. I was in San Diego training recruits for about two years. From there they put me in a DI school to train Marines to be Drill Instructors. That was even harder. You had to be in really good shape. We'd take in about seventy people and end up with about forty. We were looking for the cream of the crop. You have gone into the Marine Corps, and you have earned those Marine Corps emblems with hard, cold sweat and blind obedience. They make you what you are. Now, when you become a Drill Instructor, you're still eating dirt. They've still got you. It's a machine that's so precise. It has a cutting edge that just won't quit. Those that are too weak or can't handle it, they're gone.

We'd get recruits in from all walks of life. I had one platoon which were flunk-outs from Officer Training Academy. These were intelligent people. The only thing that was lacking in them was hard turds. They were shitting soft when they came in. The ones you had least trouble with were farm boys because they were pretty solid—physically and emotionally. The city boys who were raised by a mother would never fit in. All of them were treated the same. It doesn't matter if you're Indian, black, Jew, or white. You all have to do the same shit, and nobody slacks off. I had a roster, and whoever I disciplined during the day, I'd remember them. My DI would remember them, too. Every evening we'd go down the roster and find out who had been disciplined, and we'd put a check mark by their name. All of those who hadn't been corrected, although they been doing their job, I'd line them up and accuse them of the smallest thing—and they'd admit to it.

I never neglected a soul. They couldn't blame me for being prejudiced. The Marine Corps has its laws that you can't mistreat them. You don't really have to kick their ass. You can put them in so goddam many exercises and positions to where you've got them begging to stop. It's probably worse than being in a concentration camp. You set the example. You're running, they're running. They don't do anything that I don't do. The only time they got in trouble was when they didn't do what they were told. That's easy enough. The officers would come around and corner them. They'd give them a sheet, and they were to say if their Drill Instructor even hit them or threatened them. We used to tell them, "Hey! All you got's me. We are all together. *Those* guys are the enemy." We'd get them all squared away—the officers would say, "You must run a tight platoon. I know you're kicking their ass." When the recruits would leave, they'd make a collection. They'd want to give us money, which was against regulations.

When the Vietnam War came along, I was training reserves down in Nevada, so they wouldn't let me go. Then about three months later, some other orders came in, and I left. They said, "Hey! You haven't had your shots for about two years. You're about eight shots short." I said, "Give me four on this arm and four on this arm." They did. They then gave me my orders, and I got on a plane. When we got to Okinawa, they took our names and gave us seabags. You dump all the stuff you don't need, all the nice stuff, and they tag it and put it away for you. Then they issue you what you need, and then you're on another airplane off to Vietnam, to Da Nang—this was in 1966.

GABE GARCIA

I was born in Texas. I went to Catholic school and was an altar boy for five years. When I graduated, I was waiting to go to a seminary in Pennsylvania to become a missionary. While I was waiting, I got drafted . . . I was eighteen. I told Father Smith and Father Pugh I would be back in two years. That's all I had to serve since I was drafted. I don't like to think about my childhood . . . I was involved with the Man upstairs . . . I was heavy into the Word upstairs. If there were a real God, Vietnam would never have taken place. The government tried to murder me . . . they scarred my brain, and they got away with it . . . I got cheated out of a life. They stole me from my home, and they lied to me when I got to Vietnam.

I don't want nothing to do with nobody until they fix me the way I was . . . before they took me from my home. Today, fuck God, fuck Jesus . . . fuck the fucking government. I don't have any feelings about nothing and nobody . . . I don't need to love nobody. Since I've been participating here at the PTSD program, I haven't been saying the things that these people want to hear, like "I love you" . . . or this or that shit. I don't need to love anybody . . . I don't even love myself . . . I know what they created.

The reason I am talking to you students right now. . . is because I want the fuckin' public to know . . . what the fuckin' government done to us. They promised they would make a man out of me . . . and I'm still waiting twenty-one years afterwards. All they did was create a fuckin' animal. The government gave us a good fucking . . . for what? I still don't know . . . I don't know what I done wrong.

BOB SWANSON

I was born and mostly raised in Grandview, Washington. I had a little trouble being socially accepted by the local kids. I was teased a lot because my mom was overprotective and insisted on walking me to school until I was nine years old, even though we only lived a couple of blocks away some of the time. She was also a person who taught me not to fight. For a long time, I wanted to join the service. She didn't want me to join, but I made her promise me, finally, that I could make up my own mind when I turned seventeen. From what I understand of my father—though I don't know too much about him—was that besides being an alcoholic, he was also an abuser. Those memories are blocked for me. I was raised pretty much by my mom until I was eleven. Just before I turned eleven, she was married to my stepdad.

Leading up to going into the service, I had a lot of trouble with the police. Not being socially accepted, I finally found a place where I was somewhat accepted, and it happened to be with the wrong crowd. I had my first police record when I was eleven years old for second-degree arson. This friend and I tried to make a fort out of the basement of a vacant house and decided to burn the cobwebs out with torches. When I was fourteen years old, I called in bomb scare to the police station, just to get the local schools out for a day. We ended up being out for an hour, first thing in the morning. It was ice cold, and I was in gym shorts because PE was my first-period class. Then they let us back in, and then somebody who had known that I did it, who was supposed to be an ally, squealed on me. I was on probation for that for a year and a half.

Later on I got a record for car theft, which was a car I didn't steal. A kid came by and asked me if I wanted to go cruising around in this car he was going to buy. My mom and dad were in the yard, and I got their permission to go, and we got in the car . . . and it turned out it was stolen. I spent pretty close to five years probation for that. Some other kids and I started a gas ring. We broke into a farm shed and took quite a bit of gas. Two of the guys got arrested. They told the story on everybody else. My probation officer called me up—and he believed I was not really guilty on this car theft thing. After that, he really had something on me and said we would just keep everything the way it is. You know, "I got you now."

When I was seventeen, I was having trouble in school for being a nonfighter and running from fights. I had a bad reputation for running around with the wrong kids. I was on probation, I felt unjustly, and for something I didn't do, so I was quite resentful . . . and was causing quite a few problems. So when seventeen got there, I went back to my original plan of joining the Marine Corps. My mom didn't want me to

Backgrounds 61

go, but I held her to her promise. Then she begrudgingly signed a waiver for me to get in. I had to sign a waiver to get out of probation and to get into the Marine Corps.

I was stuck on a 120-day delay. During that time period, I got arrested for violation of probation. The local police weren't aware that I was off probation yet, and I stayed out one night too late. They picked me up and wouldn't listen to a thing that I was telling them. So they sent me up to a detention home again. And I got up there and saw my probation officer, and he said, "Oh, we really got you this time—violation of probation!" I said to him, "I'm not even on probation." Then he goes, "What are you talking about?" I said, "I'm enlisted in the Marine Corps and have already been sworn in, and this judge took care of it." My probation officer had been on vacation and didn't even know about it. So I got out of that and went back to the police station and told the arresting officers what I thought of them.

I reported to the Marine Corps boot camp in San Diego in September '66. We hit the San Diego airport, and the drill instructor came to meet us. He marched us outside and had us line up on these footprints out in front of the air terminal waiting for the bus. He was walking around yelling and screaming, and I turned to the guy next to me and said, "What the hell is this guy's problem?" I found out that I had the problem, and the DI didn't. We got into the boot camp area, and I was kinda set back by the sound I kept hearing. I kept hearing this weird sound, and I found out later it was the drill instructors calling cadence. I was pretty successful at controlling my attitude problem and I felt more or less accepted by the units I was in. I didn't care much for basic and AIT, but I got myself through. I felt pretty good about myself—about getting through and being in good shape.

DARREN GATES

My dad's a teacher in Santa Maria, outside Santa Barbara. He's teaching sixth grade right now. He's a good teacher and has been for twenty-five years. He was teacher of the year in his district last year. My mother's a secretary at the college I went to.

I went for three and a half years at the university back home. It was just a lot of work. I was working forty to fifty hours a week, plus going to school, and I was getting burned out. I was bored with college. I decided for a change of pace, I'd join the army. I started looking into it and decided I wanted to do something exciting. I didn't want to be a truck driver or something boring like that, so I talked to my recruiter, and he said, "How about the Rangers?" I didn't even know what a

Ranger was. I started looking into it, and I thought, "Heck—looks like I can get a lot of experience in a short amount of time." I've been in the army for two years now. It's been an exciting two years.

Basic Training was pretty much a joke. Looking back now, it didn't really help me for what happened down there. After basic, I went to Jump School—that was fun—I thought that was exciting. Jumping out of airplanes—I like doing it. Jump School was three weeks alone, and it's kind of hard. Then you go to RIP, it's called the Ranger Indoctrination Program. You go there for a month, and basically, they try and get you to quit. They run you into the ground. That really weeds out a lot of people, and after that, you join your unit.

I wanted to go to Fort Lewis because it's closer to home in California. I'd been there with the unit about a year, and we got called in to go to Panama. Within that year, I got a lot of training—stuff that really helped me out in Panama. We knew something was going on, we didn't specifically know where, but you could feel the tension at work every day. Something was going to happen soon. We had gone on a deployment. We were gone for a week, came back, cleaned our gear, turned everything in, and then they were going to release us to come home. We were still on two-hour recall, which means you can't go anywhere farther than two hours away to get back in time in case something happens. We came home, and my wife and daughter were in California at the time, visiting my parents and her parents. I came home, threw all my clothes in the washing machine, and sat down and was watching TV, and I get a phone call—"Gotta come back in."

All my clothes were in the washing machine, soaking wet, and I thought, "Great." So I waited until everything was dry, and I got back in to work, and everybody was rushing around, packing gear and drawing weapons. We left the next morning and flew back East. We went over what we were going to do down there. Nobody knew it was for real until we got there. Everywhere you looked, there were pallets of explosives—ammunition. We knew it was for real at that time, and everybody's jaws kind of hit the floor.

So we flew out the next morning, the twentieth—the twentieth of December. We flew into Panama. It was a pretty rough flight, we flew pretty much over the ocean the whole flight. We were in our chutes the whole time. From where we flew out, it was about a five hour flight. It was hot—sweaty—it was miserable inside the plane. Guys were getting airsick. We got about an hour out, and we started rigging weapons, just double-checking everything. Basically, everybody was just trying to keep busy, trying to keep their mind off what was going to happen.

CHAPTER 4

Horror, Abjection, and the Experience of Contemporary Warfare

> What you really needed was a flexibility far greater than anything technology could provide, some generous, spontaneous gift for accepting surprises, and I didn't have it. I got to hate surprises, control freak at the crossroads, if you were one of those people who had to know what was coming next, the war could cream you . . . and all you could feel of your whole life was the entropy whipping through it. . . . I went there behind the crude but serious belief that you had to be able to look at anything, serious because I acted on it and went, crude because I didn't know, it took war to teach it, that you were as responsible for everything you saw as everything you did. The problem was that you didn't always know what you were seeing until later, maybe years later, that a lot of it never made it in at all, it just stayed stored there in your eyes.
>
> Michael Herr, *Dispatches*

> Throughout the night without images but buffeted by black sounds; amidst a throng of forsaken bodies beset with no longing but to last against all odds and for nothing. . . . Nothing is familiar, not even the shadow of a memory.
>
> Julia Kristeva, *Powers of Horror*

For the combatants, contemporary war is a claustrophobic, chaotic, technologically violent, exhilarating descent into the dark side of human nature. The "1,000 yard stare" is the outward sign of the psychological ordeal inherent in this grueling, decidedly postmodern rite of passage. The most obvious parallel within these narratives is the limited scope of contemporary wars. Nations take pains to limit their political and military objectives. The Rules of Engagement limit the soldiers' ability to protect themselves. The time line of a tour is perfectly linear narrative. Each day is important only because it is a day nearer departure, each firefight only one more battle they will not have to fight. American army and navy personnel served twelve months in Vietnam, and marines thirteen. Russian soldiers were in Afghanistan for two years. The new "short and dirty" wars such as Panama and Kuwait-Iraq are designed to be over in a matter of weeks. In each case, there is a terrible finality about these wars, signifying either survival and the return back into the world or the terrible finalities of death and maiming.

There is a psychological dimension to a soldier's passage along the timeline of a tour. It underlies the stories that follow and is a perfect example of the inchoate—the tacit, private, and metaphoric—quality of the soldiers' knowledge. The narrators of war stories hover between reportage, imaginative reconstruction, and inductive analysis. Parts of their knowledge, such as their initiation into combat, are told as vivid, tacitly understood anecdotes. Other parts are metaphoric, the most important being the vortex metaphor for combat. Helicopters circle into landing zones, and a "hot LZ" is a particularly brutal experience in chaos. Emmett Finn's description of being overrun is another variation of the vortex metaphor. At the more abstract extreme of this continuum lie Dave Nelson's "concepts," which are more explicitly defined but still not fully articulated understandings.

As their narratives proceed, they describe three critically important psychological phases or stages in a tour. Within the first sixty to ninety days, they are initiated or "blooded" into combat. During the balance of their tours, the full horror of war registers itself in their minds, and they learn to numb themselves to the horror of war. As time passes, they experience abjection, a response to meaninglessness that Julia Kristeva in her studies of the Holocaust calls "the ultimate coding . . . of our most intimate and serious apocalypse" (p. 208). In abjection, as Nelson's story has demonstrated, they either achieve "the edge" or go "out of control" and plunge into "the dark side." In the final phase of their tours, they become short-timers, experienced and respected, yet even more anxiety-ridden about the odds against their survival.

BLOODING

In order to understand the origins of this psychology accurately, we must remember their extreme youth, their belief in their government

Horror, Abjection, and the Experience of Contemporary Warfare 65

and their culture's war myths, and the triviality of their basic training. To use a well-understood American figure of speech, they find they have gone "too far"—they have ventured outside the security of their homes and culture and out into a world that does not conform to their expectations. Suddenly and violently, they participate in killing for the first time. How they react to the exigencies of combat determines in large part how they will behave for the balance of their tours, and hence their place in the Brotherhood. Since there are few stories of cowardice in these narratives, it is reasonable to conclude that most soldiers make it through this stage successfully.

HORROR

During the first six months into a tour, Fucking New Guys (FNGs) become veterans. With experience, they gain a measure of control over themselves and their environment. They learn field-expedient survival techniques and rehearse them until they become "second nature"—automatic survival responses. They have assimilated into the culture of combat, and membership in the Brotherhood enhances both their self-esteem and their chances of survival.

Meanwhile, routine exposure to death and maiming results in what Madden has called "horror." Horror is the blank, terrifyingly fatal quality in events gone completely out of control—in the carnage of war, natural disasters, rape, the Holocaust, and so forth. The horror of an ambush or mortar attack would traumatize any normal human being. It emanates from the charred arm Mike Mitchell found hanging in a tree in the A Shau Valley. It causes the revulsion that swept through Chuck Simms when he realized he was wading through decomposing bodies. It prompts the impotent rage of Henry Talmadge as he collected the bodies of men who died because the new M-16s jammed.

ABJECTION

Gradually, they are overtaken by what Kristeva formulates as "abjection." In Vietnam, Afghanistan, and Panama, abjection is the abiding sense of meaninglessness and loss of self that results from prolonged, traumatizing exposure to the horror of contemporary warfare. Herr identifies it with the responsibility associated with what you see that stays there stored in your eyes. This collapse of meaning is not merely nothingness, oblivion, or a void. As Kristeva emphasizes, abjection is an omnipresent "something"—oppressive, crushing, profoundly significant—for which there are no adequate signifiers. Abjection is at the very core of the inchoate, hermetic mysteries of the Brotherhood and survival code. Kristeva says, in "a reality that, if I acknowledge it, annihilates me, [the] abject and abjection are my safeguards" (p. 2). Whereas the lesson of horror is the acceptance of others' deaths, the lesson of abjection is the acceptance of your own. As Kristeva implies, awareness of this collapse of meaning becomes a way of surviving psychologically. Nikki Nicol remarks that "Don't mean nothin'" was a favorite cliche in Vietnam. Talmadge now realizes, "In Vietnam, I lost my sanity, I lost my humanness, I lost my trust . . . I lost my faith."

THE EDGE

They are now at a critically important threshold. Under ideal conditions, they achieve what Nelson calls "the edge." "The edge" is a synergism of mortal danger, field-expedient techniques, adrenaline, sensory acuteness, and animal survival instincts. Men perform astonishing feats of bravery and skill in the heat of battle. Finn rushes helmetless to save a man hit in an ambush. Ron Mitscher flees back to his tank through AK-47 fire and evaporates the rifleman with a single cannon shot. Fortified with beer, Gabe descends into the tunnels. Nikki calmly softens the clothing stuck to her body with dry blood during the Tet Offensive of 1968. These amount to peak experiences, which can be recalled in incredible detail, even years later, because they exemplify what Philip Caputo calls "the compelling attractiveness of combat" (p. xvi).

On the other hand, the soldiers can go out of control and over to the "dark side." Nelson says it was what he had to do to preserve his sanity—"what I felt forced to do in order to cope . . . to use violence as a way to express my anger and frustration." Still, he knows that "to go out of control is wrong." Going out of control may be a means of surviving emotionally, but "going over to the dark side" violates the soldiers' submerged, private values. There are many examples of out of control, "dark-side" behavior in these narratives. We agree with the veterans that while such behavior is morally repugnant, it is a part of war, and it must be understood. If it can be understood as the effects of horror and abjection, it can be forgiven.

MIKE MITCHELL

I got pretty fired up on the beer my mom bought me and said good-bye to her, and the next thing I knew I was on a commercial jet flying to Vietnam. All of a sudden I saw the land, the coastline of Vietnam. It was

Horror, Abjection, and the Experience of Contemporary Warfare

beautiful. The water was blue, and the sand was white on the beaches. We landed at Cam Ranh Bay early in the morning Vietnam time. We still didn't have any weapons—which I had expected to get right away. The heat and humidity were double Hawaii. There were guys on mopeds everywhere, and I could see people surfing. Off in the distance I could hear artillery, and I could tell we were in a war zone. It took six days to get my assignment, which was with the 1st Air Cav. A sergeant said, "Buddy, you couldn't be in a better unit. The 1st Cav. really kicks ass up there. They take care of their own. You'll probably be coming home."

I was then sent to An Khe. It was a smaller base—no mopeds, more helicopters, and there was a village in the center. I got ten days jungle training, and I paid attention. I've always thought it was real humorous, because out of the ten days, nine days they told us about everything that could kill us in Vietnam, and we hadn't even touched on the enemy yet. The snakes, the heat, the bugs, the water, the malaria, the diseases. And then on the tenth day they proceeded to tell us about Charlie—the VC or the Viet Cong. We learned, "if you don't see him first, you're history." By the time this ten days of jungle training was over, I was afraid to take one step outside of the wire. Charlie might not get me, but all these other things might. The fear built from then on.

Then I went to LZ Sharon, about ten or fifteen miles south of the DMZ [demilitarized zone]—it's up to Quang Tri Province. There was the question of my MOS. I was trained in mortars, but there were no mortars. I had to go back to the infantry, down to a platoon, and then to my squad. The sergeant was a child, he was only nineteen, and the oldest guy in the company was twenty-three. I had a choice: carry a radio or an M-60. I decided, "I want more firepower," but I didn't realize until later that a radio actually has more firepower than a machine gun.

I was an assistant machine gunner, so when I drew my equipment, I realized I would be carrying four hundred rounds of ammunition, water, an M-16 with ammunition, plus my regular pack. We sat around for thirty days, which everybody realized meant that somebody was conjuring up some big mission. We trucked down through Hue to Phu Bai, and I realized I still didn't know what Vietnam was like. We were shuffled around and sat a while. Then one morning, we saddled up. The Hueys came in and picked our company up, and we made my first air assault into the A Shau Valley, along with the rest of the battalion. The sound of a Huey means more to me than anything else . . . and I have such respect for the pilots.

We went into the A Shau Valley. It is very thick jungle, triple canopy, and at noon it's just like night. There had been no friendlies in the A Shau for two years. It was an NVA R&R spot. It was a classic Air-Cav assault—helicopters everywhere—which all the major networks were covering. We had a cameraman on our Huey. By the way, I'm scared to death of heights, and one of the first things I noticed was that vets got the seats at the back. I was sitting right on the edge with my legs hanging out of the doors. I may be afraid of heights, but I was more concerned about the area we were flying into. It's a long, huge valley. I was on the first helicopter to go in from our company, and our squad was the first one in. Jets were blowing the hell out of the hillsides. We moved out toward an old air base. Cobras were demolishing the area so completely that it was like walking through a fog with dust and smoke. The cameraman was the first one out, and he was running backward to film us as we fanned out.

Vietnam for me was like 365 days of camping out, with one big hitch. Someone was looking for us, and we were looking for him. If you fuck up, you were history, and if he fucks up, he was history. It was my first action, and I was definitely baptized. We became involved in A Shau for two and a half months. We went in to search this area in the jungle. It was fairly thick—not real thick—but it had a lot of ground cover. I found the arm of a GI. It was just burnt to a crisp. It looked like a charred piece of chicken. I never found any other part of the body but that arm. That really sunk in. That was a real eye-opener, and at that point and time, I really realized that I could really get hurt. As long as I was there, I wanted to be as good at my job as I could be. I realized I was in a real war—real combat.

We did a lot of humping in the A Shau, and sometimes it seemed like we just crawled around on our hands and knees and stayed off the trails. Then Charlie would hit us—always when we least expected it. Always. Most of the medics were COs [conscientious objectors]. When all hell breaks loose and nobody is running around, the medic will come to your aid. We got ammunition resupply, but no hot food and no showers. I had five showers all the time I was in Vietnam. After about two weeks, a crust would develop on your skin. We would stink so bad we couldn't stand to smell each other—or ourselves. All I thought about was, "How am I going to get myself home alive?" I wished I hadn't slept through all the training, because there had to be a reason for it all.

After A Shau, I decided to play the game as it was supposed to be played. I was a good soldier. I *never* let my guard down. I became very, very close to the guys in my squad. I became real, real serious and was given the rank of sergeant and became squad leader. I thought, "I wish my 1st Sergeant in Germany could see me now!" A while later I was voted into the Blue Bandanas [a special brotherhood]. Then it settled into a routine. We would fly into an LZ, patrol the area, dig in for the night, fly out the next morning, patrol another area, dig in for the night, and then fly out again. That's why I say it was like 365 days of camping out, except that I was humping ninety-five pounds, and the VC were always out there looking for us.

My biggest fear was, "When is Charlie going to hit?" We rarely found Charlie. He could smell us. Some of us felt the C-rations we had to eat caused our body odor to be easy to detect. He *always* hit us when we least expected it. Once he hit us while I was taking a crap in a bomb crater. He was everywhere and nowhere. He always knocked on our door first. One morning our company had a big skirmish against three or four gooks. Three hours later, out of our company of 120 strong, there were fifty-six of us left. We used all our ammunition and called the jets right down on top of us. When it was all over, we went looking for body count. All we found was one puddle of blood. They got sixty-four of us, and we got one. It was always that way. It seemed like they got the upper hand. It didn't make any difference how big or well-trained we were, it was still chaos—hit the ground and fire in the assigned direction. The VC/NVA did the damage and then took off.

Patrolling villages was a break. The saying was, "The enemy doesn't hang around villages." If there were men between the age of fourteen and sixty, they should be in the military services. If you found any men between those ages, most likely they were VC, but you could get beers in the villages, and beers were nirvana. There were always little girls selling beers and Cokes in the villages. One day four little girls came out to where our company was sitting around taking a break. They squatted down in a little circle with their gunny sacks in front of them pulling beers and Cokes out of their bags and handing them over their shoulders and selling them to us for a dollar apiece. After about an hour, they left and headed back towards their village. About ten minutes later, two guys in our company walked directly over the position they had been sitting in. There was an explosion. One died, one lost his leg. This just confirms that no one could be trusted, not even women and children. While they were sitting there selling us Cokes and beers, they must have buried a live artillery or mortar round as a booby trap. If someone would have stepped on that any sooner, we probably would have had the opportunity to retaliate. Those four little girls would have been dead. War stories hurt me a lot. The atrocious ways people are killed in war are beyond belief.

CHERYL "NIKKI" NICOL

It is important to remember the time frames of the war, because the experience changed. From 1954 to 1966, we were there mainly in an advisor role. We tried to take over the war from 1966 to 1968, then we were withdrawing and "Vietnamizing" the war from 1968 to 1973. I was there from February 1967 to February 1968. Where you were was also a differential. My experience was also unique because we went in as a unit. We built our own hospital in six weeks. We had to learn together. Each time I speak in public, I emphasize that there were male nurses, too.

In Tuy Hoa we lived in tropical buildings. The cubby-holes were divided by plywood. The walls were plywood, and we had burlap windows. We got a cot, a footlocker, and an army air mattress. You can't sleep on an army air mattress because it's all hills and valleys when it's hard enough to sleep in. We had our trunks for tables. Tuy Hoa was on the beach, which was nice, but it also had terrible humidity. We slept in wet sheets. I went up to Qui Nhon one time, and the nurses' quarters had air conditioning . . . unreal.

We got our training on the job, too—in a different sense. We had to learn how to do triage on our own, because at first if a casualty came in, we took him straight into the ER [emergency room]. Pretty soon we saw that we needed to prioritize the wounded. We learned that all we needed to do was stabilize them, then do surgery—or send them to another hospital. We didn't have all the supplies we had expected. Some of the bandages we had to reuse, so we had three barrels filled with water. You'd put bloody bandages in the first one until it got full enough. Then you'd swish them around in there and transfer them to the second and third barrels until they were at least cleaner.

Later I was transferred to Nha Trang. The housing there was adobe, and it was filthy. The showers were moldy. We didn't dare use anything electric. We even had a pet rat named Charlie. I worked the ER all the time. Funny, but it was only seven years ago that I realized I only went into another ward three times. I still haven't figured that one out.

During Tet, when we were in the OR [operating room] for five straight days, we were using bennies to stay awake. We knew there were patients coming, and they just kept coming. We kept triage and the OR going full time for that length of time. My psyche was stretched like a rubber band. We tried to shoot Charlie the Rat one day during Tet, and so help me it was funny. Not so funny was that one of my superiors ordered me to mop the floor. I didn't notice until I went outside that blood was running out of the building onto the walkways. I was ordered to clean it up. I had to change clothes . . . and when I tried to take the stuff off that I'd been wearing all that time, the dried blood had glued it to my skin. I had to pour water on it to get it off. In the end, everybody was swabbing the OR floor—doctors, nurses, everybody.

We worked twelve hours a day six days a week as long as I was in Vietnam. Day after day we saw these kids—eighteen-year-olds in excellent physical shape with arms and legs blown off. We didn't see that many gunshot wounds because modern bullets tumble inside the body, and most men who were shot died. We saw a lot of shrapnel wounds from mortars, grenades, and booby traps. On the Wall [the Vietnam Veterans Memorial in Washington], less than 50 percent of the names are KIAs. The rest were accidents, snakes, diseases—that kind of stuff.

Bob Broyles says that being in a war is like walking into a room with carpet on the floor and nothing else. You creep into the far corner and lift up the rug. What you see is horrible. At the same time, it's exciting and a thrill. There is that duality about war. I really didn't want to see it. My letters home are made up beach stories. If I had one wish, it would be that there will be no more wars. I'd choose famine over war . . . but when I talk about it, I get that rush again.

I couldn't admit it for a long time, but it's a kick to be so busy under such circumstances. Whenever we had two or three hours off, I said to myself, "I wish somebody would come in." I knew that in order for me to feel good, somebody's got to get hurt. The soldiers get their kicks when shooting at somebody who's shooting back. It's hard for us to understand. I accept it now . . . but the conflict in your mind makes you want to get it over with.

I still can't believe some things we humans do to each other. Take flechettes. *We* developed them. When you fire them, they break apart into thousands of little darts. We saw captured VC and some of our own people who had been hit by flechettes. They look like a mass of hamburger. *We* worked hard to develop these things. Bouncing Betties pop up from the ground and explode at crotch level. The least that happens is you get your legs blown off. Napalm was horrible for the Vietnamese, who wear a lot of silk. Women wear an *ao dai* with a tight blouse. Napalm burns silk into the skin, and you can't get it off without pulling a lot of skin off, too. We had to give them morphine because they were screaming so loud . . . it was unreal. We usually sent Vietnamese to their own hospitals, which were filthy. We took care of Americans first. We kept back supplies when we were treating Vietnamese. It was a choice which was no choice.

Then there's our failure to hold territory. I still can't figure it out. I went in gung ho, but we'd keep getting these guys who would say, "We had to take that hill again." By early fall, up here in my head, it said, "This just isn't right." It was so screwed up it was unreal. Later there were issues like race and sex and drugs. All I ever saw or heard about was marijuana, but by 1972 people said it was outrageous. After 1969, the number of rapes of American women was phenomenal. Many women owed the army time because they were in student nurse programs. I was twenty-seven when I got there, so I was old. The young ones—

sometimes we said, "They won't make it." They did. It gives me great faith in the American people. Vietnam was the same as a disaster anywhere—like San Francisco. People pitch in.

We had a phrase over there. "Don't mean nothin.'" It was widespread and appropriate to that time and place. We were about to pull out the day we lost the chopper crew. Dave, Pineapple, and Ron, the crew chief. Their plane went down, and they were KIA. It was an honor to be a litter bearer. "They're ours, and we will carry them." There was not a mark on them. They died when the chopper hit the ground. They died from broken necks.

DONALD NEPTUNE

And so I went home on a short leave—about seventeen days—and reported to Oakland and went over. I didn't know anybody on the airplane. When I went over to Vietnam, I didn't know anybody. I arrived in Vietnam in September, and I remember we had to circle for a couple of hours over the South China Sea because the runway was getting mortared. They had to repair it, and finally we landed, and I remember getting off the plane, and it was a hot, sticky feeling. The climate was so much different than I was accustomed to, and the smell—the smells were so pungent—kind of a sweet smell. It was kind of sickening sweet, and it was all new to me.

And I remember having to pull KP duty for a short time in the mess hall, that first day in-country, before I went to the 90th Replacement Center at Long Binh. I had to hang around there for a few days because my orders hadn't been cut, and I didn't know where I was going. So I was just in limbo. Then I got orders to go to the 121st Evac. Hospital, at Cu Chi, and it's about forty-five miles northwest of Saigon. The 25th Infantry Division Headquarters was out of Cu Chi, so that's all I knew about the place before I got there. It was a big firebase, quite large—a lot of infantry—a lot of guys, seasoned veterans. They all looked old, a lot older than me, though they were—some of them were—probably younger than me. They had rucksacks on, different types of weapons in their rucksacks and web gear. They wore their boonie hats or headbands, whatever. It was quite—I wasn't used to that. What I pictured, you know, coming out of AIT or Basic Training, everybody with helmets on looking all the same. Nobody looked the same even though they all had the same type of uniforms on. A lot of them had their pants tailored to where they fit tighter so you wouldn't catch them on brush out there. And they'd have bandanas tied around their legs, upper and lower. And it was quite an experience. They had a real faraway look in their

Horror, Abjection, and the Experience of Contemporary Warfare

eyes . . . and later I came to know it, as we all did, as the 1000 Yard Stare.

I remember I was assigned to go to work in the emergency room that following day, and I showed up there early. I remember relieving the other shift that was coming in. I got to meet people there—the nurses, doctors that had been working in the emergency room all day—and the medics. Pretty large ER. And I was standing there and hadn't been on shift maybe ten minutes and heard the sound of a helicopter coming—approaching. I didn't know where it was. I thought it was just flying on up ahead somewhere. It was overhead, but it was landing, and it had wounded on it.

They brought 'em inside, and I remember it was—they were some ARVNs and NVA. I got to work on the NVA all by myself. I was in the back portion of the ER, and some guy handed me a couple of shots, syringes, to give this guy a couple of shots, and this guy was screaming. He was shot in the face and down the neck and through the chest and in the arms and down the legs and in the feet. I was cutting—he had shoes on, and he had boxer shorts—and I was cutting off these green canvas-looking boots. I didn't know at the time it was part of their uniform. And I got one boot partially cut off . . . and . . . he screamed and . . . he died . . . real hard . . . thrashing. He died real hard. That was it. And I just went white, I remember—well, I felt—I mean my hands turned white. And just call me yellow—chain-smoking. But . . . I remembered that. He—I remembered what he looked like, and his hair was shaved real short up to the top of his head, and he had a shock of hair right on the top of his head. Later I came to find out that's why they called them Zips. Just the shock of hair right on top of his head, like one of the Three Stooges, you know. But it was a lot less.

The next four people they brought into the medical unit were Americans, and they were forward observers. Their company got off course by about two thousand meters. The VC/NVA came up on them while they were eating dinner. They opened up on them with everything they had, and they ran from them, and then they swam across the river, and when they were swimming across the river, that's when they got hit. They all got hit. One guy got hit in the butt, and I think another guy got hit in the leg, and one got hit in the back. And he was—he was screaming, and his lungs were filling up with blood. He had a sucking chest wound. He was drowning in his own blood in the ER. And he—I had a chest tube in my hand to give him a chest tube, and the doctor came up to slit him open so he could insert this chest tube, and the doctor froze up. He couldn't move. And this other doctor pushed him out of the way and said, "Goddam it, if you don't know what you are doing, get out of the way," and slit him and opened it up. This other medic—I was just standing there, still kind of in a shock—grabbed the chest tube out of my hand and put it in him. And I felt like, "Will I be able to do this?" I didn't know whether I was going to be able to handle it. But I seemed to manage all right after that. That's where I came to stuff things . . . choke these incidents down . . . try to detach myself from feelings about other people.

The hospital was closing down. Anybody who had less than six months would be transferred to another outfit, and there were no orders cut on me specifically as to where I was to go. So I remember going back to the replacement center down at Long Binh and hanging around there for a day. They asked me if I wanted to volunteer for dustoff—medivac [medical evacuation helicopter]. And I asked them, "Why volunteer?" And they said, "Dustoff is an all-volunteer outfit." That was the only way you could get in. And I said, "Why not?" He said, "Well, they have a very high mortality rate." It was like 95 percent or something. It was real high.

I thought it might be better. I was real small and questioned myself out in the field—whether I would be capable of helping someone who was downed out there. And so I thought maybe I'd volunteer for dust-off. When I got there, there were four medics in the unit—and all of them were real short [on days remaining in their tours]. And so when I told them I was a medic, they started saying, "He's my medic! He's my medic! No! He's mine!" I was the replacement, and they were fighting amongst themselves as to who I am going to be replacing. So I replaced a guy named Charlie Martinez. He gave me his M-79 grenade launcher. I went on a few missions with Charlie.

I flew later that week with him, and we went into an LZ that was hot. We were flying out of the LZ—we were taking fire, we were returning fire—and we were taking still more fire. All of a sudden Charlie grabbed the pilot's armor plate—slid it back and got back behind it . . . and the pilot screamed, "Push my armor plating forward!" And Charlie was saying, "Fuck you! I'm short! I only got a few days left, and I ain't going to buy one for you!" The pilot yelled, "What if I get hit?" And Charlie yelled, "Well then I'll kick your sorry ass outa there and fly it home!" They taught us how—later on, they taught us how to fly—all the crew chiefs, all the medics—in case the pilots got shot. So anyway, Charlie was laughing—the pilot was so scared—he was a newbie pilot. He didn't say much about it, and Charlie never got into trouble.

One day we flew into this paddy, surrounded by a tree line, and we were taking fire on the way in. The chopper got hit . . . I jumped out and ran about fifty feet away, picked up a guy, threw him over my shoulder, and ran back and threw him into the helicopter. About the time I reached the helicopter, my crew chief was throwing a guy on from the other side. And I remember running away from the helicopter after another wounded man—and I saw three. I changed direction and went after the third one because he was farther away. And I kept going . . . almost got to the three guys, when all of a sudden . . . an arm reached up and snatched me. We were in grass about calf high, and he pulled me down. He was shaking as bad as I was. He told me those guys were dead . . . the three men were dead . . . and I turned to look and the helicopter was taking off.

We were pinned down under heavy machine-gun fire at that time . . . we couldn't even move. We had fifteen wounded men on the ground, all spread out, and two on the helicopter, and he was the only one who wasn't hit—the guy that pulled me down to the ground. So in about—it seemed like forever—twenty minutes or maybe thirty—our helicopter comes back in . . . low again . . . fast. It slowed down, but it never stopped, and I ran out to catch the helicopter, and the other guy stayed in the field. I told him, you know, we'd be back. And I jumped onto the skids, and the crew chief jumped on, and he had a guy over his shoulder. He was hanging on with one arm. He's about the same height as me—five foot eight and about 150 pounds—and I'm hanging onto the skids . . . and I pull myself into the helicopter and crawl across to the other side. I try to pull him in—and the other guy. But he's got this guy by the ankle now. There was no way I could pull him in. So . . . I looked at him, and I looked at the other guy, and looked back at my crew chief. He let him go . . . we were about one hundred feet off the ground pulling close to about three *g*s . . . dropped him. I pulled Darryl up inside.

He pulled his pistol and was going to shoot the pilots. Then he started pistol-whipping the pilots . . . and they were crying, and they were asking for forgiveness for leaving us. And they said, "Well, what should we do? Should we go back in now?" And we screamed, "No! Let's get some gunship protection before we go back in there!" So we did some circles, and finally two Cobra gunships showed up. And we're coming into the LZ again. And all of a sudden, about twenty feet off the ground, and I look back, and there's an F-4 jet, and he's the same height as we are, maybe ten feet off the ground now, and the pilot's waving at me as he's going by. I was never so happy to see those guys in all my life, especially after being pinned down and not knowing what was going to happen the second time in.

I'd like to share one of the experiences I had with the wounded. I remember going into an LZ, and we picked up eight wounded. They were really bad, and they had just got hit, and they really didn't have any time to put dressings or anything on them . . . threw 'em in there, and they were all stacked in a pile on the middle of the chopper floor.

And I began to work on this guy . . . he was . . . he had both of his arms blown off, and he had both of his legs blown off, below the knees. His . . . his hands were . . . his hands were blown off, and both his legs were blown off below the knees, and he was . . . he had a crease along the side of his head, and his brains were . . . coming out. And he was wide awake—he was talking to me—and he didn't want to live any more, and . . . he was a . . . when I tried to put a tourniquet on one of his legs . . . he started hitting me with one of his stumps. In the face. His stump went in my mouth . . . in the eyes . . . and . . . I began to . . . uh . . . I began to slap him . . . in the face . . . and . . . uh . . . he looked up at me . . . like a scolded child, and he began to cry . . . and he died . . . and I began to work on the other wounded. Just left him. And . . . uh . . . never felt like I had enough hands to do the work. I remember so many with their arms and legs blown off . . . and . . . it got so I . . . just when they died . . . I began to get bitter . . . and I prayed.

BORIS VOLKOV

I was in the army from age eighteen, and from that time on, I was in Afghanistan. I left about August of 1988. I was there in the same type of unit as the American Special Forces. The two months of training I had before I went to Afghanistan were useless. We had not fired some of our weapons, and we did not know which ammunition went with which weapon in some cases. When we got there, we found a different war than we expected, and that led to a lot of casualties—needless casualties. We had every kind of operation. We learned to change the tactics. Most of what I learned was from seasoned troops who were already there and learned by experience by fighting against the Afghan guerrillas. We simply were not trained in guerrilla warfare.

During the daytime, everybody seemed peaceful—there was hardly a way to tell who was the enemy with everyone around. They infiltrated during the night. These people set mines and traps, and they had all sorts of weapons. It was hard to tell who was carrying weapons and who wasn't. From talking to U.S. Vietnam veterans while we have been here, it seems just identical to what went on in Vietnam.

It was kind of easy to subvert the Afghan people since their life expectancy is only forty-two years. We didn't have to pay them much money to do whatever somebody wanted done because they were trying to sustain their families. You could only tell by little details who was friend and who wasn't. The response from civilians was varied, but as I know, feelings can be hidden. They can be smiling at you and keeping a stone in their pocket for you—as the Russian proverb goes.

I can't really give you a description of a typical mission because there were so many varied ones in a day's action. We would do a number of things, like land with the helicopters or proceed with vehicles—or on foot. It all depended on the terrain, what was available to bring us in with—mechanized or helicopter—but then we would always have to go on foot into action. Nothing was typical in Afghanistan. We were trapped a lot of times. We might get lured down a road that led to a mine field, or we might get hit from long distance with rockets . . . any kind of trap.

There was one action I can tell you about that was pretty bad. We got up for breakfast one day, and we were alerted to go and rescue an outfit that was under fire. We took off in our helicopters, which carried fourteen men on board. We got there and fought with mortars, grenades, and our automatic weapons for over three hours. Many people were annihilated on both sides . . . including some women and children. When the action was deemed to be all over with, we flew back. Our helicopter had fourteen people on it. The other helicopter thought that four of their men, who should have been on their helicopter, were on ours. They took off and left these four soldiers behind.

When we found out they left those four men out there, we turned around immediately and went back. Naturally we found that they had been annihilated. They were murdered. One of those men . . . rather than being taken prisoner . . . killed himself by falling on a hand grenade . . . there wasn't much of him left for us to pick up. We lost four men for no reason.

RON MITSCHER

I left Fort Lewis, and I flew to Anchorage, Alaska; Anchorage to Kyoto, Japan; Kyoto to Cam Ranh Bay, Vietnam. I remember very distinctly arriving in Cam Ranh Bay. Cam Ranh Bay is a very pretty area. It was all white sand and weedy grass growing near the big Air Force installation. It was very pretty. They flew us in and put us on these Air Force buses. The funny thing about the buses was they had wire mesh on the windows on the outside so nobody could throw a hand grenade through the windows. As I was riding in on the bus to bunk overnight, I thought, "Well, you're here." I didn't know if I had made the right decision or not. I took a look at myself and said, "Look, unless you can walk on water, it's a long swim home." When I got to the field, I found out there were no tanks, so they just made me a gunner. Actually, I was supposed to be in the platoon sergeant's tank, but he was on R&R in Hawaii. Three days after I was in-country, the tank was coming back in to get replacements. It got hit with a B-40 rocket, and everyone on the tank was killed. The first lucky break was for me.

We had a lot of field operations along the Cambodian border, and we stayed out in the bush at that time for about four months. I experienced everything from small-type ambushes to artillery coming in and a loss of a few APCs [Armored Personnel Carriers]. A lot of my war experience is jumbled. It is hard for me to remember what happened when. The main reason for that is that until I got home from Vietnam, I did not know what the major cities were like in Vietnam. The only thing I had seen were what they called field maps—small gray maps that distinguished the area.

As far as giving you a taste of what it feels like to be in Vietnam, I have two incidents. The first takes place at what's called Dak Ya-Ayun Pass. It was quite an historical area. French Mobile Group One Hundred had been wiped out there during the Indochina War with the French. They had lost a complete mobile battalion. We came in from the bush, and we're going to go on road security. We found out in the morning that we had actually slept in a French graveyard. There were a lot of tombstones, with a lot of small undergrowth about them, so we really didn't visualize it as a graveyard until morning. We were supposed to be guarding resupply.

One morning about ten thirty, I was looking for a couple of pieces of bamboo to make a shelter. I must have been fifty to seventy-five yards into the wood line, and I got into a clump of bamboo that was the right size I wanted. I wasn't armed, and I didn't have a machete. As I turned to go back, there was an NVA soldier there. He apparently thought I had seen him and was going back to warn the others. What I actually had done was prematurely set off an ambush. All I can remember covering that last fifty to seventy-five yards going back was . . . all I can remember is taking the final two steps to the tank. Looking back on it, I went into tunnel vision. It only allowed me to see what I needed to do to get back. The soldier was firing at me, and I could see and hear his AK-47 rounds going by me. I jumped on the tank and . . . I turned it toward the NVA I had seen . . . and when I pulled the trigger, he disappeared. He completely disintegrated.

In the meantime, we had a truck convoy coming up behind us. I fired down the wood line. What happened was they fired a couple of B-40s at us. A friend named Carl Singleton dove under the tank and came up on the other end trying to find a place to get in. I got him in the driver's seat. It wasn't a minute later that we had a B-40 going underneath our tank. A B-40 is an armor-piercing weapon. As I think back on it, I still find it hard to believe that guy with the AK-47 could have missed me. I have nightmares about it. I see his face in my dreams. One major issue for me is letting that go, trying to get rid of those nightmares. No matter what nightmare I have about Vietnam, no matter what situation, his face is always in the situation.

The next incident happened when we set up in the wood line, which is unusual. Normally, the tanks and tracks are not set up in a wood line if they do not have to be. We had been running sweeps all day long. A little before midnight, I was woken up for my watch. I checked the radio, checked the batteries, and I had just stepped inside and checked my watch when the tank next to me caught two B-40s. The guy on watch manning the guns was killed right away. I can still see the flash . . . the shrapnel cutting the back of his head. There was a guy sleeping in the rack, which was like a carrier rack on the back of the tank. He was hit severely with shrapnel. I had three AK-47 slugs go through what I was using for cover, which was just some dirty clothes and stuff like that in a bag. Those three slugs stopped in my ammo kit, which I was using as a kit for my tooth brush and personal belongings.

The situation brings up a lot of anger in me, because we had a captain in the field at that time who was out there to make himself look good. Basically, the career officer in Vietnam learned from his NCOs. If you didn't know what you were doing, you looked to the next guy down. It didn't matter what the hell your rank was. You had to learn from being in-country and being there a while—like setting up in tree lines. Some people in authority didn't learn. It cost people's lives.

I wish there was more I could do to help explain the war. The feeling of a lot of us guys who went was whether what we were doing was right. We questioned that once a day or at a certain stage of the war. We questioned the resolve of the people who sent us. I've seen what the North Vietnamese did inside the villages to people or to the local population if they did not cooperate. They would go in, and if they were in a village that was not per se friendly or cooperative, they would actually pick out the chief or whoever in that village and kill him or take his wife and have twenty guys jump her bones and then fuck and kill her, and the same thing with his daughters until somebody in the village would cooperate. It's terrorism, just plain terrorism. You can't blame people for cooperating in situations like that.

I've talked to some people after the war who fought with some fairly decent South Vietnamese units. I, at the time, hated the little beggars. I felt they wouldn't fight for their own country. One of the things that I've heard since is that if you were an ARVN and you weren't in such an elite unit—if you were in just, per se, a regular army unit, you may not get paid because your battalion commander or company commander steals your pay. You may never get paid or get just enough to keep you going. If you get your leg blown off, Saigon may not pay you your pension—whatever little bit it was. It's very hard to work in the rice paddies with no hands and no legs. I think some of the ARVNs just wanted peace. They were just tired. They didn't care who ran the damned country. Our big mistake there in the beginning was that the ARVN and the American soldier should have fought side by side. That would have instilled a type of spirit.

I think Bobby Kennedy had it right. We should never have committed troops to Southeast Asia . . . but on the other side, I believe that what I did was right. When my president and my country asked me to go to war, I went. I thought it was wrong for people to withdraw their support without withdrawing the troops. We didn't decide government policy. We just did our job, just like the guy who may not have liked the war had a job, too. I think that when you volunteer for something, as I had, I think you're always going to be more shattered than any other person. Some of the younger people got back from the war and said, "Hey, this damned thing wasn't any good. I'll protest the war." I got sucked into something. What was I going to do—go out in the street and hold a protest sign? What I felt like was, "You're a damned fool," because I didn't have to go. So those values inside of me were just as difficult as the younger guy who really believed at seventeen.

PHILEMON PEARSON

We was on the ship out of Oakland for a total of twenty-three days. On the way, we stopped at White Beach on Okinawa. While we were there, there was a fire in the brig. The guard was outside the door to the brig, but he didn't have the key. A sergeant had the key, and he was off the ship. We lost three soldiers inside the brig from smoke inhalation.

Finally we got to Qui Nhon, and they said we could get off the ship. "Here we go!" My job was to stay with the KW-7 [classified communications equipment], so I didn't have to carry all that junk on my back. In full gear, we're getting off the ship on these nets made out of really thick ropes. We're climbing over the side of this doggone ship, and I'm ready to fight. I had an M-14, as did all of us in my battalion. We climbed down into these Mike Boats [landing boats], and they're telling us, "Lock and load. Pay attention to detail, and you guys on the KW-7s, whatever you do, don't leave them." Now then—this is the truth of the matter—the Mike Boats got to the beach, dropped the front . . . and goddamned if it wasn't an American band on the beach with some Vietnamese girls with flowers around their necks. I said, "Well, there goes the John Wayne part of it."

I was really expecting to dig in. We was going through the pass between Qui Nhon and An Khe—they did tell us that, but what they didn't tell us was that there was going to be American troops over our heads on the hills. We did not know that. We just knew we was going through the pass, then they said, "Lock and load," so I loaded my weapon . . . scared to death. Finally we got to An Khe, still scared to death. This was where our base camp was going to be. We was adopted by the 1st Cav. Division Headquarters at An Khe. The reason we was adopted was that our guns was so large, it took them four months to catch up to us. They was vehicle-mounted and could fire twenty-six miles. Meanwhile, we really were adopted by the 1st Cav. Patrols—you name it, we're doing it. We had no training with helicopters or the 1st Cav. tactics, so when the duty roster started coming down, we just did it—we just did what we had to do.

So that went on for a while, then we got hit one night, and yours truly couldn't put his magazine in his weapon. I just couldn't get it in there. So we had this little bang-bang. We never saw a target—never . . . just never saw a target. Whap! Whap! all around you, and you Whap! Whap! back at whatever you think is shooting at you.

Then, all of a sudden, we got pulled out of the field to go to Camp Holloway, which was an army base. There were a lot of helicopters there. I thought it was going to be a cool set at Holloway. We'll get some beer and whatever—*wronng*. They put us over by some helicopters. We was physically loading GI bodies in the Con-Ex storage containers. It was Con-Ex containers with metal doors on them. Our main job was just to get them off the army mules . . . whatever they were on . . . and put them in the containers. God only knows where the Army took them. When we were putting in bodies, we didn't have time to lay them neatly. This is dead weight, and you're doing what you're instructed to do. In some cases, you heard a moan or something. One of the guys I was with said, "Look, if you threw a bunch of bodies on a guy back there who's got some air in him, it's got to go somewhere." I went for that then . . . but it bothers me to this day. We had got hit real bad . . . somebody was wiping out Americans like you wouldn't believe.

We stayed in An Khe approximately four months, right by Hong Kong Mountain. There were snipers on that mountain, no doubt about it. Somebody would get shot every once in a while. We were allowed to go to An Khe Village, which I don't think was wise. It only lasted a couple of weeks. I did go down and get a haircut, but you had to travel in groups. One night they hit the radio station on top of Hong Kong Mountain. I didn't think much about it. They usually took their bodies out with them, but we did find some bodies, and damned if the guy that was cutting my hair wasn't one of the VC they found on the mountain. I thought it was like the neighborhood back home, but that told me how serious things was . . . I had trusted this man.

Finally we got to Pleiku. Our base camp area was a big grassy mountain with a statue on top—I think it was St. Christopher. It wasn't Mother Mary, and it definitely wasn't Jesus, or I'd have been up there constantly. We had to build a base camp. We dug in bunkers, we laid a mine field. It was Bouncing Betties in diamond clusters. God, there was a lot of mines.

We had an early-warning fence, which is to keep cows out. Then we had a second warning fence, and then there was the mine field, so if you came through that first fence—if you're smart at all—you turn around and go back. If you came through the second one, you was in no-no land. The VC did that—came right through the second wire, through the mine field, and booby-trapped the little airfield we had for the bird-dog aircraft, and they went back out. Diamond clusters—can you believe that? That's four mines in the shape of a diamond, one at each corner. Bouncing Betties—three prongs sticking out of the ground, and if you look at one too hard, it's going to come out of the ground and WHAMMO! Those VC went in *and* out.

A brigade came over from the United States several months after we got set up, and they decided they wanted the mine field dug up, so we contacted the people that would take it out. They said, "Where's your map?" We said, "What map?" They said that we were supposed to have a map of the field, but we didn't, so they wouldn't touch it with a ten-foot pole. The battery commander, Captain Solomon, said he would not have his men doing anything he wouldn't do, so we had guys finding mines and digging them up. Myself and Sergeant Poe was detonating them. I didn't really know too much about it—if it wasn't for Sergeant Poe I wouldn't be here today.

We was detonating the Bouncing Betties, and we were having a smoke break on the other end of the mine field, and WHOOM! I said, "Oh, shit! It's one of the mines!" We go back to where the captain was at, and we got three guys on the ground from one mine. Two of the guys was bleeding like hell. In fact, two of them didn't make it, and one was the battery commander. His feet had reversed—like his shoes was on the wrong feet. That's what that damned mine did—it just reversed his legs, and his feet was just like they was on the wrong leg.

So we would go out to the An Khe Valley as part of the 1st Cav. It was a pass that we were supposed to keep open so we could use the road. We would go out and harass the VC, and then they would harass us. We'd stay there two weeks, and then we'd just leave it—just leave it—

Horror, Abjection, and the Experience of Contemporary Warfare

then we had to go back and take it back again all over again. We would integrate with other outfits sometimes. You never did know who you was going to be with or what the mission was. Your job was to be at this point, with this vehicle, and this equipment, at whatever time, and you would fall in. You just never knew where the hell you was going, and this went on for the rest of the tour.

That tour basically confused me. That's where my nightmares start—at An Khe—but I got out of there in one piece. I was glad to get back home. On the way back, we landed in Hawaii, and I tried to call my mother and tell her I was safe and in Hawaii. I went home, and me and Mom cried for seven days. I went to Augsburg, Germany, from there. I was married to a Korean wife, and we went to Augsburg, and damned if I didn't hit another levy to go back to Vietnam for fourteen months—can you believe that?

Here we go back to the fucking Nam. I was assigned to the 86th Signal Battalion in Cu Chi . . . that's Rocket Junction. That's where I found out how to get nervous. Cu Chi's my base camp now, then they assigned me to Team 99 Advisors with the 25th ARVN Division in Duc Hoa. That was the beginning of the end if you want to get all screwed up. Cu Chi was already bad enough because of the 122 rockets coming in. We couldn't shoot back, because we wasn't on the perimeter. Cu Chi was very large—citylike. So all you could do was wait for that monstrous BANG! Then I was transferred to Duc Hoa as a radio sergeant, and I was working in the ComCenter [communications center], which was superinteresting. I had the radio. If our ComCenter got hit and went out, our backup was the KW-7—Morse code, teletype, or whatever we could get on the air. A lot of information that was coming across is classified, so I can't give that to you.

But the incoming in Duc Hoa was bad . . . very, very bad. The 25th ARVNs was there next to us. When I went to look out my bunker when we had incoming, the bunker line was an L, and at the end of that leg was the ARVNs. We're taking incoming, and I'm looking through the window of the bunker to see that nobody is coming in behind the mortars, and I could see muzzle flashes from small weapons on our left—at the end of the short leg of the L where the ARVNs were. The ARVNs were shooting into *our* compound! That happened more than once.

The incoming got to where I couldn't handle it. The VC would normally hit you when you were asleep. When you slept, if you were smart, you slept with your clothes and your boots on. You'd take off your web gear and your weapon, and you lean it against your bed on an angle. You have your weapons, your pistol belt and stuff, wrapped around each other, so when you get up and grab for it, you get everything in one motion as you roll out of bed. If you miss it, you just miss it, because if you stop for it, you may not be around. I missed mine more than once because I'd have to get to the bunker—*first* to save your life, and *second* to hold your position. The incoming got so bad I was on medication. It felt like things was crawling inside my head.

The 25th ARVNs—they go on patrol with geese, ducks, dogs—and you're trying to teach them how to fire an M-60, trying to teach them to use their radio. You have to use correct procedures, and you want to make it short and clear. Of course, I didn't really know what they were saying because I didn't speak Vietnamese, but I did have an interpreter. We were sent to a place to patrol, and we got briefed by the war room. Here these guys are on patrol, and there's an air strike—B-52s dropping bombs. The coordinates we went to was an air strike—they had to have known that when they sent us. It was me, a forward observer from the Air Force who rode around in the Bird Dogs, and the ARVNs. The air strike hit, and my kneecaps hurt. My nose bled, and my kneecaps hurt really bad. The air pressurized, and I was confused. We got back to Duc Hoa . . . I don't even remember coming back.

I got interested then in Special Forces—I'm getting hit every night, anyway. I talked to the colonel and told him I wanted Special Forces because they needed me as a radio man. I went to personnel in Long Binh, and damned if those people didn't send me to an MP battalion—can you *believe* that?—in Saigon, at that. That MP battalion kept me busy communications-wise. They sent me to Can Tho, in the delta. We had an MP detachment there, and it was required for them to have radio where they could fire up in a secured area and communicate with the outside. It was supposed to be on the air base—Can Tho Air Base—or in a hotel somewhere. What I did was install the radio on the top floor of the hotel, which had an iron door into it. I had to bribe the utility people with beer to get them to put the door up. I finally got the door up and all the equipment in, and it worked pretty well.

In this communication business we had KW-7s, which is a classified piece of equipment. It was mandatory equipment to be in certain outfits. The KW-7 is used for anything except voice. It's beautiful. We can communicate with other people that have that setup. Unfortunately, it was only as good as your signal was from radio to radio, and it depended a lot if you was in a dead space. At An Khe—at the base camp—there was a dead space, for God's sake. We can't get out with any of our equipment. Sometimes we could communicate a little bit, but usually we couldn't even communicate from our camp to Firebase Hong Kong—that was less than a mile.

If a KW-7 went out in the field, regardless of whose it was, it was my responsibility to take another box out to them and take that box and get back on any helicopter I could find. In many cases, the pilot said, "I can't wait." That was great. Only rations enough for so many people . . . and you just don't know nobody . . . God only knows when you'll get back. I ended up hitchhiking a hell of a lot. The whole thing sucked, as far as I was concerned, because Mister Charles was trying to hurt people. If I was going to die a good ending, I would like to be with my own outfit. I felt weird because I didn't know anybody. They didn't know who I was, unless I would say something. If I said something, then they could say, "What outfit you with? What section are you?"

I kept getting a fever that I couldn't break for some reason. I don't know to this day what caused that. On my first tour, I got a fever, and they sent me to a hospital which didn't have a name yet. They had a Quonset hut, which we couldn't stay in. Finally, on my own, I got two blankets on this canvas cot, and I stayed under the blankets as long as I could. It worked, and the fever broke. On my second tour, when I was with the advisory team, the same thing happened again. This time, the blankets didn't work. We had no trucks going to the 3rd Field Hospital, so I had to hitchhike to Saigon. When they got the fever down, I had to hitchhike back to Duc Hoa, mind you, calling the 1st sergeant every day and telling him what my location and the situation was. Sometimes he doubted it. I didn't feel safe. I had nowhere to go. I almost went back to the hospital, but I finally got a chopper ride back to Duc Hoa.

My third tour . . . 1st Cav.? Duc Hoa? See what I'm saying? Remember when I got here today and you was sitting on the porch and I was looking at you and asking for you? I didn't know it was you. I didn't remember what you look like. This shit's for real. It's difficult to keep it straight . . . my third tour was nineteen years ago. First tour, An Khe—second tour, Cu Chi and Duc Hoa—third tour, 39th Signal, Red Carpet, Mars Station. Oh, that was a gravy tour. I was at the plantation. We would call LZ English and places like that—on weekends, especially. The guys on the LZ, we'd patch them on to their families at home—on the radio. I felt so good doing that. Some of the regular troops in the area had the opportunity, but I was trying to get in touch with the guys who didn't have the opportunity. One guy's wife just had a baby, in fact.

We wasn't in the field, but we had to go to Cu Chi once in a while with the chaplain. Once we was going to Cu Chi, and we got shot at. It's lucky we didn't get wiped out, because we had a bottle of whiskey, and we was drinking out of it. We got shot at, and the chaplain asked, "What the hell was that?" "I don't know—I guess it's rocks or something." We got all the way to Cu Chi before we found out we got shot at. I almost got sent to Laos—*wronng*. What's right next to Vietnam? Cambodia. See what I mean? I damned near got sent to Cambodia to set up a radio station. If I hadn't been buddies with the 1st sergeant, that's where I would have went to, too. I had a little less than thirty days left, so he just wouldn't have any part of it. I beat that trip to Cambodia. I finally went to the repo depot, and I caught that smoking bird back to the good old U.S. of A., and I've been here even since.

One thing I'm positive of, I wasn't sure why I was over there. We was restricted from firing when at times we were fired on first, so I wasn't sure what I was supposed to do. If you defend yourself, you could get court-martialed. If you fired first, you could get court-martialed. That put a lot of stress on me. I began to feel angry without reason. Not only with the enemy—I got angry with my superiors, too, because we would get our hands smacked if we did what the hell they trained us to do.

CHUCK SIMMS

I went to Vietnam to serve with the volunteer corps to work with a Military Assistance Advisory Group [MAAG]. I was really discriminated against because everyone there was Special Forces, and I was just a low-ranking security guard. They would not even let me stay in the compound with the Special Forces. I stayed in a transient hotel in Cholon. Somebody finally came around and said I would be training security guards. I got in pretty good with the Vietnamese I was training. I had a rapport with them. I was going to their homes and dating one sister. In fact, I dated two of them. I ate with them, slept with them, talked with them, joked with them. They reminded me of people on the reservation. They had a good rapport.

I had an old black jeep they had given me, and somebody went out and painted an Indian head on the side of it about three days before I got hit. One night we went out and got to the spot we were supposed to be guarding. We were sitting there, and I was teaching them lots of stuff. I had brought along some things that were like Doritos, and I was talking with a guy who was sitting on the front seat drinking beer. I gave him the bag of chips, and he gave me some fish and rice rolled up in a big leaf. I still like it very much. A rocket came in and hit the jeep right where the Indian head was. It had a hole in it that looked like a bulls-eye, and I couldn't figure out who painted it there. I was knocked out. I could hear voices around me. One of the Green Berets kicked me and said, "This fucking Indian is still alive." I woke up and was in a dispensary in the compound. After three days they sent me back to the place I was living. I went over every four hours for morphine shots. I was out of it. They patched up my arm where I got hit, and the wound was taped shut. When I came to, a medic told me that two of my Vietnamese friends had been killed. It was just like what happened with my friends at the Presidio. Death was following me around. My whole first tour just seemed like that.

I got sent home and had a hard time getting back to Vietnam. On my second tour, I was in the military sea transport service branch of the Merchant Marines. They have other branches—freighters, tankers, and people who like to load things. They put me on riverboats. That was right before Tet 1968. They put me in a French hotel in the Cholon district that really got hit hard during Tet. I was guarding the building at night until they had me join my boat. I remember one of my trips from Saigon to the villa in Cholon. We were coming down the street. Tet had started. I was on the back of a stateside truck, and a Vietnamese was driving me over to the villa. The civilians had a habit of holding onto the back of a military vehicle or any vehicle so they didn't have to pedal. It was really crowded, and this guy was hanging onto the truck back there, and somebody shot him in the head. It was a gory mess, splattered blood all over the place. That was my first bad experience with the Merchant Marines there. It was a hot summer afternoon. Every time the tire turned over, I could still hear the sound of that tire sticking on the pavement where the blood and brains were. It reminds me of the time in my first tour when I was hit at the MAAG unit and my Vietnamese friend was killed. He threw up Dorito chips all over me. I can still smell that smell. If I get near somebody eating Doritos, I get sick. The smell coming off the truck tire wasn't the Doritos, but it was something very similar. These things have bothered me all these years.

When I started pulling duty on my riverboat—my first day out there—we went out on the bay from where they picked me up on the river. I was shaving in the little room where I was with another guy above deck while the rest were below deck. Most of the guys were ex-military. They had been in Vietnam and decided to go for this job after they got out because it was pretty good money. They paid a lot more money than the army did. The VC started firing at us the very first day I was out there. A big BOOM!—and a big wave came on the porthole by me—and I was half-shaved. I ran into the galley where the other guys were sitting around and said, "Hey! What the hell do we do now?" They said, "Go finish your shaving. They do this all the time." I went back and finished shaving, and they didn't shoot at us any more that day.

We'd go up the rivers towing barges sometimes. That got pretty hairy because we'd tow a lot at night because it was too hot during the daytime. We'd tow general cargo—a lot of ammunition and grenades and stuff like that—up to the firebases. We'd tow up beer and cigarettes. The VC knew this. At night they would come out with their boats and board the barge behind us, which was on a long towing cable. We'd see them breaking into the cigarette cartons and lighting up cigarettes. Some spots were so bad along there that we'd let them get away with it. They never did take much. We found that if we let them get away with it, they wouldn't snipe at us from the banks.

I always carried on my private little war. I was there three years doing that. It's all a jumble, but I'll tell you about it. Vietnamese would give me information which I would pass on to Army intelligence. I made good friends with the villagers, but I had a bad habit of liking to snipe the few guys who would light up cigarettes back on the barge. I sat back on the stern of the boat, and I prided myself on putting out cigarettes. I can't tell you how many I did. I had another kick when I was on the wheel at night. The fishermen in the bay were told to keep lights on their boats, but they didn't because they couldn't afford lights . . . I really feel bad about this now. A lot of them were VC posing as fishermen. They would carry ammo and stuff to supply the other VC—things like that. They were told that if we ran over their nets or something, the U.S. government would replace them. I didn't try to miss them. Some of them would get out there with their little Zippo lighters and light it when we were bearing down on them . . . but too late. I got to the point where I didn't even want to turn. Anyone who got in my way, I'd smash them . . . I'd run right over the boats . . . and I could hear them screaming. After I hit them . . . they'd stop screaming. That was a source of a lot of nightmares . . . I hear screams of those guys I ran down a lot.

Like I said, I made some friends in my intelligence gathering. There was a young girl I called Linda. She seemed like a sister to me. Linda ran around with a skirt and barefooted, nothing on from the waist up. After I was there a year or two, she started getting some nice tits. New guys didn't know her and would start ogling her, so I got her some clothes, including a bra, out of the Sears-Roebuck catalog—which did wonders over there. She started wearing the bra and blouse and miniskirt. She liked miniskirts. She was just like a sister to me. I kept the other guys from bothering her.

One night we were told to be at a certain spot at first light. We got our orders over the radio. We never saw anybody giving orders—they just came on the radio. We were there by first light. Only the captain and I were up. Everybody else was asleep. We pulled up along the bank, and there was a big barge they told us to bring back down. It was up near Chu Lai, and they told us to bring it to Da Nang. The captain took the wheel, and I ran around back to hook the boat cable on the tow. I jumped from the stern of the boat to the barge. There was a lot of gravel on top . . . I ran across the gravel and sank down to about my crotch . . . when I got in the middle. I didn't know what the hell I was doing there. Flies started coming up . . . and the stink and smell was terrible. I looked down around my waist . . . and there were eyeballs staring at me . . . and rotten flesh and bones. I waded out of the gore and jumped into the water and washed it off. I scrambled back on the boat and told the captain, "Let's get out of here." He said, "Why?" I said, "Let's just get the hell out of here. I don't want to mess with this one." We took off, and I went back to the shower . . . and I must have spent an hour or two trying to clean myself off. That was my initiation to bodies. I never ran across a pile of gravel or sand on a barge again . . . I found out what was under it. They usually had a cargo net on the deck and then the bodies on top of it, and then sand or gravel over the bodies to keep the stink down and the flies off. A chopper would gather the corners of the cargo net, pick them up, and fly them over a hole and just drop them. They were Vietnamese bodies. Once in a while I'd see a white body. They are wondering where all these MIAs [Missing In Action] are—I know where some of them are. They are covered up in a mass grave—especially during the Tet offensive. They didn't take the time to sort American bodies out from the Vietnamese if they were blown to pieces. We towed bodies quite a lot.

We got sprayed quite a bit on the river with what they call Agent Orange. The choppers were trying to knock down the cover along the river to keep the snipers back farther. They just sprayed us, too, when they went over us. The first time I got sprayed, I asked an older guy what the stuff was. He explained, and I didn't pay it much attention after that. We towed barrels of it up the river to different places where the choppers took it out to spray over the jungle. You know, when you hear about tanker trucks going out in the desert at night and letting these toxic wastes out over the road. I'm sure that a lot of what they called Agent Orange or Agent Purple was just toxic waste. They sold it to the government back then. It was just toxic waste. It didn't kill anything along the river. Now they are having trouble disposing of it after the war. They dumped it over Vietnam back then. Now they are having a helluva time disposing of it. They can call it Agent whatever they want to, but I know that's what happened. A lot of crap like that was going on.

DONALD HEDGES

I landed in Da Nang, after a real long flight from Okinawa. We got our orders for where we were going to from a guy that looked about twelve or thirteen. He looked at me and looked at the orders. It was 9th Marines—he just shook his head. I remember that real clearly, because he was like, "You don't have a chance in hell." Dong Ha was the next stop, and I thought, "This is Vietnam." There were mortars coming in and machine-gun fire. I remember the airstrip got hit with mortars right after I first got there, and it was about four hundred meters away. All us new guys ran and jumped in the trenches, and all the old guys laughed at us. The stuff's coming in, but it was four hundred meters away, so we didn't have to worry about it—but we didn't know that yet. Later we got to know the difference: some things you have to get down for, others you didn't. You just get accustomed to all this shit coming in all the time.

Then we went to the Rock Pile, which is an artillery base much smaller than Dong Ha—closer to the bush, but it's still not the bush. We spent a couple of days there because the company was still out, so we waited there. The first night they set us in on the Rock Pile, and I wasn't worried about communists—I was worried about tigers. I said to this guy who was showing me my hole, "Did you ever hear about the guy who was dragged from his hole by a tiger?" He said, "Yeah, his hole was right down there by that river." I wasn't looking out for communists; I just watched out for tigers. Still nothing happened. The company came into the Rock Pile. I got with my company, and we went to Camp Carroll. I spent Christmas at Camp Carroll. Still nothing happened. The only impressive thing there was the troops, but they put on a Christmas show for us, and it was really neat. I was real homesick and hurting and lonely . . . the most miserable Christmas I'd ever spent.

I think I probably landed in the best outfit I could ever have been with. Captain Conger and Gunny Muldowny would just go up into the DMZ—just go into it, to say they were there and chase the NVA. They had a reputation for that, but we went back to the Rock Pile and stood lines. This was January 13, 1968. Our company was going to move down the road to Ca Lu, toward Khe Sanh. Our platoon got selected to stay back—we were going to catch up with them later. The road sweep came in from Ca Lu, so our company jumped on the trucks and went on down the road about a quarter of a mile. The NVA had set up an ambush in that short a period . . . and totally annihilated our company. Not everyone was killed, of course, but a lot of them were, and nobody walked back. We sat there and listened to it. We couldn't see it because of the terrain, but it was on the radios. Muldowny, the first sergeant . . . everybody was just completely gone. So my company went from 180 to 30 in just a few moments . . . but I skated it. A lot of feelings were left over from that, because I felt like I should have been out there . . . but, of course, that wasn't my choice.

We weren't able to do much because we weren't an effective fighting force. We stayed on OPs [Observation Points] for a while, and then we moved to Ca Lu. The Khe Sanh siege had started by that time—which was six miles farther on down the road. We were pretty much relegated to watching that small perimeter, and it was really a spooky place. It was small and vulnerable, but we never got hit while I was there. Not too long after the move, Kilo Company was on patrol between Ca Lu and Khe Sanh. There were NVA everywhere, and they were hit real bad. So we went to help them, and that was my first contact. I walked point up to the hill to where they were. I walked past Kilo's sentry. He didn't see me, and I didn't see him. But my squad leader was the third one back, and he saw him, and he opened up on him, and these two are having a firefight, and I looked over and could see I got two Marines fighting each other. I just stood there and watched it until someone finally yelled to cease-fire. I'd walked point before on routine patrols, but we never had contact. It was real serious . . . real scary. I was able to walk as slow as I wanted to walk. I felt kind of good about it, but being a virgin, I was real careful and real tense. I thought it was a big responsibility and was proud to be doing it.

They sent us in on the lines where Kilo was cut short. They were just trying to collect the dead and withdraw. I heard the choppers coming in—then my teammate comes running in and tells me to fire. Well—I could see *nothing*. In training I was taught to shoot what you aim at, but in Vietnam, you just fired, and hopefully your guys will keep their heads down, and you might even hit an NVA—if you're lucky. So I just fired, and we had a firefight, and I didn't even realize it. It seemed like we were just sitting there—just an exercise. The helicopters couldn't get in, but I wasn't particularly scared because of that. I didn't really feel it. We decided to carry the wounded out and left the dead . . . there were six. I hate that word . . . dead.

We packed up the wounded, and I had one guy that was slightly wounded. I had to support him—kind of John Wayne–ish. I had my arm around him and was helping him down, and artillery was coming in behind us, and we had flares in the air. It was a really spooky feeling. It was all new to me. We had two short rounds. It seemed like they exploded in threes. The guy in front of me and the guy he was carrying . . . they were both killed . . . I remember now. The guy I was helping was wounded again, but not seriously, and I was knocked down. But still, I didn't really understand what happened. It was my second friendly fire. I had been there about three months and seen friendly fire twice and enemy fire once.

We left those dead marines up there for two or three months. I don't have a very good sense of smell, but when the wind was blowing right, guys could smell them. Recon went in about March or April and got their bodies . . . all their heads had been severed. And I remember thinking, "Oh! This is the way we play the game!" . . . and it just filled me with terror. I realized there were no rules there—just whatever it took . . . and I remember the fear that put in me. I did that sort of thing later on . . . much later. Even today, I know I don't have to hit you to get you, and that's the way it was . . . they didn't have to shoot me to get me. I learned from that—it was real effective.

We went down to Khe Sanh in about May or June. It was just a mindblower. I mean—Johnson said we would defend it to the last man, and a couple months later we go in and tear the sucker down. It just made no sense whatsoever. They said the siege was over, but I think they forgot to tell the NVA that. We didn't make ground contact, but everyday, artillery—big stuff. It was so weird because Khe Sanh was so big. You could lose a couple of guys and not even know it. We lost two guys on our squad that way, on a garbage run. We didn't find out until a couple of hours later that they were gone. The whole time there was real intense. We were there until July. We had a great Fourth of July. We lined up every gun on the perimeter, and it was a real bombs bursting and rocket show.

We were sitting in trucks ready to go, and the NVA decided to give us a royal send-off. We were just sitting there with this shit dropping around us, and finally the trucks got going. I was sitting in the right-hand rear corner of this truck, and I heard the gunfire, and I said to myself, "There it is." And I hunched down in the truck as far as I could go, and a round hit about seven yards away. It was like . . . THE FORCE . . . I mean, I had had rounds come close to me before, but we were sitting up high. When it settled, I could hear somebody scream on the other side of the truck. We just got off the truck and pulled people off the truck . . . and I found an identification. There was one truck behind us, and they just barely got around the wreck of our truck. Other guys on the truck were wounded . . . there were only three of us who weren't. This attack was on the CBS video with Walter Cronkite. They showed that and the remaining evidence of our presence at Khe Sanh. They sent a truck and a tank back for us. When I got back, people were really surprised to see me because I had been reported as MIA. At the time, I felt like, "What makes you think that I'd be dead? What's the big deal?" I can see now . . . looking back.

By this time I had carried the radio, I had carried the M-79, but I had never been squad leader—then I was the squad leader. I was an E-3 at the time. There were three of us left. We were so small, I was attached to other squads. We borrowed guys from other squads. I didn't really have any skills. I'd been RTO [Radio Telephone Operator], so I knew radio procedures. It's just that I had never been in a command position before. It was my niche. I really enjoyed it.

I got a bunch of new guys from the 27th Marines, from down south. I met this corporal and introduced him to our squad. He was going to take my place, and he knew some of them because he'd come up with them, and he went back to the LZ to get his stuff. A round came in from the DMZ, and he got wounded and medivacked, so I lost my squad leader in about twenty minutes. All these guys had heard about the north and were so afraid of the north—because we fought the NVA, not the VC. Well, we felt the same way about the south—they got booby traps. I was trying to tell them it wasn't that bad, and then the squad leader gets blown away. I told them, "It's not like this every day," and it wasn't. I mean, there were long periods of time where nothing happened.

We got back from a patrol a while later. My flight had come in . . . DEROS [Date Eligible Return from Over Seas]. I was so tired . . . I had a can of beefsteak and potatoes I had been saving . . . I ate it. The next morning they cut an LZ, and I got a chopper and went out. As I was looking out of the window of the helicopter, the crew chief said, "I bet you're glad to be out of there." I said, "It's not that bad." He said, "What! Are you crazy?!"

I had signed on for a second tour, so I went home for thirty days . . . I was in the Crystal Ship in Eugene . . . I had this coat I'd bought in Okinawa—a nice suede coat. This guy says, "Where did you get that coat?" I said, "I bought it in Okinawa." He looked at me . . . I . . . I still looked like a kid. He asked if I was in Vietnam, and I said, "Yeah." He starts saying, "Don't you know the CIA is running drugs and getting rich?" I said, "Where you coming from?" He goes on and on like this, and I thought he was a commie-pinko . . . but he put the question in my mind.

Toward the end of my leave, I started getting antsy. I had several girls I was writing, but one I took out. I came home, and all I wanted was a cheeseburger with fries and a milk shake, so we went to the A&W. I had heard the "baby killer" crap, of course, but there weren't any babies up where I was, and at A&Ws back then they had a Pappa Burger, a Mamma Burger, and a Baby Burger. I'm sitting there with her, and I said, "Oh! Baby Burger! We have those in Vietnam all the time." I was just joking, but it wasn't until a year or two ago that I realized she might have taken me seriously, because she quit writing after that.

I was getting antsy being at home. I can't stand what I call "static cling." You know, people were more worried about static cling—polishing their cars, unimportant stuff—than guys getting hit in Vietnam. I was just having a hard time seeing what Portland—it was like I felt I was on a different level, you know? I had lost my best friend just a few days before, and they're worried about static cling! It just seemed that everything was so shallow. When it came time for me to go back, I wasn't afraid, I wasn't going to jump plane or break down or anything. I was still afraid of getting killed—actually, more worried about getting mutilated than killed.

One of the things I did when I was home, too—I bought a bunch of canteens. I went to a sporting goods store in Eugene and bought a bunch of canteens—they didn't give us enough canteens in the bush—and three or four packs. I couldn't buy any magazines, but we needed magazines for our rifles. I bought an air mattress—extra weight, but I couldn't get one in Vietnam. I hauled all this stuff back with me. Everyone was real glad to see me, and—BOY!—it was like coming home—real comfortable.

I got back just in time for Dewey Canyon. I was feeling confident of my ability to do my job at that time. Something happened to me while I was home . . . I still can't figure out what it was. Maybe I just got rested. I had one night I slept twenty consecutive hours and missed the Super Bowl. I slept right through it—I didn't even get up to urinate. Maybe I was just rested, but I had all this energy. I was real aggressive, and I needed it all, because I was in the A Shau Valley . . . and it was really the enemy's home. I had never heard of the A Shau Valley until I got there. I didn't really know what we were getting into. We were there fifty-two days, and we had some sort of contact—some heavy, some real light—every single day for those fifty-two days.

I don't remember much about 1969 except the A Shau Valley . . . that was *real* traumatic. I didn't lose anybody through 1969, except the one to appendicitis. I do know when I started to get short again. We were out on an operation where Khe Sanh used to be with an army mechanized unit. It was like six o'clock in the morning . . . all of a sudden I woke up restless—I was just waking up, and I heard a pop flare go. I could hear people screaming on the radio. The firefight was kind of incidental. It didn't last very long, maybe half an hour or so, but it was a turkey shoot. We were with an army unit, and they carried extra wire, extra machine guns, extra claymores—all this crap out in front of us. The NVA hit us just directly, and it was a turkey shoot. We lost one dead to a rocket, and we had an LP [Listening Post] out that got hit in the cross fire between us . . . all four of those were seriously wounded. But our casualties were really low, and we killed a lot of NVA.

This incident was a big turning point for me personally, already feeling antiwar. As a matter of fact, I was writing a column in the high school newspaper, and my letters turned from *telling* what was going on to *asking* what was going on. I had written some letters to the editor—one was published in the *Portland Journal*. I was getting letters from people asking my permission to send it to different places. I wanted it sent to every Senator, every Congressman, the President, and the Vice-President. So I was doing a lot of writing, and we were doing a lot of thinking and just trying to stay alive.

Horror, Abjection, and the Experience of Contemporary Warfare

After the firefight, we went out to sweep the lines, and my partner found a body. I went up to cut his ears off—some of the guys had been cutting ears off—and I just wanted a souvenir. I had already done some decapitation and stuff, not so much for souvenirs as for terror. I thought everybody was doing it. I really did. I'd cut their head off and put it outside my hole at night. I carried it with me for a while, actually, and then just dropped it along the trail. They'd find the head and not the body. This was a kind of carryover from when they decapitated those six marines on my first tour, near Ca Lu. But the ear was something I could take home. So I went up to cut his ears off, and I had my M-16 under my arm, and I had my knife in my hand . . . and I pulled him over on his back. He was laying on his face . . . I pulled him over . . . and he was conscious and alive. He had a little nick on his neck. I think he wanted to be captured. I took my M-16 off my arm . . . and I stuck it up in his temple . . . and I started to squeeze off on him . . . I had pressure on the trigger . . . but he was looking right at me. Something happened there . . . and I just pulled my weapon back . . . and didn't say anything. We had a tank with us, and I told the tank driver, "You make sure this one gets back alive."

That was the end of my motive there. We stayed in that spot for a while, but the energy was gone. The Laotian border was no place to be losing motivation. I had to find someone to stand my watch so I could sleep . . . I just couldn't . . . I mean, that was standard operating procedure, and I always did it . . . but I just gave up . . . and I realized these were human beings that we were fucking up every day.

Now at the same time, there were eight bodies in front of this one army position, and they'd been burned with napalm, and they were stinking, and we very rarely buried them. I always wanted a skull, but I didn't know quite how to go about it, because they usually had meat on them. I told one of my platoon friends, "I'm going to cut these guys' heads off." And he says, "If you cut them off, I'll carry them." It was no big deal over there—I really did think everybody was doing it—that it was normal. And this is something that has bothered me for years—because it never bothered me to do that, you know? It was actually a real effort, because they were decomposing. They were actually moving, the maggots were so heavy. I had this machete, and I always used a knife before. It's a much better tool. I was chopping and chopping . . . and I couldn't get them off. It was like I had to put so much effort into it. We put them in empty sandbags.

There were these army guys sitting up on a track, looking at me with just disgust . . . like I was real weird . . . like it was sick . . . I was sick . . . that they were going to get sick, and that bothered me a little bit . . . the way they were reacting to me. I got back to my hole, and I'm not sure I did this to both of them or just one . . . I know one, for sure. I took my knife and cut all the flesh off—took all the organs out . . . and I remember scraping out all this tissue on the inside of the skull . . . and reaching through this little hole where the spine goes in with my knife . . . to dig it out. I could kind of sympathize with that scratching on the inside of my own skull . . . and I totally forgot about that until maybe four or five years ago. Just for some reason, it came back to me one day . . . and now every time I talk, I want to hold the top of my head . . . because I feel that. But that's the only feeling I ever had about it.

Well, I had asked to extend—this was after I captured the NVA. My heart felt this big, knowing full well I was in no mental or emotional state . . . I didn't have the military mind to extend. What I think now is that news of what I had done with those heads had reached the command structure. I remember them looking at me kind of out of the side of their faces, going, "Well no, we think you've had enough, Sergeant. As a matter of fact, the full regiment's going out to Okinawa. You can still go on R&R if you want, but you'd just have to come back here for a week or so. If you want, you can just go over to the Battalion, then go home with them." So I said, "Okay."

I went over and chose Bravo Company. It seemed appropriate that if they were going to let me out early, it would be with Bravo. I knew all the people—they were the walking dead . . . they were just the most hardened men. I walked in there, and everybody's got their heads down, and nobody looks up. I can remember one sergeant welcomed me. This LZ had been getting rockets every day, and I'm sitting with the walking dead, and I can tell you, I was just going nuts. I wanted to run so bad . . . I have to say it's probably the most afraid I've ever been. The last day, we were sitting in trucks—they had the whole battalion lined up bumper to bumper. We pulled out—I couldn't *believe* the NVA let us go. Boy that was a long ride. Let me tell you, I was just going nuts. After we got to Ca Lu, I felt a little better.

In Da Nang, they had these pretty little Vietnamese girls in their long silk dresses—they gave us flowers and put these ribbons around our necks. They had a band playing. I thought, "Let's just get on the boat and get the hell out of here." I was totally demoralized at that time . . . I was exhausted . . . physically . . . spiritually. Every day was just like dragging myself through it. I felt like those guys I saw were dead . . . disillusioned. We got on the boat, a carrier of some sort. I can remember as we left Vietnam, there were a bunch of us standing on the tail, watching it disappear . . . we had this weird, relaxed state of mind . . . we just cheered . . . that's when we felt relief . . . we had a real rare blessing.

VLADISLAV TAMAROV

I was Blue Beret. You know this type of soldier—in your army, you have Green Beret? We have Blue Beret, and this is paratrooper's army—Special Forces. I was a sergeant in minesweepers' platoon? Bigger than platoon? Company—yes, company. The base was at Kabul, but we went a lot of places. I was there from August 10, 1984, until April 24, 1986.

What did I think when I come to Afghanistan? My training did not help me. Some kind of special training was good, but just physical training to get us physically prepared. I jumped three times, but for what reason? We didn't jump in Afghanistan. Everybody knows this is because when you come down, you're such good target for snipers. So why did we do it in training? Where I needed to go is Special Forces Blue Beret training in Soviet Union, not to war. This was a specific war, in mountains and everything, but they didn't train us. One time we came to a special kind of camp in mountains—maybe two times just. They tried to say for us to see what we see in Afghanistan—like this and that. But, you know, this is so fast—for a couple of days, that was all.

The real training was in Afghanistan. When we came to Afghanistan, I became a minesweeper because the commander of my company came to base and says, "Okay—this one will be in my company . . . this one . . . this one." He came to me, and he said, "Oh! A minesweeper—you!" He put a finger on me and said, "You will be a minesweeper." Okay—you don't know what they can tell you to do. They decide.

In our army, they tried to make us shit from the beginning. You're shit—rolling cubes and carrying balls, fighting—you're shit, you know? I don't want to talk about combat. I don't like to tell you about this. Maybe I can write or take photograph, but I cannot tell. I didn't know how I could do this type of work. It was dangerous . . . fighting those who were fighting.

I was always stationed on the edge of Kabul—the outskirts. This commander came to the embassy and brought us new movies, including some from America. It was our life on the base. Where can a man meet a woman—you know—the way people are just walking or working—just can do things the way they want to do things, not like they were soldiers at the base? Some way so you can forget for about two hours where you were. He tried to help us like this. The lieutenants tried to teach us to be stronger, to learn our profession as minesweepers.

The minesweepers—everybody thinks minesweepers are just testing the road. That is not true—no. Each car that was going away from the base, they need to go anywhere—each line of a lot of cars, convoys—at all times, these can only go with minesweepers. Mines were everywhere. All groups of soldiers that were going into the mountains had two minesweepers. On the road, minesweepers are the first in line. In the mountains, no, since if I am going first and there is an ambush . . . you know what I'm saying? The minesweepers couldn't come first, because if they are both killed . . . the platoon may come to a mine field later on.

My detector was only for metal mines. The detector is so heavy from Soviet Union. I test one, found this one—North American, and we had a German one—it's so light. So I have, ah, this kind and second minesweeper has one for other mines, and we have a special kind of blow-up substance, you know? Blow up—like this! There are two minesweepers—one sergeant who had spent a year and one soldier who had spent six months. The officers would send in "Greens," since they needed to learn fast. A new man is called a Green.

You want to know about first combat? You want to make me story talker! I don't like stories. I must tell about feeling, not about stories. I just can tell . . . I was with a man who was there six months longer than me, and he teached me everything. At first, everything was from surprise, and I can't understand anything. I thought, "I can't believe this! This isn't real! In six months, maybe I understand. A lot of noise and explosions . . . what this means?" I ask him, for example, what was this and what was this? I didn't know anything because I just came, after ten days, to combat missions. How does he know all this? I didn't know anything. He told me, "Just look what I'm doing, okay? After six months, you understand."

Actually, about after the third combat mission, I began to understand, because I can feel who will fight, how to fight—what happens, and what I can do to do this and this. You learn quickly, because you don't want to die. You must learn because you want to stay alive, and you must learn this quickly. He teached me a lot of things. I want to give you his name—Sergei Artemiev. He teached me a lot, you know? Everything was surprise for me. For example, some motherfuckers try to say I was afraid . . . I was scared. They tell stories in Soviet Union about these kind of people, and you know . . . that's not true. You're scared because you don't understand. You cannot understand how scary it is. You're a soldier, you know? You cannot feel afraid—afraid to die or this and this. I'm afraid because I don't understand. We were young boys. We were eighteen, nineteen, some of us twenty. This was interesting—the experience was interesting. For example, bullets were so close to you. You say, "Oh! I'm afraid!" Your body . . . sometimes feels this. You say, "My back doesn't want to go away from the storm." Just like glue . . . my body felt this. I listen to bullets that are just ten feet high or twenty feet high. In this kind of situation, there's a lot of fear.

The first combat mission, I was not too afraid. I just could not understand anything. I just looked at what everybody else was doing. I could do what other people did. This was real dangerous, real dangerous, but I didn't understand. In the action, I didn't understand why people were suddenly so happy until I learned our military cars and tanks were coming. We came on helicopters, much faster than the cars. We came maybe a day ahead—twenty-four hours—since the cars needed to spend time to come, you know? The helicopters are very fast. I didn't understand why everybody was so happy, in such feelings, when they heard this when they just started fighting. After that, I understand.

The enemy was all around us, everywhere . . . I didn't know this . . . I didn't understand this. When the convoy comes, the enemy goes away. I didn't know this. This is one of the first times when our leaders decided to start us from helicopters. They can't see you very well, can't say, "The Russians are coming! The Russians are coming!" You can go through the mountains very quickly. I was nineteen. It was probably my eleventh or twelfth day in Afghanistan. I didn't know it was dangerous in this firefight. I just saw people fighting.

I can give you one story. It was so cold in the mountains that we didn't want to go there. This was a special operation. My platoon supply sergeant, he wouldn't give me water, "Hey you! I need water for tomorrow!" "No! You can get it yourself!" Three of us ended up in the mountains, not so high a place. The three of us were in a fighting place, but the others have to find it, and they cannot come up there. I'm just . . . this was a feeling that I just don't know how to say. We didn't think about us dying . . . we just thought about how to stop these enemy soldiers. Many men were killed. Out of this group, one of three of us was the supply sergeant . . . I have very strong feelings about this. After a time of very intense fighting, we can finally stop. I cannot talk about that. . . .

I came out one way with some of the soldiers, and he came another way down. This was the other part of the group that was still alive. He was wounded and came to the hospital, and he is given the Red Star. I know if he was not wounded, this Red Star must be mine . . . but this kind of shit comes back always. The Red Star was only for if you got killed or did something very brave. That's why I want to put his name in the book: Victor Serchenko.

I answer for my wounds. I knew I could not fight him since I know I will have a lot of problems with officers after that. He was afraid to go into the mountains. One of my friends that was killed was given the Red Star shortly after he died. That's why I am so angry . . . it's not like this supply officer deserved this kind of military order. That's all I want to tell you about this . . . about my feelings.

When they train people to march, why do they train like this? Why do we do this stupid stuff? To show the high officers how good we are? How good we learn the life of war? The reason why we are good soldiers is to save our lives. We learn to save our lives.

They treat you like shit. No drinking, no anything . . . rolling cubes and carrying balls. Marijuana and alcohol—some soldiers on some special patrols in the city buy these kinds of stuff. When your home's a long way away, you cannot live this way. I don't know anyone who didn't test these rules against this and this. People used hashish. It was so easy—there were these boys around our bases—one dollar for a lot of hashish. A lot of people use this like I use cigarettes. This is so easy in Afghanistan . . . when you live like shit, sometimes you want to feel like you're not shit.

I had maybe six months—five—before I went back home. I really started to be afraid. I served fourteen months in Afghanistan. Now I know Afghanistan—I know this war. I can feel everything. I know what is this, what is this. I listen now to bullets that are just ten feet high or twenty feet high. You're afraid, real afraid, not because you're afraid to die . . . you're afraid you'll die with home so close. You feel home . . . you smell it. In this situation, there was fear, since how many soldiers are killed like this . . . just at the end?

You come into villages, and they're just people . . . just people. They look . . . who knows what they are doing? But I need to say in the English, my English—strangely, we came to Afghanistan to defend this land from people who live in this land. In the daytime, he's just working on the land, and at nighttime, he's your enemy, not because we have aim to fight him, but because he must fight us. In this war, we didn't think about a defense of our land, of Soviet Union—you know, our southern borders. We thought not about helping for some kinds of dreams for revolution. We just fight . . . we just fight like somebody sent us here, and we have aim to stay alive . . . that's all.

JIM GOLDSTINE

I went to Fort Bragg for the Special Warfare course and Fort Bliss for a Vietnamese language course, and about seven or eight months later was off to Vietnam. I was posted to an A-team in the I-Corps area located on the Laotian border about 150 kilometers from anywhere. As luck would have it, it was one of those places that nobody wanted at the time.

There were three captains that came in together. Two of us went to I-Corps. I got assigned to this detachment that was way the hell and gone out there in the middle of nowhere, and the second guy went to Khe

Sanh. This was March 1967, before the marines went into Khe Sanh and took it over. He'd been there about ten days, and the bad guys came through the wire one night, dropped satchel charges in all the bunkers, and blew his. I don't know what went on with him, but he came running out of the bunker and got blown away by AK-47 fire. Just another one of those little footnotes that cause you to pause and scratch your head, "How come I went where I went instead of Khe Sanh?" You never know about this stuff . . . if you try to figure it out, you go crazy.

I got a case of scrub typhus from a little bug out in the elephant grass and spent about eighteen days in the hospital at a Naval Support Activity Hospital in Da Nang. And that was an event in and of itself. I learned two things in that hospital. One is if you go in, you're damned lucky to get out. And whatever you do, don't ever go to the GunShot Ward. The pain and suffering is indescribable. When I got out of the hospital, I spent about ten days recuperating before being reassigned just on an A-Team southwest of Chu Lai. My area of responsibility butted up against the back edge of the American Division. I suspect the thing that is most vivid in my memory with that is one day we got to go into a VC area and play Billy Sherman. We started at one end of a valley that was inhabited by people who were obviously living in that in-between land that belonged to the VC. They grew cows, chickens, pigs, and rice. The food went to the bad guys. When we went into this little valley, we started at the north end and worked our way to the south end. When we got done, we turned around and looked back, and all we could see was smoke. It was like marching through Georgia. It was also a measure of my naivete in some respects. We did end up catching a couple of women that we evacuated the next day. It took about two months for me to find out what went on with my Vietnamese troops that night. I . . . uh . . . like I say, it was just a mark of my own innocence at that point.

Prior to Tet '68, there were many indications that something was going on. The intelligence buildup that I was listening to indicated that there was movement—activity—capability—but nothing that was happening. That "nothing was happening" commentary was quickly disavowed one morning about four thirty when a spread of about four mortar rounds blew up just outside the walls of the building I was sleeping in. Our offices were located in the compound of the province chief of Quang Ngai province, and it was like—CRUNCH, CRUNCH, CRUNCH, CRUNCH—the shrapnel flattened every damned tire on our vehicles. And I was lucky that whoever set that mortar up didn't turn the deflection knob a bit, or it would have been in bed with me. As it was, we had about an eighteen-inch brick wall between us and the fire, and everything worked out lovely.

In our own location, there was a walled moat that ran around the province chief's compound. Our building was located on the back edge of it. Just over the wall and over the moat was a street and on the other side of the street was a two-story school. And the bad guys had gone into the school and were up in the second story. We had gunships making runs on them. It was close enough that when the Gatling guns would make the final revolution to clear the barrels, we'd catch those rounds into the compound. We had a Con-Ex container set up on the wall. When we got to the top of it, we were able to shoot M-79s into the windows of the school with open sights—about sixty to seventy yards.

A while later, I went out on a heliborne assault, and just when we were getting ready to go onto the LZ, the pilot broke the other way and started making circles. About the second time around the circle, my stomach filled with butterflies, my knees turned to mush, and I got this overwhelming feeling of fear. To the point where I didn't think I could control my sphincter and my bladder. I was just ready to fall apart. When we broke out of the pattern and went into the LZ, and this internal conversation in my head way saying, "Goldstine! Stand up! You cannot sit there! You cannot *not* go! And you cannot be the last asshole off! GET UP!" And by force of will, I stood up—and I'm telling you my legs weren't working. I picked them up and drug them along. And I went off the end of the tailgate of the CH-46, and here's some VC in the tree line shooting at us—actually, they were shooting at the helicopters. Well, at that point, training takes over, and you do what you do.

I didn't understand that experience for what it was at the time that it happened. It took me eighteen years to come to grips with what that was about. Somebody was telling me something. So this business about intuition? When anyone tells me they have an intuition about something, I listen to them. And it took me a long time to come to terms with that and what was going on. I don't know how many other people had that kind of experience, but those experiences exist—there's something associated with them that's important. And in our culture, we ignore them—especially if you're male. So I've found, since I've had the opportunity to look at that—to deal with it—I listen to my intuition a lot more.

I came back from my first tour and went to the Artillery Career Course at Fort Sill and was there until around March of 1969. After a brief leave, I went back to Vietnam, specifically having volunteered to get into the 101st Airborne Division. Again, I wind up being fairly naive about things. When I got in-country, I found out that on all field-grade officers, the 101st had a veto. And they didn't take people they didn't want. They had some very specific management criteria for people to get in. If you were an infantry lieutenant colonel, they were command qualified, Army War College, and previous command experience. In my own case,

Horror, Abjection, and the Experience of Contemporary Warfare

I believe what happened was that there were some people on the G-1 staff who I knew, and with my background and those connections, they sent me on up.

I spent the next five months working on the Commanding General's special staff in charge of the perimeter of Camp Eagle at Phu Bai, which consisted of about two hundred bunkers and fourteen kilometers of perimeter. I was in and out of the office on a continual basis. My place of operation was located in the tactical operations center, which was an underground bunker. I was relatively junior, and yet I was required to associate with the primary staff on an ongoing basis. It's part and parcel of the way the Commanding General commanded the division. He required that all his general staff eat in the general's mess every evening. If your duties took you somewhere else or if you had something special going on on any particular evening, that was fine. Over the long haul, he requested your presence for a very specific reason. More business got done at the thirty-minute cocktail hour before supper than got accomplished during the rest of day. If a question came up, it was very simple to turn around and beckon someone to get into the conversation. Things were resolved on the spot.

I arrived at the 101st in the early part of May '69. I found that there was a tremendous amount of planning in process for a major operation that was to kick off in June, and that operation would insert one of our brigades into the A Shau Valley for the dry season. A little background information would be appropriate. The A Shau Valley sits on the northwest border of South Vietnam. The entrance to the valley is from Laos, just south of the DMZ. It's a series of trails that cross over the ridge of mountains that separate Laos and South Vietnam and debauch into a rather wide and open river valley that probably runs about fifty kilometers in length. In the earlier days of the war, the NVA ran the valley. They had caterpillar tractors out there doing roads, and it's always been a place of strategic importance in terms of logistical support for the bad guys in the South. As I'm sure you're aware, 5th Special Forces Group had a fortified base in the A Shau. It's where Donlan and Fisher both got their Congressional Medals of Honor when the NVA decided to take over the valley in force.

There had been no allied presence in the A Shau since the fall of the A Shau camp. Some of the information regarding intelligence becomes important at this time, and it fits in with the 101st strategic plan for control of their portion of I-Corps. When I left Vietnam from my first tour, it was about a week to ten days following what was the end of Tet. They were still flushing the bad guys out of the local village here and there, and the Marines were still involved in the Imperial Citadel at Hue. But it would be fair to say that the allies did not have control of the towns and cities along the coastal plains. When I went back in '69, there was *no* question that the 101st had that kind of control. They did it by having a series of platoons detached and operating on a daily basis with the RF–PF [Regional and Popular Forces] units in their respective areas. They went out, they did ambushes, they did patrols, *and* they controlled the night.

The move into A Shau had several strategic and tactical advantages. First of all, it created a situation in which that control of the coastal lowlands would be perpetuated by putting the NVA and the main force units' support mechanism even further away than it was. It specifically put allied forces on both sides of the hill mass just to the west of the coastal plains. And it put major units across the lines of communication of the bad guys who were in those hills. It essentially cut off their free-flowing routes of supply and caused them to have to deal with the troops that were cutting off those routes. The continuation of the Ho Chi Minh Trail through the A Shau and into I-Corps was cut off also, so that to supply their people in the south, they had to go further south in Laos and then cut back to the east along the gray area between the I-Corps/II-Corps border. All of this information had been accumulated and gathered and processed through the intelligence community and was supported by the results the 101st got when they went into the A Shau Valley. That supporting information came from captured documents and POWs that were captured out on the plains and were having trouble getting ammunition.

The insertion of troops into the A Shau Valley kicked off somewhere around the fourth of June. Essentially, we inserted two battalions of U.S. infantry and a battalion of Vietnamese. And we put another battalion of U.S. infantry in on a subsequent lift, with supplies and support going in. The artillery had been moved into position earlier in the week. The 155s and the 175s from corps artillery were moved around where they could be in range of the valley. Several days later, another battery of 155s was put in, so that nobody was operating at the long end of an artillery range, and they were always in a position to be covered fairly well with minimum range dispersion.

The battle that was so delightfully named Hamburger Hill by our journalistic friends was cited in the official history of the war as being the battle for Dong Ap Bea, which was the name of a mountain for which the battle was fought. The fight was precipitated by a classic meeting engagement. The troops had been in the field about three or four days and had kicked nothing out of the bush. On the afternoon of the day the fight started, the point man for 506th Infantry ran into an NVA regular at a split in the trail. The point man had been in some doubt whether to take the left fork or the right fork, but the bad guy broke and ran, and that answered the question as to which way they were going to the top. The NVA ran a few hundred yards and wound up getting some support from two or three others in his unit. The point man called for assistance. They maneuvered a fire team and over the next several minutes, every action generated a response by a larger unit on the other side. By about 1600, the entire battalion was fully engaged along its entire front with an NVA unit. They had no idea of the size of the unit at the time, but they knew it was flying hot and heavy.

The brigade's Tactical Operations Center [TOC] for the assault was located on a ridge line that essentially made up the eastern boundary of the A Shau Valley, and from it you could look about five or six kilometers across the valley at the hill—and at the same time monitor the command nets for the brigade and the companies. Walking through the TOC, one had a sense of what might be going on, but at the time, no one could really get a feel as to what was really happening. The evening briefing was such that we knew there was an engagement—we knew there was contact. There was no sense of the size. It was an ongoing thing and was briefed as such.

That evening at the cocktail hour, there were several of us standing around, eating chilled shrimp and drinking Jack Daniels Black Label and listening to the commanding general, who had been out in the Valley in his command and control bird for most of the day. The G-3 came rushing in and rendered a report that sounded something as follows:

> The 506th is in heavy contact. It's believed to be major elements of an NVA regiment. The regiment has the high ground and dug in positions on the hill mass, but Cobra and helicopter gunship support is on station on an ongoing basis. Our artillery fire is effective, and the battalion commander wants to take the hill.

The general asked several questions on details and then said, "Take the hill." As far as I was concerned, that was one of the most historic events of the war in I-Corps, and it certainly was one of the historical focal points that I had been around.

After the initial contact, it was obvious the fight was going on for a considerable period of time—it wasn't going to end in a day. The division responded with every piece of firepower they could muster on the hill. During the first four days, they put something like twenty-four arclight strikes up on top of the hill mass. It went from looking like a lush jungle ridge line—which it was—to a piece of cratered earth on the moon. They literally tore the top off the hill. There was artillery on the hill almost continuously. About the fourth or fifth day, our people had advanced far enough up the hill that they could make an assault on the top of it. In preparation for that, every CS gas artillery round in-country was procured. CS is a tearing agent used for riot control. It is a nonlethal gas. As part of the artillery preparation for assaulting the hill, the CS gas was fired in heavy concentration for all calibres for which rounds could be obtained. This was done in conjunction with high-explosive and white-phosphorus rounds. When the hill was finally taken and the bunker complexes were searched, they found several individuals who had died, not necessarily from CS, but from the lack of any oxygen to breathe, demonstrating how heavy the concentration had been.

The battalion commander of this unit was a megalomaniac. All of the stereotypes you hear about people in Vietnam who were there for the ticket punch—this guy was one of those. He had little demonstrated respect for his people, and that lack of respect was probably typified in the way he addressed them and talked to them. When they charged up the hill, he was above them in his command and control bird, which certainly wasn't inappropriate, but about every third word out of his mouth was a four-letter expletive. Again, nothing unusual in that day at that time. What was unusual was that it was coming from a commanding officer, and it was in a manner that was personally demeaning to the people he was addressing—and there was no doubt that he was demeaning them.

There are certain individuals who, by their manner and their composure and their deportment, convey confidence and calm and bring forth the best out of people that they command. This guy was the antithesis of that. As for his tactical competence, I suppose he was adequate. It was difficult to tell how much of the battle was him, how much of it was the Brigade Commander, and how much of it was a result of input by the Commanding General and his two ADCs [Assistant Division Commanders]. Having said that, it's very difficult to have a sense of how many of the casualties that were incurred in the fight for Dong Ap Bea were because of the battalion commander's judgment and lack of sensitivity for his men, and how many of them were generated because of the order of battle that was faced.

EMMETT FINN

I was a second lieutenant assigned to A Company, First Platoon, 1st of the 8th, 4th Infantry Division in the central highlands of Vietnam around Dak To and Ben Het. I was actually relieved of my command at about five and a half months for being too close to my men. Essentially, I guess, I would have to go through my tour to get a lot of things you want to know, including why they thought I was too close to my men.

When I first got to my unit, I had been sent to Panama to Jungle Survival School, so I'd had additional training. I trained with the navy SEALs [Special Sea, Air, Land units] down there. I felt pretty well trained. I volunteered for Infantry Officer School, volunteered Vietnam, volunteered for 1st Cav.—but when I got there, I was assigned to the 4th Infantry because they'd had a lot of losses. They needed lieutenants.

When I got out to my company, they were at a firebase they were just digging into, and I was introduced to my platoon and digging bunkers and setting out the perimeter. The platoon leader before me was relieved for cowardice, for going into a hot LZ and staying on the chopper when it left. His people and his RTO did get off the chopper. He was relieved of his command. I was kind of fortunate in some ways. Shortly after I got with my platoon, we dug in that day and the next day, and then we were told we were going on a company combat assault into an LZ, which they didn't know if it was hot or not. I ended up being on the lead chopper going into the LZ. It wasn't hot, but at the same time, it was an operation, and I was pretty nervous about being accepted by my men and how well I could lead. I had an experienced platoon sergeant—I kind of deferred to him in our talks and told him I realized my training was without live ammo and an enemy in place, and I would need his help as much as possible until I knew what the hell I was doing in combat.

Five days after I got there, coming back to the firebase, my platoon was walking rear security for the company. We passed through a low area starting up the hillside. The point man for the company I guess had sensed some movement and stopped. I didn't feel comfortable where we were stopped because the end of my platoon was just barely up out of this low creek bed area. Just as we stopped, I had my people move off to the side of the trail. The ambush opened up on us. My platoon sergeant was hit first, and two other people were hit. I was at the front of my platoon, he was at the rear. I didn't really know the guys' names yet.

I remember throwing my helmet off and running down the trail to try to get to them. The bullets were going through the foliage, and I knew I had to get to the back because I heard the call for the medic. The medic . . . I was trying to get him with me down the trail. I got him down there and saw that Kuda was down. He had been shot through the legs. I started trying to get people to move out and establish a perimeter and starting laying down some fire because we were still taking quite a bit of fire.

I remember the machine gun jammed and this Black kid, Kokomo, was the machine gunner. I ran over there, and he had put the ammo in that he had been carrying with him. I told those guys when we went out that that was the last resort ammo. I wanted them to use the ammo out of the can because you can double-feed sometimes. It jammed on him because he used the dirty ammo that was convenient. There was so much small-arms fire going through the foliage that his ammo bearer couldn't get the can open. I ran over there, and I remember standing up and kicking him, hollering at him to get . . . I remember he was so nervous. He was looking up at me, and I opened the machine gun and got the ammo unstuck and they started laying down fire with it.

Just as I did that, this one kid, Bridges—Willy Bridges—he . . . Kuda was behind me and up the trail a little bit, and Bridges stood up and started running to get him, and I was just ready to holler at him to get down because we were laying down fire, and he was shot through the heart. He died right there, immediately. We called in some artillery and air and secured the position. We couldn't get a medivac to land anywhere close by, so we had to have them send a basket down through the trees to get Kuda out, but the dead we had to carry with us . . . we carried Bridges out.

That was in April, and we went to another firebase, Hill 826, and we did a lot of patrols out of there. There were two companies on this hilltop. They kept bombing a lot, all through May. A lot of B-52 strikes were between us and the border. Then they started really fortifying the hill. They set out concertina wire and beefed up our armaments.

We all were getting kind of spooked, and May 22 and 23, the attack began . . . the night of May 22. We were overrun. They reached the perimeter around eleven. Midnight was when they overran C Company. I was in A Company, down on the lower part of this hill. The battle . . . we had been receiving a lot of incoming mortar rounds and 122s and RPGs. I had a machine gun bunker with Harris and two other people in it, and it was to the left front of my bunker. I told them to take—there were two kinds of ammo. The duplex rounds with a green tracer—every bullet was a tracer—I told him to make sure he didn't use that unless we were getting overrun, unless he saw troops coming through the wire—to use regular ammo otherwise, in which every fifth bullet is a red tracer, and to fire in short bursts, so they couldn't get a fix on us.

I saw him open up with the duplex rounds—we were getting some RPGs from another hilltop—and as soon as I saw it was duplex, I started running toward the bunker. Right before that the mortar platoon had come down to my position . . . they didn't have bunkers and asked me where to go. I told the sergeant to take his men to Harris's bunker. As I was running down there, an RPG came in and blew my helmet off and knocked me down into the trench, and it dazed me. The next two RPGs went through the bunker window . . . two RPGs went through the window . . . killed everybody in the bunker.

We fought all night. They overran C Company, and we had two Puffs [the Magic Dragon gunships] on station all night long and flares and five artillery batteries firing in support of us. They were coming in up through the trenches. C Company was on the high part of the hill, and we were on the lower part. There was an LZ out in front of my bunker line, and then the hill dropped off again. I heard them massing on the other side of the drop-off at the end of the LZ. I could hear the NVA . . . they were coming up individually and starting to establish positions and starting to probe and getting into our end of the hill. We could hear them fighting hand to hand in the trenches in the platoon next to mine and on the other side. They . . . .

My call sign was Stingray. We were all fish, and Gator—he was a lieutenant from Florida, the 4th Platoon leader—he came running over to my position and said that he needed volunteers to fight back through the trenches, to try and take the hill back. At that time, I asked for artillery—antipersonnel artillery—to be walked in over my position . . . because I knew they were massing down there. I started directing artillery fire and walking it up the hill, and they started coming in up over the end of the LZ. We were just throwing grenades at them. I got everybody out of the bunkers because the RPGs were mostly hitting the bunkers.

Then I walked the artillery in, and there was a lot of explosions. As soon as I heard the pop in the air, I would tell everybody to get down in the trenches. They got down, and the antipersonnel rounds would come in, and they walked them over the top of our position. We kept firing. One artillery battery blew out its tubes because of all the support fire they were giving us—we lost three tubes of the 155s. They had two Puffs flying all night long for us, and they kept pulling the fire up around us. We finally took the hill back about seven thirty or eight in the morning. We were still fighting outside the perimeter, though. We were still receiving a lot of fire. They were retreating, trying to drag their dead back and everything. We tried to get out and bury the dead that day and started doing the body count. We encountered a lot of . . . .

I guess when I really lost it was the next morning when I went up to sign the verification tags for the dead. When I went up . . . I passed Gator. He was coming down the hill. We didn't speak . . . but I saw the look in his eyes. It scared me. I had to go up and sign the verification tags. I got to Harris and my men . . . . then I remember walking off the hill. I remembered seeing Gator's face when I went up the hill. I think when I came off the hill . . . I had the same look in my eyes. I don't remember anybody coming into my platoon as replacements after that. I don't remember any names . . . I don't remember any faces . . . I just saw all my dead and all the dead NVA.

We spent that day and part of the next burying bodies, and then the afternoon of the next day they realized the bodies were beginning to smell badly. There were just too many of them for us to bury. They realized that we . . . the people on the hill . . . they realized we were going crazy. They sent in the 101st Airborne to relieve us on the hill. They had bulldozers to dig a mass grave to put the NVA in. The body count was 685, or whatever.

A lot of times I thought—this comes only in hindsight from going into brigade headquarters later—a lot of the intelligence information was bogus and bullshit. We had horrible intelligence on the war. The job they did on intelligence . . . it wasn't necessarily bad military information . . . it was posturing military forces from this information, which was developed by the CIA—to justify their funding, or whatever. Everybody had a different war, of course. In the war I fought in the central highlands, I felt that what they did was use the 4th Infantry Division as bait by putting some of the companies out on hilltops. If there was no activity, they would move you on to another hilltop. They'd use you as live bait . . . they'd drop you out on a hill like bait.

I can remember they sent us to Rocket Ridge, and we did more patrols . . . and then I started changing patrol routes and telling people how to stay safe and still do their job right. I didn't always literally follow . . . a company commander heard me once changing the patrol route, and he told me I was too close to my men. In the field, I felt fortunate in that I wanted to be an infantry lieutenant. I volunteered for it and was fortunate that circumstances dictated that I was lucky enough to . . . for my men to develop a sense of trust in me. There were always things that happened—that they didn't go out on patrol sometimes, that they were hiding—and I never court-martialed them for it. I just explained to them how important it was to do that—that everybody's life depended on everybody else doing their jobs. It's not easy . . . I was caught in the middle.

I was actually relieved of my command at about five and a half months. In some ways, I guess my company commander was right in relieving me, but in other ways, I didn't think he was justified . . . I wanted to kill him. I have a lot of anger about that. I can remember his name . . . but I can't remember the names of my men. I have an amnesia about them. I try to remember their names . . . but I don't remember much.

Not everybody's a hero in a firefight. I had a platoon sergeant that had been in Korea, and he had been in World War II—when we were overrun that night, Sergeant Panger . . . the next morning, I told the captain, if he didn't have Panger off the hill in ten minutes, I'd kill him . . . because he hid in his bunker all night. I had to do his job and mine, too. I understand him now. He was done . . . his cup was empty. I just . . . he'd take the SP [Sunday Packages] packets—I wasn't aware of this at first—he'd open them up and take all the Salems. I had a lot of black guys in my platoon—finally Harris and Kokomo came up to me and said, "You know, Stingray, we're not getting any Salems. He's taking them out." I had to go to him and explain that the way I ran my platoon was you open the SP pack and supervise the men taking out what they want. All my guys smoked Salems. If there's anything left, we get it—me and the sergeant. I don't like Chesterfields, but that's what I ended up smoking, because that's how my platoon was run. I wasn't trying to buy anybody's loyalty, that's just what I thought was fair. These guys were going out on patrol more than I was. We shared things. My RTO, Joe de Felice—his grandma would send him all these dried salamis and stuff.

I had a real good feeling in my platoon. The Brotherhood I saw—I was there in 1968 . . . real hard times. I remember sitting on that hill where we were overrun, crying . . . because Martin Luther King had been assassinated and Bobby Kennedy was assassinated in that one year. I remember saying to Kelly and O'Neill that I didn't even want to go home because they were killing our leaders at home. What were we fighting over here for? It's like I thought I should just stay where there's war . . . a war makes *some* sense, rather than go home where it doesn't seem to make sense any more. When I was there and in control of the situation, I felt okay. I felt that everybody was going to be okay. Even when I lost people, I knew that I could do something. If it was giving my life for my men, then I was definitely prepared to do that.

I was sent to another infantry company. They were short of lieutenants. I didn't know anybody in that company. I spent about a month and a half with B Company, at 1st Brigade headquarters as a liaison officer. I coordinated operations between the Special Forces and Arc Lights in our area, coordinated intelligence, and flew to Pleiku to inform the commanding general of the Fourth Division on our operations and intelligence. I had that job for about three weeks, and then I was the Company Commander for a LRRP [Long Range Reconnaissance Patrol]. Their commander was killed, and the colonel asked me if I would take over. I said I'd gladly do that. We operated in two-, three-, four-man teams in long-range recon—did most of our work along the border areas in the west. Sometimes we were in Cambodia and along the Ho Chi Minh Trail above and below the Special Forces camps in the areas of heaviest infiltration. I was there for a month and a half . . . then I got sent home on emergency leave.

HENRY MINCEY

We got off on the flight deck of the *Minotaur*, and they ran us down into the hull, to the check-in place. I got my linen and all that stuff. This guy showed me where I was going to be sleeping. I was assigned to an aviation supply unit. That pissed me off, because I wondered where all this aircraft mechanic stuff was that I was supposed to be doing. I didn't realize where I was at. We were on station, but I had no idea we were on station off the coast in the Tonkin Gulf. Our station was called Yankee Station—we was in a war zone, you know? Gilman told me, "Well, we're in combat, so you'll get seventy-five dollars extra—combat pay." I said, "No shit? Where am I going to spend it?"

I used to think we were doing something really productive, but it wasn't that. We had something like thirty-five hundred men aboard our carrier. There was a lot of tension . . . a lot of tension—racial tension, tension between young guys and old guys—but not really any tension between units. It was just basically this new crop of individuals who was hardheaded and questioned authority. We told them we was going to work their asses off, but those fuckers didn't have *no* military behavior. I got 3.8 on my work performance, but military behavior was like 2.0. I guess it was because I never did truly grasp the meaning of it . . . I wanted to, I really wanted to, but I saw that it didn't mean shit . . . it didn't mean shit.

If it hadn't been for the racism thing, I probably would have been a damned good sailor on a military level, because I use work as an outlet. That's my way of keeping from going crazy or hurting somebody. That military stuff I just couldn't grasp because you see a guy that the book and boot camp tell you you're supposed to respect, because this person will protect you and help you out, and then you see some of the stupid stuff they did and you . . . at first, I thought it was just me, like I'm doing something, but then you see other Black sailors going through the same thing. It just seemed like no matter how hard you worked, what you tried to do to be positive, it wasn't enough—it just never was enough.

Then I saw, looking at the rank structure, there were no Black officers. Why were there no Black officers? Then I started looking at our jobs. Why do they always want to do this shit—why are we always doing the shit that has no reward in it? So I started looking at all the aircraft pilots, and I just learned as much as I could about what I was there for. I got really enthused about what was aboard that ship—stuff I never would have learned if I hadn't been there. I never knew a helicopter blade was pliable—I never knew that it was a wing rather than a propeller—actually, it was more like a wing. I used to look at all kinds of aircraft parts, trying to figure out what was the difference. Why was it this? Why was it that? I guess really, the whole time I was on station, it was just like going to school. I never did give a thought about it being in war.

But then you start talking to guys that have been to Da Nang, guys that have been on the riverboats and have really been into some heavy-duty shit. A lot of it was bullshit, but when you looked at those guys, you could see them really hurting, and it made me feel kind of guilty. Here I am, Johnny Badass, living the life of Riley, and these guys were really suffering—got head problems, you know? I started looking at it that way, then I decided maybe I was contributing in some way. I saw a lot of aircraft come back that was damaged. I just thought the pilot didn't know what the fuck he was doing. Then you see the results of war. I think the thing that really got to me was one day when I realized this shit's for real. A helicopter came in with body bags. You add two and two together, and somebody's going to . . . that's a real body there. They took them and put them in a damned meat locker where all our meat was kept. The navy carries a lot of frozen meat, but they were put in the same locker with it. To me, that was kind of weird, but what other logical place would they put it? I was kind of squeamish about eating—definitely squeamish.

We thought those helicopters were making mail runs, that's how stupid we were. They would come back riddled, and I guess what the fleet had done was lying to the people back home. The pilots and crew were assigned by unit to the carrier as part of their regular stateside duty. I got talking to myself and started thinking, first of all, that the water here was too shallow—no submarine was going to be there. It's too fucking shallow, so there goes the antisubmarine warfare crap. A lot of the time, all we did was move just enough to keep the wind speed up so we could launch planes. We were probably doing some bombing and doing some recon flights—whatever you do in a war . . . it wasn't until the guys started coming back, telling me what it was like, and I saw those body bags, that I began to think about all this. When I went on R&R, I felt guilty about that because the only thing I had to do was go in a bar, and I go back fine. These other guys got to go back and deal with this shit. A lot of those guys didn't resent it. I guess they saw planes coming in and saving their ass.

I had no idea what we were doing. All I knew was I was working my ass off, but you'd think at least somebody would tell you why you're here. Nobody's telling you strategy . . . I guess maybe an E-2 shouldn't have strategy, especially if you're aboard an aircraft carrier. I had no idea, really—I really didn't. I could not tell you what we were doing. If I was a POW and somebody had stuck a gun to my head and said, "Tell me what you do," I would have had to make something up. They would have beat the shit out of me, but they would not have gotten anything, but still . . . you were still there, you were still there.

I still felt guilty—I felt guilty for a lot of reasons. For one thing, I wasn't in combat. I felt guilty because there were guys out there getting blown to pieces . . . for the same motherfucking seventy-five dollars a month I was getting. I felt guilty about that and because I wasn't doing anything to improve myself. It was like somebody just scooped you up and threw you on a vessel and said, "Bye! If you make it back, fine. If not, no loss." I think that was the feeling you join the service with. You really pick up on you're expendable. You don't see yourself as a human being. The only reason you're a human being is because it gives you the ability to obey orders and be able to respond verbally. That's the thing I saw most imbedded in all of us—we was just flesh.

I'll tell you one other thing I really picked up on overseas was the way this country treats other countries—the citizens of that country. We think we are God's gift to this planet. Actually, we are some of the dumbest folks on planet Earth, considering what other countries are going through.

YURI KIRICHENKO

Different units trained for Afghanistan in different ways. The different ways they were prepared depended on the desires of the commanders—how they were trained. I served in Kabul. I was there from '81 to '83. I was in the infantry and the noncommissioned officer in charge of my squad.

There were a lot of commanders who were lazy about the military. There was a definite lack of understanding between the officers and soldiers in the field. I wouldn't call it animosity, but it was a definite misunderstanding. Some of the officers were the same age as the soldiers. It didn't happen often, but there were some soldiers—some officers—who were hated because the soldiers knew the officers could care less about what happened to their own men. I met an officer like that, and a very strange situation comes up here. These officers' sense of military values was to survive themselves, to eat well, to have something to smoke, and to sleep as much as possible. There was actually a lack of things for officers to do, but they demanded a lot, and it wasn't always justified.

This produced a situation where feelings were aggravated, and it was counterproductive to the sense of the group's spirit that ought to have been produced. At first there was anger, but then a kind of gratitude that they forced us to do this because maybe that was why we survived.

There's a Russian saying, "Laziness was born before I was." There was a joke that, for young officers, Afghanistan was the ladder to a decent career back in the Soviet Union. And young officers, before they understood what was going on in Afghanistan, would try to be sent there. They thought it was the quickest way into the Soviet Military Academy.

In spite of that, there were good officers. My first commander was a really decent person who wasn't that great of a career man—but this man really took care of his men. However, the feeling in any Soviet army is the feeling of dislike and mistrust of those who were back in Moscow. The general feeling was that those guys in Moscow were living well. They didn't have to fight. They weren't even in combat. They had plenty to eat, and they had no idea of the conditions that were going on in Afghanistan.

The first thing you need to know is that we went down there in the time of Brezhnev and came back in the time of Andropov. Until '85, nothing was discussed in the press at all about Afghanistan. Until the end of my service, I was personally convinced that I was doing the right thing by serving there. Only upon returning, after a certain amount of time, did I become conscious of what war really is and what that meant. The experience of soldiers who served in Afghanistan varied particularly according to what period of the war they spent in the country. During the period from '79 to '85, the soldiers believed they were correct in serving in Afghanistan. And they even had a feeling of pride that they were fighting down there. As I said, we believed we were part of an International Peace Brigade.

After that, when the troops were being told about the facts of the war before they went, they themselves began to realize what was going on. They became more reserved and began to hold back within themselves. Then in peacetime, after they got back to Russia, they understood they had been deceived. It was a lot more difficult for the soldiers after '85. They began to have doubts—maybe this war was a mistake. The hardest period was for those who were sent towards the end who already knew before they went down there that the war was wrong. Their feeling was that it was an obligation that was forced upon them, and they had no desire to be there. When they arrived, it was with anger.

There wasn't any alcohol, but there was marijuana and hashish. The war was strange enough. The whole idea of the enemy was very abstract. I saw captives who had their Communist Party card in one pocket and their Afghan guerrilla card in the other pocket. If you asked them, "What are you doing here?" they would answer, "We came here to defend ourselves."

War can never be noble. It's a very ugly business. Man is such a strange animal that under strange conditions—in strange situations—

you can't tell what he will do. Even before I got to Afghanistan, there seemed to me to be something—a strange sort of power of necessity in war—something awful that you can't do anything about. And then—toward the middle of the war—I was sucked into it. I thought I would spend the rest of my life in those kinds of circumstances.

Every year of a two-year tour is divided into halves. The first six-month period everything is novel and interesting. Then what I had been playing all this time became real. Along about the ninth month, it all came clear to me that it was an obligation—and also necessity. During the first year and a half, I had absolutely no fear about killing men. In that last six-month period, a certain horror set into my mind. I became aware that there was not much time until I returned home, and I got this horrible feeling that I was going to be killed. All of us who survived until we didn't have much time left struggled with this fear. So we threw ourselves into combat in order to push this fear away. There was one positive thing about officers. When they knew that someone didn't have much time left in his service, they would try not to send them into combat. These were desperate people. Still, men in the last period had a sort of eager daringness, wanting to be out there in combat.

HENRY TALMADGE

Within about two weeks after I left the States, I was in Vietnam—leaving a nice, warm bed for someone trying to shoot my ass off. That was really a fast change from me—a storage depot in Nevada to Vietnam in around fourteen days. Your mind is still back in the United States. It was confusing as hell—you know, your diet all of a sudden changes, and all that bullshit. I was assigned to a rifle company. The more I went out on sweeps, the more I relaxed, even though we were taking fire. All of a sudden they made us a Special Landing Force. They helicopter lift you to all the trouble spots. That's when we really got hit. There was a lot of setting up of the perimeter at nighttime, a lot of patrols in the daytime . . . setting fires in villages, shooting at anything that's not American.

Vietnam *was* different from World War II and Korea. I went over there alone. It's like walking into a chicken coop—a strange chicken comes in there, and the pecking order starts. In Korea, we went over with a draft, and I ended up with a lot of people who I knew. I really wasn't alone. We had some things in common, being new people. You still got the short end of the stick when you walked in, but that's to be expected. In World War II, we all went together. A ship is just like a little town, moving from place to place, seeing eight hundred people on a day-to-day basis. We had a lot of togetherness there, and in the Korean War, the same thing.

Vietnam was different. Even though they were the same rank and lived together, I think they were afraid of making friends. They were afraid of having a real togetherness—a real closeness. I think they learned really fast not to get attached, because that attachment wasn't going to last. We couldn't trust a person because he wouldn't be there—he'd soon be gone—DEROS, killed, wounded, POW—they'd soon be gone. We carried this over when we got home. Most Vietnam vets are in their third or fourth marriages. They don't trust anybody, and they don't like to get close to anybody. That was a lot stronger for me in Vietnam than it was in World War II and Korea. For me, one of the biggest differences was just being alone.

You'd hear guys in the rear say they went to a house of prostitution, they had a lot to drink, they were doping, or whatever. I didn't experience that . . . we just had constant bullshit. You're making sweeps, you're in the jungle up to your ass, you're going here and there—it was just constant bullshit. We didn't have a safe perimeter to go in. Another big thing was the constant fear. In Korea we had the Main Line of Resistance, so you could take a break behind there when you're not on patrol. On the ship in World War II, you could kind of kick back and tell a few jokes. A ship is just like a house. We had hot food and regular showers. Some days all hell would break loose, and some days it didn't, but you were getting to the destination you were going to. You knew the ship was going to be on station, so you kind of expected it, and you geared yourself up for it. Then you'd cool down.

In Nam, you were charged up like a battery, and you stayed charged day and night. It had a toll on me. It was one of the most difficult things I ever encountered in my life. When we first got there, we started sweeping villages. The Vietnamese would be sitting in front of their hooches. They were scared of both us and the NVA. To me, it was really traumatic, because we go into these villages that had been there for I don't know how long. They were beautiful, peaceful, and quiet people. We'd go in with our Zippo lighters and burn everything. We'd shoot the pigs and oxen. They didn't have many possessions, but their furniture was all carved. You became numb to that. You start losing everything that is important to a person. Sometimes we'd go on an operation in a sweep, and we wouldn't see anything. It seemed like they always eluded us. In some way—they *knew* we were coming.

Then there was the treating of the individual fighting machine all the same, no matter what his name is. It was just like he didn't have an identity—just a body. You didn't want to identify it. It was just something there for you to utilize to the best of your ability. That was a difference. But you could tell when they weren't going to make it. They kind of had a shadow over them . . . it was like a grayish shadow. After they were dead, then they really turned gray. This is how I saw most of them—this is how I felt about them . . . I couldn't tell them or explain it or say they had that shadow on them.

Another thing that was really hard, being that you are in a position where there's all this bullshit daily, you get to the point where you have a lot of hatred. Any time something's going down, you want to do some big things. I think all this brought on a lot of our atrocities. That kind of enemy doesn't have any identity. That kind of constant pounding definitely has an effect on your humanness. You lose respect for humans, then you come back here, and there's nobody doing *nothing*, and people are treating you like shit to begin with. It pissed me off, but then again, I didn't give a fuck about it. It wasn't too long before I tried to get back into society and function like a civilian and tried to gain back all the bullshit I had before. How the fuck do you get it back—or do you ever get it back? In Vietnam, I lost my sanity, I lost my humanness, I lost my trust . . . and I lost faith.

The incident that was very important to me was when we were up in I-Corps on the hills above what became Khe Sanh. They herded us in there like a bunch of cattle. We finally got organized and were making our move up Hill 881—they later called this "The Hill Fights." We had just traded the M-14 for the M-16, and I was the Gunny [Gunnery Sergeant]. This is in April of 1967. The M-16 would fire a round or two and then jam up on you. You're operating an M-16, that doesn't operate, against an AK-47 that's going to tear your ass off. You could only get two rounds out of the thing, and then it was like you were in Kentucky in the Civil War. You had to assemble this three-part ramrod and punch the round out in order to fire again—this was bullshit! You can't fight a war with a weapon like that. For America to put us in a predicament like that—it was a fuckin' slaughter.

Those NVA up there had brand new uniforms, new boots, clean goddamn haircuts. They were big. I think they were from a different area of Vietnam. They were lean and mean. They were dug in up there. We gave them everything—we gave them artillery fire, we gave them mortar fire, we gave them napalm.

I didn't like the son of a bitching M-16 to begin with. It was like a plastic car—you scrape anything on a plastic car, and you're going to have to replace the whole fender. Back in the old days, you just banged it out and painted it, and you drove off. You can drop an AK-47 in the mud and stomp on it and pick it up, and you can fire it. Somebody made a lot of money on the M-16, and it was at the expense of our lives. It's bad enough you got to go over there and really kick ass, but Jesus Christ!

Don't give me a bean shooter. We had so many casualties . . . we had so many bodies . . . that we ran out of body bags . . . and we were using shelter halfs to cover them.

This officer came up to me and gave me some bullshit about the men not having their rifles clean. I said, "Here is my M-16. It is clean. Fire it." He fired two rounds, and it jammed. There is this book which has the dealings as to day by day what went on. There's only this small paragraph saying something about how we encountered problems with the M-16 in the Khe Sanh area. That little fuckin' comment was a slap in the face. They were responsible for the death of those kids over there . . . then they'd say, "If anybody asks you about this, it wasn't the weapon. It's a dirty ass Marine behind it." It was only a paragraph, but to me it's like a whole book.

I don't remember what happened after that, but I think I just got tired. I got burned out. I remember talking to a doctor who had a lisp. I don't remember drinking water or eating or going to the bathroom. By this time, I had a year and a month to go. When I got back out to my unit, this guy says, "What are you doing back?" I said, "Well, I've still got some time left." He said, "Your tour is over. You get the hell on back. You've put your time in."

When I got to Hong Kong, I met this guy who had been a 1st sergeant in Korea. He said, "You can stay with me tonight. I've got some cold beer." I had brought nine guys with me from my unit. I said, "When do we leave here?" He said, "In a day or two." I said, "Goddamn! I'd like to get the fuck out of here right now." He said, "If you're not picky, you can ride in a transport. They had these Con-Ex boxes in them. There's about four feet of room between the Con-Ex boxes and the top of the airplane, so you can put your troops there." We got to Okinawa and would have to wait three days to get out of there. I said, "Can't we get out of here sooner?" The transportation clerk said, "Sometimes we have seats available, so if you'll be around . . ." I said, "I'll be around." We got on a 747 that was full of nothing but army guys coming from Saigon, and that was weird.

GABE GARCIA

When they drafted me, I wasn't pissed off. I was excited . . . I felt good. I used to respect that fuckin' costume. Today, I will never salute the flag as long as I live. I'll piss on it. I thought when I went into the service in 1967, that in 1987 I would be able to retire. I'll always be a warrior. They created me . . . they pounded that shit into me . . . KILL! KILL! KILL! I was in Hue . . . the rubber plantations. I was in seven firefights, two ambushes . . . I don't know how I survived them.

Did you know that when you got ambushed . . . you shit and pissed your pants? You're walking along in the jungle, and all of a sudden they're shooting at you. You don't know how to take it, and you lay there . . . for what seems like hours. The impact is so heavy . . . you don't even recognize . . . that you've shit and urinated in your pants. You can't move until you hear the choppers . . . then the enemy will leave. In my first ambush, out of the seven of us . . . only three survived . . . and I shit and pissed my pants. Anybody who tells you he didn't is a damned liar.

I was a tunnel rat. I'd go inside tunnels at night. I came back a hardcore alcoholic . . . I never drank till I got to Vietnam. I never went sober inside a tunnel . . . I went with a buzz. I never encountered people, just stuff from Russia . . . medical supplies . . . rifles that snipers used. It was against my religion and all that shit . . . but I couldn't go in a tunnel without two or three beers in me, and . . . to me, alcohol is poison.

The Vietnamese were very good people. I got a lot of respect for Oriental people. They were very good because they been fighting for centuries. I love them more than I do our fuckin' government . . . our fuckin' government got away with murder. We had no business in their backyard . . . how could the fuckin' government send people out there? The government murdered 58,000 motherfuckin' Americans . . . and they got away with it. Right now there are over 160,000 of us who have died from suicide. That's all we know . . . how to die. I've been dying since 1967 . . . I got cheated out of a life.

I didn't get wounded; I broke my leg. I caught malaria twice. In 1968 when I came back . . . I weighed eighty-nine pounds. I was mad at the world, and I still am. I'm not badass or a macho guy . . . I just don't know the difference. They created me . . . now they don't know what to do with me. They told us we were going to stop the communists . . . that's a fuckin' lie. Don't believe the books. The government noticed that our generation was ahead of its category. We were a step ahead . . . and that bothered the government. We were too alert . . . too bright . . . so they decided to create a war to get rid of us sons of bitches. Today, I still can't stop people from fuckin' with me . . . but I can break them of the habit.

When I killed my first person in Vietnam . . . I kneeled down next to him . . . and I felt bad . . . and I cried a little . . . and I kept wondering, "What's going through his mind? What is he thinking?" A couple of weeks later . . . I saw my first dead American soldier . . . and that really pissed me off. We weren't allowed to shoot at them . . . unless they shot at us first. Sometimes it does bother me that I'm immune to pain . . . yet that's all you hear coming out of me. We aren't this way intentionally . . . we just realize what a fucking we got in Vietnam . . . that we were used and abused. When I die . . . if I ever do again . . . I'll die fighting the fuckin' government.

BOB SWANSON

Out of the first six months or so, only three of our guys got wounded. One guy lost part of his skull from shrapnel. Another guy took a piece of shrapnel in the leg, and one other person's hand got burned from white phosphorus. I've never been a superstitious person till I got to Vietnam. The guy who lost part of his head, his last name was King, and he got his kicks out of chasing down chickens and chopping their heads off—and he lost part of his skull. Then another guy named Billy Mason . . . liked burning lizards and toads over heat tablets. He ended up dropping a cigarette into a box of unused powder. He reached in to grab it, and it started up, and he got third-degree burns from the waist up. After those two instances, I realized there was a spirit of nature that I hadn't been aware of before.

One night I remember, I went out on an LP into a cemetery. It was myself, a guy named Murray Lawrence, and another guy named Kimbro. We did an LP about 150 yards out beyond the wire, which they called a double length because listening posts were supposed to be within seventy-five to one hundred feet. The first night they went out seventy-five, and there was activity farther out. Then we went 150 meters, and that night the NVA got between our LP and the perimeter . . . and all hell broke loose . . . and we couldn't do anything. We were stuck out there . . . hiding behind this grave with a poncho over us, and tracers—our own bullets—flying over our heads. If we raised up and fired, we'd be giving away our own position, and hell, our own guys would be shooting on us. It was a real freak out, and all of us were shaking. Murray and Kimbro were both black guys, and I swear to God they were white. We were just freaked. And all we kept thinking was, "I hope they don't retreat this way." Luckily, they retreated the same way they came in—laterally. They brought us back in, and I was really shook up.

We later went TDY to 2nd Battalion, 4th Marines, who were called the Magnificent Bastards. We got into one pretty confusing action. We went into a village that we had just fired on and pretty much liberated it. It was miniature Hue, I guess you'd say. There was a building—pagoda—and a big church there that had been taken over by the NVA. It was right on the river, and they were controlling everything that went up and down. The fact is that they controlled it so well that there was a week and a half that we went without food or any kind of supplies. We couldn't eat what was there because it had all been sprayed. To eat one day, we finally went out and threw hand grenades into the river and sent a couple of guys out on air mattresses to scoop up the fish. We didn't know which fish were edible and which weren't, so we just ate them all. They tasted real good.

Our captain, who wouldn't let us kill any livestock—chicken or pigs or stuff like that—was later found out by the sergeant that he had two cases of C-rations in his tent that he was eating off of while we were out there going hungry. And my first sergeant went in, and he saw it, and he just walked up, and he kicked the little stove in the captain's tent over, and he grabbed the two cases of C-rations and split it amongst the outfit and told the captain if we didn't eat, he didn't eat. Course from then on we had very ill feelings about that captain. We didn't kill him. He didn't become a frag victim [an officer assassinated by his own soldiers] as much as we just talked about it. We had a mortar platoon that pulled in next to us for a while, and they fragged one of their officers while they were there.

Anyway, we moved to My Loc, and when we first came in, the first thing we saw were bodies all over the place. Andy and I had a chance to bury the dead, so our first detail when we got there was to bury these people. One of the things that I remember doing—and I really had trouble accepting this about myself afterwards—when we were digging the graves, they passed out food, and this one guy and I took turns sitting on the body to eat our rice while the other one dug. In afterthought, I had trouble accepting myself as being what I saw as animalistic.

We didn't even get the dead totally buried, and we got hit by our first mortar salvo. Between our outfit and all the others, there was only about 232 of us in this camp. The AmTracks [Amphibious vehicles] were gone, and we didn't have trenches set up or anything. We just had the guns sighted. So we fired over probably twelve hundred rounds within a three-hour period. Combinations of gas, white phosphorus, and high explosive. We were firing within fifteen to twenty-five meters from the perimeter. There were bullets flying off—ricocheting off the guns and everything else. We just had to function through it. We came out of it, and out of our whole group there was only about sixty people that were either hurt or killed.

We thought it was miraculous. We didn't even know what was hitting us until afterwards. And then, of course, they gave us the statistics. It was flat level, and we could see out there beyond the perimeter and see what was going on. We could see who we were shooting at—what we were hitting and stuff. And we could see bodies flying, so we knew we were making contact. The only part that happened during the battle that kinda screwed us up for a while there was a slight wind shift, and it blew the gas back right on us. And then the wind shifted again— WHOOSH—and we're all trying to fire, and our eyes were burning from the CS gas.

We moved over to Camp Carroll, and things calmed down for quite a bit—for about three months. I guess it had to be the last part of April to the first part of August. We got an occasional incoming—artillery fire coming into the base. We were so used to the bush that our first day there—we were at the mess hall—it was our first look at real food for almost two months. And I remember these trays of pineapple upside-down cake. All of a sudden . . . artillery! The sirens went off. We hear a couple of rounds land inside the camp, and everybody—the mess sergeant and all the mess hands—went running around outside getting into the trenches. We looked around, and we were the only ones left, and we ran over and started scooping it up! Afterwards, the mess sergeant came in and really gave us hell. He said, "Whenever that siren goes off, you *will* get in the trenches!"

Anyway, I got stuck on mess duty while we were at Camp Carroll, and I ended up getting into the supply part. I had to ride once a week to Da Nang and back with a group called the Rough Riders. We never got hit. We got sniped at a couple of times, but we never really got hit as we were going down and back. But I remember, we were at the supply depot, and there was a bunch of grape juice, and we were picking up eight cases—I think it was eight cases—for the mess hall. I saw that it was from Grandview, Washington—none of the other guys knew much about Grandview—there's a lot of grapes grown around Grandview. This grape juice just happened to be canned by the Yakima Valley Grape Producers. I don't even like grape juice, but I stole a whole case of that stuff just for a taste of home. Plus I was able to show the other guys, "Hey, look!"

I think the worst thing that happened to me then was what could happen to any soldier in Vietnam—I learned to see the Vietnamese as people. And I began realizing that we were out there fighting because we were told to, and they were out there fighting because they were told to, and I felt that somehow if we could get together under different circumstances we'd probably be sitting around drinking beers and having a good time together. From that point on, I had to be stoned even to fight. I had to get to the point where I didn't think of who they were or what they were—just do it.

When I was getting short, they moved us down to An Hoa, which is south of Da Nang again, and God we were elated. "Oh, boy, we're going south of Da Nang—we're back in clear country again." I was due to rotate on October thirteenth, so I was under a hundred days when I got there. One of the things that really hit me there, and I think it really put a capper on not being able to fight, was there was a dump there in An Hoa. We used to have to take stuff out there about every day, and I got on the work detail quite a few times. And there were a couple of kids out there I had made friends with. One was a little girl that was about six or seven years old, and the boy, I imagine, was about ten or eleven. They weren't brother and sister—they were just two kids that hung out there. And one night we got hit fairly hefty—we were getting probed— and we caused quite a few casualties. And the next day, we went off to the dump . . . and this little girl came running up to me . . . she was crying. Her father had been in the body count, and so he'd been VC . . . that tore me up. From that point on, I was gone. When that happened, I had only about three weeks left. They just sent me up to Da Nang, because I had given up.

DARREN GATES

When we flew into Panama, we got about ten minutes out, and I think it really started hitting everybody. You know—we were going to jump into a combat zone. About two minutes out, they gave us the two-minute warning before we came over the beach. You could have heard a pin drop on the plane . . . it was real quiet. Right when we got over the objective, the pilot came on the intercom and said we were taking fire. We were supposed to jump at eight hundred feet. They pretty much dove for the ground and hit the green light, and everybody went out as the plane was coming down. The plane started taking hits from anti-aircraft fire. It was weird though, because I knew we were going to jump into that shit. It was tracers flying everywhere, the planes were getting hit, and guys were falling down around you. I didn't see one guy hesitate. They gave us credit for that. I think that's the quickest we've ever unloaded an airplane before.

I felt better jumping out into it than sitting in the airplane, getting shot at in the air, but it was just pitch black outside. It was about one in the morning. I got out of the plane and looked around. All I saw was tracers flying everywhere—just like the Fourth of July. It turns out we dropped out at about five hundred feet—maybe a little less. It didn't give anybody any time at all to get oriented. Our job down there was to take over an airfield. I guess it was one of their major military airports or air bases. It wasn't very big, but it was major for them. They had two companies

Horror, Abjection, and the Experience of Contemporary Warfare   125

that were supposedly their best crack troops—that's what we were sent in to take out.

I hit the ground. I landed right in the middle of the runway. It was pitch black. I couldn't see any of my friends—nobody was around. So I'm sitting there, laying on the runway, trying to get out of my equipment, and all of a sudden I start seeing these tracers, bouncing off the runways. After the planes had flown over, they trained the guns on the soldiers on the ground. They were strafing the runways—I just saw tracers hitting the runway and bouncing off. They started walking rounds in to where I was at. I said to myself, "Holy Shit! I'm gonna get shot."

I threw my rucksack out in front of me, because there was no place to hide. You know—it's one thing to be in the mountains or jungles fighting—I've never fought there, but you've obviously got something to hide behind. I remember thinking, "Christ! This is like being in the middle of the mall parking lot having someone taking potshots at you. There's no place to go!" So I threw my ruck down in front of me, and sure enough—the tracers started hitting my ruck. I was hiding behind that, trying to become part of the runway. I was the RTO on that mission. I had been RTO for the platoon for about five months. I never really liked carrying the radio. It weighs about thirty pounds, and it's a pain in the ass to lug around all day. I'm glad I had it, because it stopped most of the bullets that were coming at me.

The fire swept over me . . . and the next thing I know, I hear what sounded like a full can of Coke rolling up to me. I heard it hit the ground. I looked down, and two feet from my leg was a concussion grenade, sitting right by my leg. I don't remember to this day what I thought when I saw it, but I remember trying to kick it out of the way. Right when I kicked it, it went off. It blew the crap out of me. It felt like God reached down out of the sky with a flyswatter and cracked me a good one. It threw me in the air, and I hit the ground, and I was all wrapped up in my chute lines, and . . . I was kind of shocked as to what had happened. It took me a couple of minutes to figure out what was going on. I pulled out my knife and cut myself out of the equipment.

I got my weapon out, looked up, and there were two Panamanians standing about thirty, forty meters away from me. They were the guys that threw the grenade, and they thought I was dead. They're standing there, and they both got AK-47s. It's really weird when you think about how easy it is to kill somebody. I didn't think about it . . . you just do it. I shot and killed both of them . . . ran up to them to see if they were dead or what . . . and I remembered back to how they had trained me in the Rangers. When you shoot somebody, you put them down and make sure they stay down. I ran up to them. One guy was dead for sure . . .

half his head was blown off. The other guy . . . I wasn't positive if he was dead or not . . . I shot him again—didn't even think about it.

Thinking back on it now, it's a weird situation to be in, because you spend your whole life with people telling you it's wrong to kill . . . it's against the law to kill . . . you go to hell if you kill. Then all of a sudden, you're thrown into a situation where you're told to kill . . . it's okay to do it. It's a hell of an adjustment to make in a few seconds . . . and I've had people ask me if I liked doing it . . . and automatically you know that they've never killed anybody or even shot anybody . . . because nobody that has isn't going to ask you a question like that. I think that if there's somebody out there that enjoyed doing it—in Vietnam, World War II, or wherever—if they actually enjoyed doing it, they should be locked up, because it's not something you feel good about. I've had people tell me, "Well, they were trying to kill you. That makes it all right for you to kill them." I guess in a sense it does, but it doesn't make it any easier . . . I remember thinking . . . right after I did that . . . "Oh God, I am guilty." It's a shock.

After I shot that guy again, I just couldn't stay there any more, so I just got out of that area. I went walking down the runway, kind of hobbling a little because my leg was swollen. I'd been on the ground it seems like about ten to fifteen minutes by this time. So I'm hobbling down the runway, and I saw a ranger out in the middle of the runway, just laying there. I thought, "Oh shit, He's dead." I went over to him. He was alive, but he'd hit the runway pretty hard and had a compound fracture in his leg. We knew it was going to be dark and confusing, so we'd spent a lot of time learning about certain landmarks on the ground, so I pretty much knew where I was at. He couldn't walk, so I picked him up and carried him off the runway . . . I started looking for the casualty collection point.

I took him over to the casualty collection point, and by the time I got there, it was over a kilometer away. It was the longest walk of my life, carrying him. I dropped him off and started looking around, and all I saw was rangers everywhere . . . guys that had been shot . . . a kid with a broken neck had his chute malfunction and was paralyzed and dazed. He's confined to a wheelchair the rest of his life. He was banged up pretty bad. Just everywhere I looked there were guys that were shot . . . missing arms and legs . . . you name it, it was there.

So I dropped him off, and by this time it was starting to get to me. I started walking off towards the objective. I found another guy in a ditch—Air Force—he was a Combat Controller. They jump in with us and help to work with air traffic. He had a broken leg, and he wasn't going anyplace. By that time, the adrenaline was wearing off . . . and . . . I noticed my leg wasn't quite right. I walked over to him and laid down next to him. He asked if I was all right, and I said, "My leg kind of hurts." He said, "I'm a medic—let me check it out." I twisted my ankle a little bit, and I could feel the bones crunching, so I knew my leg was broken. I had blood running out of my ears from when the grenade went off—a ruptured eardrum. He had some morphine with him, so I shot myself in the leg with morphine. We sat there and watched the war go on around us. Like I said, it was like the Fourth of July, except there were real bullets—no rockets, though.

I was on the ground seven or eight hours—not very long, but that was long enough. As soon as we jumped out of the airplanes, it was wild. Sometimes I sit here and try and think of words to put it in . . . what it feels like . . . and the closest way I can describe it is, you take every fear, every time you've felt brave about yourself, every emotion you've ever had in your life, and compact it into five minutes . . . that's how it feels. It's hard to put in words. If I ever have a son, I hope to God he never has to go through that—and everybody else's kid out there. I'm sure the reasons were important why we went down there, and I'm sure the Panamanian people are better off than they were . . . so, I'm glad about that. Sometimes I just can't help wondering if there's other ways to help people lead a better life.

We finally got picked up two or three hours later, and they took us to an airplane and flew us out of there. My leg was broken in three places. They still don't know if it was from the explosion or from getting thrown in the air. My leg was broken in three places, I had a broken pelvis, ruptured eardrum, mild internal injuries—bruised kidney and stuff like that. It's amazing what you can do when other people are shooting at you. The goddanged airplane was still getting shot when we were flying out, and I remember thinking, "Jesus! We're going to get shot down. Survive all that crap, and then get shot down!" The sun was just coming up when I left.

CHAPTER 5

The Brotherhood

> It would be difficult to describe the brotherhood of men that was here established on the seas. No one said that it was so. No one mentioned it. But it dwelt in the boat, and each man felt it warm him. . . . they were friends, friends in a curiously more iron-bound degree than maybe common. The hurt captain . . . spoke always in a low voice and calmly, but he could never command a more ready and swiftly obedient crew than the motley three of the dingey. It was more than a mere recognition of what was best for the common safety. There was surely in it a quality that was personal and heartfelt. And after this devotion to the commander of the boat, there was this comradeship that the correspondent, for instance, who had been taught to be cynical of men, knew even at the time was the best experience of his life. But no one said that it was so. No one mentioned it.
>
> Stephen Crane, "The Open Boat"

No aspect of the soldiers' knowledge of war is as vulgarized in our popular war myths as the Brotherhood. In contemporary wars, the Brotherhood is not a bunch of guys sitting around, joshing each other good naturedly, trading food and sexual fantasies, and extolling the virtues of their hometowns. The Brotherhoods in Vietnam and Afghanistan served many purposes, but first and foremost they were a necessary response to a world out of control, in which their own survival was their paramount consideration. The Brotherhood was the only organization whose sole objective was the members' survival. Though these communities were spontaneously organized and informal, they developed into highly effective defenses against the pervasive horror and abjection. As Mike Mitchell says of the elite Blue Bandanas (within the elite 1st Air Cavalry), the Brotherhood was like a high school social club among a group of very young fellows who were "very, very close because we got along together." Phil Pearson points out that only in the Brotherhood could the individual soldier feel valued or express emotions.

The strength of the Brotherhood was the certain knowledge that individual survival was greatly enhanced by collective survival. The soldiers' knowledge of war is institutionalized in the survival code of the Brotherhood, which is inchoate—anecdotal, referential, and sometimes deliberately silent. The brutalizing experiences and the ambiguities in these wars reduced their lives to the narrow tolerances of the survival code. The more superficial, pragmatic parts of the survival code are explicit in the narratives. These are called field-expedient tactics, as opposed to "The Book," military procedures imposed upon them by the chain of command. Field expedients are embedded in war stories such as these, and they all promote survival. Examples abound: Don't set up tanks in tree lines. Bamboo contains water, but banana plants are more reliable. The U.S. Army Rangers have collected over twenty pages of such advice: If the enemy is in range, so are you. The tactical plan no longer applies after the first shot is fired. This is survival, not sending messages to upstart governments or taking military objectives.

Perhaps even more importantly, the Brotherhood located the troops within a close and responsive community, which seldom extended beyond their platoon or above the rank of sergeant. The Brotherhood provided an identity and that most precious commodity, collective trust, which was established by each person's behavior under fire. In the strange world of contemporary warfare—ambiguous objectives, alien terrain, and the daily presence of death—Brotherhood communities are a stabilizing force in a hostile, out-of-control environment.

Their behavior became surprisingly ritualized. There were ways, many of them nonverbal, to be invited in—witness poor Don Neptune when he stumbled into the bizarre Brotherhood of his new unit. Blue Bandanas delight in hazing REMF officers. Allowing an officer to play cards was a signal honor. Although black troops enforced the "dap" [an elaborate handshake used among Black soldiers] ritual with threats, racism and sexism were irrelevant on the field of combat.

With the advent of Nixon's Vietnamization policy and the Soviet withdrawal from Afghanistan, the soldiers became even more conscious that they were being used in a futile cause. With the added impetus of the political situation in the late sixties, the Brotherhoods evolved naturally into countercultures. The highly centralized, hierarchic structure of the military services makes the chain of command predictable—the perfect foil for a counterculture. If the chain of command put them at risk, then the chain of command increasingly became the enemy, and they had to bond even more strongly together. In these circumstances, even some officers felt no compunction about changing orders so as to minimize danger.

In the broad context of these wars, Brotherhoods are the only way to resolve the psychological and spiritual crises men and women experience from prolonged exposure to intense combat. Their civilian values are simply dashed, and military values get them into situations that traumatize them far beyond their worst expectations. They have to construct their own social order, not merely to survive physically, but also to survive psychologically and spiritually. The values of the Brotherhood eventually supersede civilian and military values in importance, providing both justification for killing and the spiritual force of an honorable moral code.

Crane is especially perceptive in identifying the talking taboo in the Brotherhood. On the one hand, men and women are bonded into a community that does represent a supreme moment in their lives. They are held together by a single, compelling issue. Communication is instantaneous, nonverbal, and "heartfelt." Talking about their feeling of community reduces it to the banal language of cliche. Their experience becomes hermetic. It is isolated in time and space, free from external influence, and unknowable to the uninitiated. As a consequence, the Brotherhood is both a boon and a trap. It saved their lives, but Dave Nelson's experience foreshadows their collective, irretrievable loss and the sacredness of their memories of dead Brothers.

MIKE MITCHELL

I got to be very, very, very close with my squad. Less so with the platoon and company. I have never been so close to anyone in my life, and I actually didn't know anyone when I got there. The Brotherhood is a bonding among men—which is amazing because we were nineteen to twenty-one years old. We became men very, very quickly, but we were also like friends at high school . . . I will always miss them. Then one guy or ten guys would get killed in one day . . . and it felt like the inside of you was completely ripped out. We lost fifty-six men from our company in one day. It's one of the things I've had to deal with because it's never allowed me to totally give myself to anybody. Friends say, "Let it go," but the hurt is tattooed into me. To this day, I have not been closer with any other person. Now, I remember a couple of the names and a few faces. My name was Stache because of the moustache I grew—like a bandito. Another name . . . Jake the Snake, a short Black fellow . . . he was the one who trained me on the M-60 machine gun. When I first got to the company, he only had forty-five days to DEROS. We hit it off, but unfortunately, he left country and went back to the real world, and I took over his job.

Later, I was voted into the Blue Bandanas. The Blue Bandanas was an organization within our company of a group of fellows. It was sort of like a private social club in high school. It was basically the same thing in Vietnam. Our company commander didn't particularly care for it, but he couldn't do anything about it. We were by no means prejudiced or racist. The Blue Bandanas had been together in our company for a long time before I got there. Anybody that got along with the Blue Bandanas could get in. It was just a group of fellows who just really seemed to all genuinely get along together. I was a friend of one of the Blue Bandanas, and all of a sudden one night he asked me to come to this meeting over at this foxhole. All of the other Bandanas were there, and they informed me that I had become a member.

Your company is broken up into four platoons, and the members of the Bandanas were throughout each platoon. How did you get accepted? I'm really not sure. I think it must have been my good looks. No . . . I really don't know. Usually anyone who wanted to be a member became a member. There was a vote. My initial friend in the Blue Bandanas was a medic. He was a passive person, and so was I, and we got to know each other and got along very well. I think he's the one that more or less got me introduced to the rest of them. The evening I became a member I was given a blue bandana, which I still have. I cherished that thing. The nice thing about a blue bandana was that it was the only thing that wasn't military issue that I carried. It was *blue*. It wasn't green.

When I went back to the rear to have dental work done or something else—I'd do anything to get to the rear—and I'd always wear that bandana as my little bit of protest to the military system. Some officer would always tell me to take it off. I'd look at him and laugh in his face. In the bush, everyone respected everyone else as an equal. I'd get back to the rear, and everybody's pulling rank on you, and you knew you were going back out to the bush, so rank didn't mean anything to you. There was very little respect by us for anybody who was working in the rear.

This one time, I remember myself and another guy in our company went *way* back in the rear for dental work. We were on some big military base, and it was very secure. There were guys walking around without weapons. Here we were, fresh out of the bush. We hadn't had a change of clothes in a couple of months. We were real funky—had beards and moustaches, and our hair was long. We were carrying our weapons, and we looked like death warmed over. We were walking by a couple of lieutenants, and they stopped us to tell us we didn't salute them. We asked them why we should, and they said to respect your officers, but we told them we didn't have any respect for officers . . . the officers where we came from usually got shot. They were very upset when we left them. We heard about it when we got back to our company a week later, but it was just kind of laughed off—no big deal.

I also remember one day when the mail came, I got notification I had received a Bronze Star. I went over and asked the CO what it was for. He said, "Oh, you remember—that day when you went out and brought back two of your guys who got pinned down." Well! My men were out there—what else was I supposed to do? It was just something you did. If someone got pinned down—you went out and got them. You didn't do it because you'd get a medal. You did it because that is what you did.

CHERYL "NIKKI" NICOL

It was extremely bizarre being older and in a medical unit in Vietnam. We formed incredibly strong friendships. We were on a first-name basis, and we really stuck together. After a "mass casualties" everybody pitched in. The doctors swabbed the floors in the ER and OR. Nothing was ever left for anybody on the next shift. If you had a bad night or a hangover, we covered for each other. People were willing to put themselves out for others. Patients got stuff for us for our hooches.

One time I had to treat a VC sniper who had hit some of our men. It was all I could do to keep from strangling him with my bare hands. Somebody else took over for me. I wanted to kill that VC sniper—I really did. He did not make it. One of the chopper pilots from the medivac came back later and told me, "We have a message for you from that sniper." And I said, "What is it?" He said, "AAAHHhhhhhhh!" They'd tossed him out. I was glad.

There were no REMFs in Vietnam. Everybody had jobs supporting the grunts in the bush. No matter what you did, if you did it well, you should be proud. That OR job was ten times easier than being a nurse in a military hospital in the States. Here you had a twenty-year-old with parents, a wife, and a baby. His right side is messed up, and he's facing one to five years in the hospital. The hospital nurse is there day after day. She's there when they see him for the first time—so she's got to help the whole family. The medical people in Japan had a horrible job. Within two or three days, we sent them off to Japan. That's where most of the hospital deaths happened. We only lost 2 percent of the men who made it to the hospital. The burns died in Japan. In two and a half to three weeks, they'd get fluid in their cells so bad they'd drown. I really pitied the women doing caskets at Dover when we went into Panama.

We had to put up a wall. We didn't do it consciously, but we did it to protect ourselves. I think you're right. Every nurse has a "one guy" story. Mine was Larry Zwitloe, an E-9 Sergeant Major. He was hit in the gut and chest. Zwitloe was a real neat guy. I was prepping him . . . he was kind of special . . . but he was what we called a "seven-tube syndrome." When you got six tubes into a guy, he still had a chance, but a seven-tube will die, mainly from infections. He got worse a couple of days later. I went to see him every day, and I couldn't tell you why. He was just that special guy. He never got off the table. His name is burned into my memory.

It's important to remember that thirty-five hundred military women served in Vietnam. Twenty-five hundred other women were also there during the war. Three Red Cross women and eleven nurses were killed, most of them in the C-5A [jet transport] that crashed when they were bringing children out when Saigon was falling. There were 265,000 "Vietnam era" women in the military. At most, we've got fifteen hundred names for a memorial to the women at The Wall. But it tells you women did form that Wall, and it's still there, to one extent or another, in all of us. It's important to us to get a statue of a nurse at The Wall.

The Brotherhood for Vietnam vets is quiet. It's nonverbal. We have shared something. We have looked under the wall-to-wall carpet in the empty room and seen the horror. I respect others' experience. There are some things I will not share with you students. I do it a lot to protect you from what I know . . . what I experienced. If you don't have to feel the pain, I wouldn't want you to go through that. I'll never forget the feeling of Brotherhood in that hospital. I get that feeling now when I go to The Wall. I have to go back there pretty soon . . . I haven't been there for a while. I can't go during the day with kids yelling around. We go at night and sit on the knoll about a hundred feet away. We just sit there and feel peaceful.

DONALD NEPTUNE

I got to the 121st Evac. Hospital, and I got shown around the hospital, where everything was. Got checked in, and I was put in a hooch with a Canadian who had been drafted. He had been going to school or something down in the States. I don't remember his last name. I just remember his first name—Jacques. I always pictured a Canadian with that name, so it just fit him real well. He was kind of a small guy, kind of skinny. And I remember walking down into the hooch—it had rooms down off to the side off the main corridor—and they had streamers going down the hall. Streamers—plastic streamers. Different colors—red, blue, green. And some had beads and what not. And in a lot of guys' rooms they had painted the walls with a Zig Zag Man, or STOP THE WAR—something of that culture or generation back home in the States—anything that was identifiable to the world.

I was transferred to a medivac unit to be a medic on dustoffs. I remember this sergeant. He was the senior medic—kinda had a weird sense of humor. Showed me to this hooch. There was just a bunk there and a mattress. I threw my duffel bag in there on the floor. I heard music coming from this hooch next door. So I just stepped in this hooch, and again the streamers—all down the hall. And I looked through the streamers into this bay, and there was some rock and roll music going. I saw people in there, and they had jungle fatigues on. Most of them had tank top shirts on because it was so hot.

One guy was sitting there with a mask over his face—it was a gas mask with a pipe sticking out of the end of it. And there was a footlocker lying there with a big pile of marijuana, about a foot high, piled there. Another guy was holding onto a rope tied to two beams that was used to hang clothes on that *mama-san* washed. He had a fifth of whisky in his hands, taking slugs off of it, and he was singing, "Ding-ding! How do you get off this trolley?" The rest of the people were just, you know, standing around listening to music, laughing.

And the next thing I knew, somebody grabbed me, and I had . . . a towel or rope around my neck. They had me pinned up against the beam and had a .45 up against my head and an M-79 grenade launcher shoved in my face. It was that quick. I didn't know what hit me. I saw this Indian guy . . . he had a thick Bowie knife . . . and his hooch was back around the corner. And I saw all these scalps nailed on the wall. They were questioning me about who I was, what I was doing there. Finally, I got so mad I told them that if they ever got out of there, I was going to kill them all. I was so mad because they were choking me, and I couldn't breathe. You know I had to do something. And this Indian guy got up, and—I later found out his name was Frank—he said, "Let him go." They seemed to do whatever he said. I never heard him talk much.

During that week, I had my first mission with Frank. We flew all day long, and we flew that night. We had to pick up a Cobra pilot that had been shot down. When they got shot down, they came down through the trees, and a rotor blade came—got bent—and came down and hit him dead straight in the face. And it mashed his face. From the bottom of his chin to the top of his face was depressed. Frank wanted me to give him mouth-to-mouth, and he didn't even have a mouth. I said, "You give him mouth-to-mouth." He wouldn't do it. He said, "Well, I'm going to tell them you let this pilot die." He just pulled a blanket over the pilot's face. Later that evening . . . a bunch of guys came in . . . to my hooch. One of them had this pilot's knife in his hands . . . and he came up . . . and gave it to me. They said, "We wanted to give you this knife in honor of the pilot you let die." That was my reception into the unit.

I continued to fly missions, and I'd like to share something about one of the experiences I had with the wounded. And . . . uh . . . I never felt like I had enough hands. I remember working on so many with their arms and legs blown off . . . and . . . it got . . . I . . . it just began when they died. I . . . I . . . began to get bitter. And I prayed—I asked to take their pain. I flew close to three hundred missions . . . and uh . . . I remember picking up some wounded, and one had a jaw blown off . . . and the skull was exposed. And other wounded had their legs blown off—gunshot wounds—severe gunshot wounds . . . multiple shrapnel wounds. And I tried to put a compress on the jaw of the man that was exposed . . . and his hand grabbed mine, took the compress, held it . . . and pointed to me to work on the others. By the time I got back . . . it was too late.

BORIS VOLKOV

One of the commanders I was serving under was wounded under fire, and I was wounded, too, for which I received the highest soldier's medal. The commander was kind of—he had a great wound, which was very painful. He kept dragging me down as we were retreating. The commander kept telling me to go on, to leave him alone, because it was very painful . . . too painful to live. I got him back to safety, and we were flown back to the aid station. When he was well again, he came back, and there was no need for words. We just looked at each other, and that was it. We felt like there was a real Brotherhood there among us in Afghanistan.

Actually, my values were changed for the better while I was in Afghanistan. We were very young, so we didn't know what real Brotherhood was—what real friendship meant—until the conditions became very bad. After being in Afghanistan, I understand much more clearly that I am an individual rather than being a part of the masses. I started watching for the effects of my own actions, which I think I'll have to pay for. Although one individual is rather small, if he is allowed to think, by his thoughts he can influence other people into thinking of other things, thereby creating something out of nothing, so to speak. That's really what I learned from the Brotherhood, plus being responsible for my own actions.

RON MITSCHER

You asked about the Brotherhood. What you're talking about is camaraderie. The camaraderie we had over there was like—there's no way to compare it—but you could probably compare it to a best friend that you had in growing up, only you have a whole bunch of best friends in a life-threatening situation. The camaraderie becomes something that you carry the rest of your life with those individuals. Sometimes you never get a chance to see those individuals again, but in your heart you know you'd do anything for them because they did that for you in a situation which could have gotten them killed. So that kinship is something that a Vietnam vet feels per se with other Vietnam vets. I think this is true for all of us who went. What happens now though, the war has been gone for so long and it's very hard to identify who was a combat veteran in Vietnam and who was a Remington Raider [clerk]. A lot of people lie about what they did over there so the kinships can be stronger. I think for the most part when you identify with or belong to an organization like the Vietnam Veterans of America, you meet a lot of people, and those kinships are increased because you get to know the guys—especially in a program like this where you get close. You may get closer with some people than others, but that's just human nature.

As far as survivor guilt, I think that's very prominent in the one-year tours. I can't relate to somebody who came from a wealthy family, but I can relate to the idea that a lot of us kids were poor and didn't have much when we went over. Survivor guilt for me is that I have seen people over there who I felt had more to live for who died—families . . . a decent, good family relationship—a wife, kids, and stuff like this to go back to . . . whereas I didn't feel I had as much to go back to. Also, there's the idea that there are some individuals who you just cared about so much that you would have rather you had taken their place and let them come back. I don't know if it's different than being in any other war, but it's a very strong feeling with us. A lot of us especially got very close to a very few people because we did not go over in large-scale units or come back in large-scale units. So once you found a friend in a situation like that, you hung onto him like he was your family.

PHILEMON PEARSON

Getting to the Brotherhood—the bond. We had fun over there. In the Brotherhood you could have emotions that the army wouldn't let you have. You talk about everything in the Brotherhood . . . foolishness, mostly. Having fun, playing cards, watching a rat steal your buddy's candy bar—and it comes after you because you have the other half. We didn't have any race problems during any of my three tours of Vietnam. Even on the third tour, it appeared to me that as troops we were closer over there than we ever were over here. Any type of pleasurable moment, anything we could do and enjoy together, it was just like magnified. We joked a lot . . . because when you lose your buddy, you can't keep that around . . . because it keeps you from functioning. It will just screw you up real good. A day at a time was what it was.

The troops were really close, especially the black troops. They had this "dap" going—which was a handshake. I didn't know the proper method of doing it. When I took an R&R to Vung Tau, I was threatened because I didn't know how to do it right. These brothers meant business. I can't do the "dap" now to show you—I honestly don't remember it all—but that shit was serious. It was like you were in a Catholic church or something, and you better be serious with it, because I almost got injured for not knowing it. They said, "Either you learn to dap, or you gonna get wasted." They was superserious. I learned it.

In Vietnam we fought for . . . if you say you're fighting for freedom, that mission is too great for you. Freedom means this whole country. The individual soldier can't do that. If we complete *our* shit, we have contributed to the entire mission. The Brotherhood contributed to the mission. You're doing the military thing, but you're also doing the survival thing with the Brotherhood. What you need is both. That love I said we needed—that was the Brotherhood. We was too macho to say, "I love you." Instead, we'd say, "Get the fuck off me, motherfucker. You a faggot?" So to keep from doing that, the Brotherhood was "Mayday! Mayday!" We'd get a call from somebody that was in trouble, and we'd say, "Hold on. We're coming." If the VC was in front of us, that's their fault, because we was going over after our buddies. If we didn't get through, it's because these VC stopped us. That was the Brotherhood.

A female vet—she might not have been authorized to carry a weapon, but she sure did know what the hell she was doing with the bandages. Our nurses—I watched them work. I went to hospitals, and I'd watch them. I watched them cringe when there was in-coming. I saw the weariness on their faces. I saw the pain . . . the patients they lost . . . it's not easy to work with death every day. We was in the field, yet we didn't see dying every day. When we did see it, we felt it, because, "Hey! That was my right hand over there that's gone. I just had lunch with him." These nurses and medics had to go through the same replay every day.

Where the hell does it stop? When I visited any wounded troop, I told them, "Hey, my man—hang in there. I'm just back here for a little while, but I want you to know I got time to come and see you." The medics—everybody did their share. I have a large, warm feeling for the medics . . . and the helicopter pilots that risked their lives . . . like Mike. Puff the Magic Dragon . . . those guys are on the top of my list. I never met any of those guys personally, but they saved my buns more than once. They can change the score of a game fast—a matter of seconds.

When I got assigned to the MP battalion, I wasn't doing enough. I wasn't in the field any more, and it was rotten. I couldn't get in Special Forces. They just stopped it. Meanwhile, I started going over to the morgue. I said to myself, "Well—I'm not in the field, and these are my buddies, and they cashed in, so I want to put my nickel in. Whatever I can do, I want to do it." The reason I went over there, I was going on R&R to Japan, and I met this civilian mortician from the base. I said, "I'll stop by and see you." What I didn't know was this was a goddamned assembly line, for God's sake! I went over the first time and found him . . . . it was something. The room to the right was the guys that was messed up too bad, and there's twenty-five tables there. You'd just walk in and see anything—I'm telling you, anything! It's a screwed up feeling . . . it still fucks me up. That's why I insisted on trying to do something. I said to myself, "Those guys gave everything they had . . . and I'm still here . . . and I'm going to help do something" . . . .

One of these days, I'm going to The Wall and give them a report: "Guess who's still walking around trying to do the best he can?" They didn't die for me to be an idiot or a failure . . . I'm one of them, and I'm still out here. I didn't give up. I'm still here, active in the community. I never forget them. In fact, I want to represent them. They didn't make it, and we were all over there trying to do our thing. If I do a no-no, I'm a Vietnam vet. These guys didn't die for me to be a jerk out here . . . you're branded is what it is. When you get in trouble, they say, "That guy's from the Nam." In my case, I hope it means, "Good. He's got his head above water." Sometimes when I get uptight, I talk to the guys, as in, "This is another fine mess I've gotten myself into." Sometimes I cry with them, and that feels really good. I can remember a picture of The Wall where veterans have their hands pressed against the surface . . . like they're touching hands with their ghosts on the other side . . . .

CHUCK SIMMS

On my second tour, on the boat, we formed quite a Brotherhood among the guys who stayed there all the time. Anybody could do anything they wanted. We just all knew our job and did it. We'd go up to the villages and get girls down to the boat and take off with them. We may be gone two weeks up the river. We'd be sleeping with them and doing what we wanted to them. We'd take their clothes and throw them over the side and make them run around naked on the boat. They didn't care. They seemed to have a good time. When we got back, we'd pay them off. We'd take them back to whatever village they came from, give them some clothes, and let them go.

I started drinking heavily over there, especially toward the end of my three years. I had to take sleeping pills to knock myself out. I'd wake up and take speed to get through the day. You could buy anything at the pharmacy, across the counter. A lot of the other guys were smoking marijuana. I never fooled with it. My drug of choice was alcohol, speed, or a downer. A lot of people were using cocaine, LSD, and heroin. I thought I'd stick with the old habitual drugs.

I liked to get a little time off and go to Saigon and places like that. I didn't like Da Nang. There was a lot of racism going on. There they split the town in half, blacks on one side and whites on the other. I had a hell of a time there, being Indian. I'd go in the black bar and somebody would pick me up and throw me out. I'd go in a white bar, and it's the same damned thing. I started hanging out with the Vietnamese and going to their bars—I had a lot of girlfriends over there.

DONALD HEDGES

You know, when I first got to Vietnam, I just didn't fit in real well. This was the time when things really started to get tight. I was a new guy with these Con Thien vets. We're talking October '68 by this time. A lot of Con Thien vets were gone by this time. Later, when I was squad leader, I got to know my guys. They were just a nice bunch of fellas. And we did—we got real tight.

We were just a bunch of kids, real kids with real guns and real bullets. The only problem was, they shot back. And we had to watch out for these American assholes . . . our own artillery . . . friendly fire . . . it was just a big game, and I felt like I was hunting—playing soldier. To me, it was real, and I liked it . . . especially being squad leader. It was such a fulfilling job, you know. We built our trust through October, and we had a couple of contacts. Then in December, I went in to stand over for Christmas, and I didn't want to do that, because . . . I was getting to know these guys . . . and I just couldn't run off and leave them.

So I extended my first tour, with the stipulation that I could go home for Christmas, and they said, "We're happy with that." Also, I was just starting to figure out what the hell was going on. I was just kinda getting in the groove . . . and they were telling me I could go home. So this was December 10, 1968, and they took me out from my squad and put me in mortars, because they wanted to save me, because I was coming back and didn't want to get myself screwed up the last few days.

My best friend Rudy took over the squad. He was a Puerto Rican. It's funny, but for a long time I never liked the guy. He was always trying to get out of the bush—he'd stick little holes in his arms with a can opener and say they were rat bites, and he got malaria. But—I don't know—we just kinda stuck together, and that really changed things for me. He was just really a nice guy. He was Puerto Rican and Black mix, so the Puerto Ricans didn't like him and the Blacks didn't like him . . . but I liked him . . . and he was a good man in the bush. It was just that he didn't want to be out there.

Well—we were just humping through the boonies, and they called Rudy and told him to set up an ambush behind us, because they thought we might be being followed. So he went out. The point [man] saw some movement, and he went out to check it out, and it was a platoon of NVA on a hill . . . they just opened up. When the firefight started, I knew my replacement squad leader was down . . . and I only had like three magazines . . . I'd given my magazines to my squad, because my squad still needed more magazines. But I still went down there, and they were still pinned down when I got there. Rudy was just ahead of the firing line . . . and he was just dead as a doornail . . . the gunner was killed, too. The NVA ran off . . . they left their packs . . . they left thirty-three backpacks. We had to get the bodies out, and we hadn't been resupplied, and we didn't have any food. We were real tired, anyway, but we had to carry these bodies several hundred meters to find a hole in the canopy. They lowered a line down through the canopy and . . . took Rudy . . . and these other guys out on a line . . . through the canopy. It was time for me to DEROS . . . so when we got back to base . . . that's when I ate the can of beefsteak and potatoes I had been saving for so long . . . then I puked it up.

On my second tour . . . it was real chaotic and real deadly. That's when my squad really came together. We were in the A Shau for fifty-two days. We were real motivated. We took Tiger Mountain in the A Shau. We walked point seven of the twelve days it took to take Tiger Mountain. I lost one man to appendicitis, and that was all. The rest of the companies suffered quite a bit . . . most of the second platoon got wiped out.

I think a lot of my energy came from—and I've just discovered this in the last two or three days of this program—I don't function very well when things are quiet and tranquil, because in Vietnam, tranquillity meant something bad was going to happen pretty soon. Presently, it means for me that if I can force a conflict, then I have control. In a conflict with enemy troops, we had some sort of control. I think that's why I hate artillery so bad—and mortars—because there is no control there. You just lay there and hope something doesn't hit you, whereas when you're engaged with small arms, there's something you can do. More than once when the rounds went off, I'd say, "First platoon, move up," and we'd move past the rest of the platoons to get up front. I hated sitting back in the column waiting to be called up. That manifests itself even today. When things are going well for me, that's the worst time, because I'll go out and create a conflict with someone else so I can fight or flight, and for me it's usually fight.

On the last day of the assault on Tiger Mountain, they called me in for a meeting and said that Lima Company was going to take the point when we made the final assault. So I went back and told my men they had pulled us off the point, and they raised so much hell—they figured it was their mountain. I went back to the company commander, and he said, "Okay." But that's just the kind of people they were. You don't find that very often. I just really loved them, and I'm sure they felt the same way. We were just friends. I can remember almost everyone's name . . . there were a couple of guys whose names I can't remember, but I remember their faces.

There was a change in the war then. I'd been home, and some of the new guys—well, Faru, he was a dope smoker and somewhat political . . . Rudy was the same way. We'd talk, but I was still a patriot and still real into the Corps, so it didn't really sink in much. But we got this new guy named Wall, who was from Portland, and he was real big on the political scene—involved in some of the antiwar stuff back home.

And we used to talk about, "What the hell are we doing?" I mean, we tear down Khe Sanh . . . we go into the A Shau, we clean it out, and then we leave. Meanwhile, people are dying all around us. And, of course, I still have that thing ringing in my ear from that guy at the Crystal Ship—running drugs, pawns for the big corporations—all that rhetoric. I'm still to this day not sure—something was going on besides running the North Vietnamese out of Vietnam—I know that. And so, after the A Shau, the attitude changed. It wasn't like we weren't so interested in running Charles off, but more in preserving each other. Matter of fact, we used to talk about maybe we could run into a patrol of NVA, and if they wouldn't fire, and we didn't fire, maybe we could just sit down and smoke a joint and talk this thing over and maybe solve it. They could go their way, and we could go our way. That never happened, of course, but that's kind of what we were thinking. I mean, these guys were just guys, you know. The only thing that got to us was the carnage . . . and we were willing to do the mission, but it didn't seem like the mission was so important, at least not to the people at the top. The mission was important to us.

VLADISLAV TAMAROV

In this kind of situation, the dark side of the man can wake up . . . the dark side can come out—but that's good, because you can understand who is a shit and who is a good guy. You can understand who's your friends and who in the mountains will be afraid, and if he will help you, or maybe he won't. This was a lot of shit, and I am bitter then and now. Only about 30 percent of our soldiers were good guys, but many officers were good because they lived with us when we were in the mountains. People are different—things are different in the mountains. Some officers were good, some were shit. I felt good when I was with good officers, good soldiers.

I was not lucky with some guys. I had a good friend, but he . . . I have a picture with him . . . he was killed twelve hours after the picture . . . here, you can see. He was a real good, *real* good friend, you know? The second friend would become like a good friend soon, but on a combat mission, a bullet got him in the leg. I felt good about that, since he is getting back to Soviet Union.

I think this happened in Vietnam, too, this Brotherhood. I was one step from finding the dark side, because I find somebody who was very bad soldier. Somebody can die because he is a coward, and he doesn't cover well for us. I was like one second from shooting him . . . not because he was bad man, but because the other good man can die because he does not *do*—you see, he does not come to cover us other soldiers.

Everybody changes. I change, they change. I don't want to see these guys I was with since just because I know they're different now. I remember how they were. I want to remember them like then . . . to remember those good guys.

JIM GOLDSTINE

After the battle at Dong Ap Bea/Hamburger Hill, the battalion was pulled out of the line and sent off to the R&R center at Eagle Beach on the coastal plains. The only requirement of the battalion was to man its night security perimeter. The bunkers obviously were manned and held by the same folks who had had to fight at Dong Ap Bea. And out of this little respite came one of the more tragic stories that I'm aware of. I came by this knowledge personally by sitting on the court-martial.

One morning about six thirty, the sergeant of the guard was out collecting the men from the perimeter. One of the troopers who was in the ranks had a verbal exchange with one of the people they were stopping to relieve. The exact nature of the words was never evident, but it could very quickly be paraphrased, "You're a motherfucker, and so's your parents!" The guy in the bunker said, "Say it again, and I'll blow you away." Of course, the guy said it again, and the guy got blown away . . . he blew away his friend. What was going on between his ears I'm not sure anybody but God knows—at least not based on what came out at the trial.

One of the ironies of war is how things sort of fall together or fall apart. There was a major piece of evidence that was not presented to the court because the sergeant of the guard was killed about two weeks after the incident at the bunker. It was a critical piece of evidence, because he was there, and he had that specific knowledge of what was said and done by both persons in the interchange. Apparently, no one else had that specific knowledge—and it made a difference. As the trial turned out, there was sufficient circumstantial evidence for the court to convict the young fellow for the murder.

Where the irony comes in is in the sentencing process following the verdict. All of the people who sat on the court-martial were very well aware of the truth of this background information. We voted for the sentence which would allow the commanding general the maximum flexibility in his decision on sentencing, and at the same time reflected some sort of sense of justice in the case. There's a portion of the trial in which matters in aggravation and mitigation are submitted by the prosecution and the defense, respectively. The defense brought in every member of the chain of command except the Battalion Commander, and each one of these people testified that this person had been, up until the time of the incident, a good soldier who had done his job, who had done his job well, had never caused any trouble, and was somebody they wanted back in their unit. The testimony on this was conclusive. There was never a question about the prior conduct of the individual. There was nothing offered in aggravation by the prosecution; in fact, both the prosecutor and the defense attorney recommended something that was totally unusual in my experience, and I've sat in on three or four dozen general courts-martial.

They wanted to suspend all confinement and return the guy to duty in his unit. After the formal portion of the court-martial was concluded, every member of the court signed a petition to the commanding general recommending that he be returned to duty. This trooper had about seven or eight months left on his tour. The sentence had been three years' confinement with hard labor, reduction to the lowest enlisted grade, and forfeiture of all pay and allowances except for about thirty dollars a month, which in the sentencing discussion was thought appropriate to leave him enough to buy soap and cigarettes—and scant little else. So the guy was facing an eight-month tour as a private E-nothing in an infantry battalion where the job that he held was probably going to be point man for the entire period of time. I can't speak for the other members of the court-martial, but my sense was that here was justice true and swift, and the irony of the thing was such that if the guy kept his nose clean and survived as a point man for eight months, he goes home alive with a felony on his record—but he survives. I know you know what the survival rate for a point man was. Some day before I die, and certainly before I finish the draft of my book, I'm going to find out what happened to this guy.

I want to reiterate this, and please keep this in mind. As much as any one human being that's not at the top of the command pyramid can do, I believe I had access to—and knew the truth—about what went on at Dong Ap Bea. And I saw it close up from the point of view of a major operative in the Brigade Headquarters. I had access to the comments of the major decision-makers who were on the ground on a continuing basis. And, not to be discounted, is that I had access to it through the informal or jungle telegraphy that operated, chiefly in the evening cocktail hour and dinner. With the exception of that one Battalion Commander, whose attitudes I have conveyed to you, I do not know a single individual who wasn't immensely concerned with the well-being of the troops who were getting shot at. I saw that evidenced on the part of the artillery men who were sitting out there on firebases that were being harassed by snipers and probed and attacked by sappers. I saw it on the part of helicopter people who were providing lift where and when needed. I saw it on the part of the Brigade Commander, the Assistant Division Commanders, and from the Commanding General. I have to tell you that I never saw anyone conduct themselves in a way that didn't exhibit the highest respect and concern and regard for *the guys who were out there getting shot at.*

There's something else I need to address, and it's pretty simple. I never really had the sense that I was in the gravest of danger—a sense of how one would feel if they were pinned down twenty-five yards from a bunker with a heavy machine gun in it and couldn't move left, right, up, or down. I've been shot at, I've had my close calls, and I've been rocketed and mortared. But no, it was never one of those deals where you fixed bayonets and went up and fought hand-to-hand with the sons of bitches. But I have to tell you that there's nothing more exciting than to have at your command the capability to call in all manner of firepower and support to do battle with somebody. It's like being shot at. You can never understand what it's about until you've experienced it, and you can never understand the ability to command those kinds of resources and to work with people who are as skilled and professional as the guys I worked with. Is it habit-forming? I think it is.

EMMETT FINN

I was naturally not let into the Brotherhood as an officer. To a certain degree I was, but I'm sure there's a lot of guys that served with me who don't even know what my name is. It was a standing rule in my platoon that everybody called me Stingray. That was my call sign, and I was comfortable with them calling me that. I felt real close to them. I hope they felt close to me, and I think that some of them did.

I think when you get a group of people together—I think this is the strange part about it—I didn't even like some of them . . . some of them just made life as miserable as possible for the old lieutenant. Even given that, I would have laid down my life in a flash of a second to save theirs. I don't know where that came from. It's a magic thing that happens. You can take guys who just had a fistfight and hate each other, and one guy calling the other "Nigger," and the other calling this one a "Cracker"—and have incoming five minutes later, and these two guys save each other's lives by their actions—and be *willing* to do it. Just the fact that they're willing to do it . . . it gets to the point in war and an adrenaline type of thing happens to people's brains, I guess.

They didn't really let me all the way into the Brotherhood. I guess the most I ever felt let in was when O'Neil came and looked me up in my hometown. We went out drinking. How he talked about Stingray to people who knew me . . . that was probably the proudest moment of my entire life. I really knew how my people felt about me. No honors—I never wanted any, never wanted a medal or put myself in for one. I thought that was just my job. There were no acts of heroism on my part, just what was expected of me as a lieutenant. I'm sure there are times that warranted a medal or recognition . . . when we were overrun or walked into that ambush. Kuda also said to me when he was being airlifted that he knew the men were in good hands. For me knowing him for just a few days . . . I felt I was very fortunate.

They were definitely a Brotherhood. I don't know how you get guys from Kansas and Mississippi, Texas and California to all of a sudden melt into a Brotherhood. I think it was more racially oriented in the later years, so I can't speak to that. It seems from talking to people here that there was a real division between the rear division people and the infantry units that I was in. I was pretty amazed that guys back there had cold beer and fans and a cot. We got hot beer when we got it, we slept mostly on the ground in the mud, with leeches on us. We had beer flown out to us once, and I think it was about a 115 degrees. They tried to get ice to us, but it was just lukewarm water when it got there.

I was worried about fragging when I got there, but I never really witnessed a fear of each other in the bush. I mean, Rivas was the biggest pain in the ass in my platoon. When we got overrun . . . he had a finger blown off, and I ran over to the position where he was, and he was trying to get the new barrel on the M-60. An hour later, Doc wrapped his finger up, and he kept on firing . . . he kept the NVA from overrunning our part of the hill. He was the first one to volunteer to fight back through the trenches to take the hill back from NVA. I was so shocked when he told me that. John Kelly wanted to go, but I told him to hold back because he was so short. He'd been with me a long time. O'Neil and Rivas and Kokomo went with Gator. I was real shocked at that . . . here this kid's being a pain in the ass—he's a Chicano kid from LA—and he does that!

But I never felt any fear. I never saw any display of that—fragging. Guys in my platoon would complain to me about the captain we had—even platoon sergeants from the other platoons. I was the only lieutenant they let in the card game. I did get in that far—I got close. The first captain I had, I got a lot of my personality and leadership from him . . . but I had some unusual things. I had a short-timers' platoon right out of OCS [Officer Candidate School]. That prepared my attitude—that was my greatest test. Here I am a butterbar lieutenant, inexperienced, and I've got my whole platoon of short-timers. They were all infantry—some tough people. To actually have them stand up and somewhat come to attention when I walked into the billet—I mean, hell! I was higher than a kite! Mostly their attitude was, "Fuck you. What are you going to do, send me to the Nam?"

We had about three Article 15s and three court-martials a month for the whole four months I was there. It was just unbelievable. They started to realize we've got to get rid of these types and started x-ing them out, sending them right back into society—because the army couldn't deal with them any more. They started the six-month early-out deal. They just kind of washed their hands of them when they came home. There was no debriefing time, no time to de-escalate their emotions or anything from the war zone. They came home, had thirty days leave—they took their back pay, and just like that they're home . . . hostile and bitter and alone.

I remember so many times . . . in the middle of being overrun—

O'Neil was scared to death. I got the 106 set up with a flechette round in it, and he was shaking so bad I told him, "We've only got one shot with this. When they start coming over the LZ, I'll tell you to fire it. Then you fire it. Then you shit your pants, and we jump in the hole!" He looked at me . . . he had shit all over himself in that ambush. He was laying there helpless, you know. He looked at me, and he laughed—then he relaxed. I never . . . later that night, we were overrun, and I was calling the artillery in . . . I was sitting in the trench, and I thought about shooting myself in the leg and rubbing the blood all over my face so I could at least look dead if we were totally overrun . . . and then I thought about my men and my responsibilities. I had to try and make sure we didn't get overrun.

The only thing I would change would be to bring all my men home alive from the war. I know that isn't realistic, but it's something—the only thing—I would change, for me. I want all of them back. None of them should have been killed . . . but they were . . . and somehow we can't allow that to just go unnoticed and unappreciated and not learn a lesson from it. People are still dying from Agent Orange . . . things like that. I don't think my pain now is any different from enlisted men's—I don't really know that for sure, but I think the pain of losing friends . . . I loved those guys like they were my brothers, but at the same time, I had to maintain a distance. It was hard, like a hidden thing with me. I think the losses are all the same. I think the mental part of the responsibility I felt in making decisions—I have suffered a lot of grief over that . . . to send four men into a bunker only to have them die . . . that's been a difficult thing for me in my life. I think our personalities are different . . . but our pain is ultimately the same.

HENRY MINCEY

You find the aviation departments aboard the carrier are broken down into different divisions, and that becomes your turf. To get away from work, everybody goes to the fantail. When you're off work and wanted to take a break, that's where everybody went. It was an open space . . . you could get a little crazy back there, but it was a small space, and everybody kept their little piece of turf. Fortunately, there were no fights back there. The only fights took place when we got to port. That's when the shit hit the fan . . . probably because you're just too damned tired . . . or probably because you just saw the futility of it all, you know?

YURI KIRICHENKO

There were good officers, and my first commander was a really decent person who wasn't that great a military leader. But this man made—he really took care of his men. Basically the feeling in any Soviet army is the feeling of dislike and mistrust of those, especially officers, who are back in Moscow. The general feeling was that those guys in Moscow were living well, while we were doing the dirty work. They did not have to fight—they weren't even in combat. They had plenty to eat, and they had no idea of the conditions that were going on in Afghanistan. From what I have heard from your veterans of Vietnam, the feelings are strikingly parallel.

I went down in the period of Brezhnev and came back in the period of Andropov. *Does that need to be explained?* As I said earlier, the hardest period was for those of us who were sent toward the end of the war who already knew before we were sent down there that the war was wrong. Our feeling about war was that it was an obligation that was forced upon us, and we had no desire to be there. Some of these men smoked marijuana and hashish, but it was very difficult to get alcohol in Afghanistan.

Actually because I am an officer in the Soviet veterans' association, I am more involved with the Soviet veterans who have PTSD. I am more interested in what happened after we got home—as a Brotherhood—how we have come together again to solve our problems. We are just starting, I know that from having met Vietnam veterans . . . we have a long way and many years to go.

HENRY TALMADGE

In the Marine Corps, you could put your wallet on top of your rack and go take a shower, and when you came back, nothing would be missing. It was honest as the day is long and as pure as it could possibly be. When I came back from Vietnam, I ended up in North Carolina, back where I started from. These so-called marines who had come back from Vietnam and knew all about it. They wouldn't salute an officer—or turn their backs. I started rapping on their ass. I became very hated. The commanding officers, including the Colonel, told me, "You're screwing up our reenlistment percentage, because these people are not going to stay when you treat them that way." I said, "Hey! I've been in the Marine Corps all my life. This is *my* Marine Corps, and I'm not going to let you screw it up! If you're going to cater to their bullshit and let our guard down, we don't need them. There are too damned many good ones who want to stay and make good Marines." So the Marine Corps has changed. That really hurts me a lot in some ways. Right now they're getting pretty selective as to who they get and who they don't.

In World War II, we would stand watches together. We got to know everything about each other. We had different divisions and our own turf, and the *only* way you got to come over to our turf was if you were invited. It was just like a town of five hundred population. The excitement brought us together—it was our baptism into combat. That lasted until November of '44 . . . after the ship was torpedoed, nothing was the same. It was like somebody burned our house down. The ship itself was a real loss to us. In the end, when we had to go and get the bodies out of the hold, that's what I remember most, because it was the most traumatic . . . and the smell. When I see dead animals in these oil spills, that's what they looked like. The bodies were full of oil and really slick.

In Vietnam, I tried not to question the political thing. I didn't want to know anything about the Vietnamese. I knew about the French—when they were there and their tactical moves—but I really didn't want to get into Ho Chi Minh and Westmoreland. For me, it was like it's over my head, I can't do anything about it, so why worry about it. In Korea, one day the Chinese would get the fuckin' hill and chase your ass off. The next day, you come back up and take it again, and then you decide you don't want it anymore, so you just walk off it. Same bullshit in Vietnam. We never occupied ground or stayed on it. I never went on R&R. I thought if I went, it would be twice as hard to get back into the swing of things again. I thought if I stayed here, at least my survival instincts would help keep me alive, whereas if I went, my defenses might be lowered, and I might get careless, and something might happen to me.

I never got close to anybody where I could associate myself with them socially. Any time I was around others, it was business. I had a company commander who talked to the men about mail from home and stuff like that. I had another one who liked to play guitar—his discipline was a little shoddy. He'd get privates and the other officers around, and they'd sing and harmonize. It pissed me off. I wasn't used to that. I never had much social life with any of the guys. I never got involved with whether they were married or single or whatever else like that.

I'm sure that the people under me probably shared something, which I think was an important feature to them. It was a good thing to hold together, although as I think I said, they didn't really get close in Vietnam because they were always coming and going. It was still a good thing to hold together. I had the opportunity to get close, but I chose not to. About the Brotherhood, you might ask the lower echelon—a regular

The Brotherhood

machine gunner or a rifleman. The teams that worked together *were* really tight. They were very careful about new people coming in.

GABE GARCIA

Somehow . . . some way . . . I want to see if they can hear the pain I have . . . every time I think of the brothers I lost over there. Me and Jerry Jenkins went over there . . . on the buddy plan. I lost Jerry on February 13 . . . but I still talk to him daily. Someday, I'll die again . . . hopefully for good this time . . . trying to get revenge on the fuckin' government. They got 58,000 of us . . . every day a Vietnam vet dies. I went to the Wall in New Mexico in 1986 . . . and I found Jerry's name . . . Lieutenant Osborne's . . . and a couple of other names. I started looking for my name on the Wall . . . I was disappointed that I couldn't find it. It still bothers me . . . that I spent three days staring at that Wall.

Nobody will ever get close to me again . . . not even God or Jesus. It's hard to believe that I was born a Catholic. Now look what the government has created . . . they don't know what to do with us. They give us pills . . . drugs . . . "Here, take these two pills and call me next year if you're still alive." It bothers me that by the time I turned nineteen over there . . . killing people did not mean shit to me. That's why I don't touch a weapon. I'm afraid I'll blow my head off . . . or take some innocent fuckers with me who don't know anything about me. I haven't touched a gun since 1968. I'm not going to die today or tomorrow . . . I'm going to stick around . . . because the longer we last the more we hurt the government. I still feel expendable as hell . . . we're tired of feeling expendable.

BOB SWANSON

The guys in the outfit and I got really close. I felt it was the first time I'd ever been really accepted by my peers. Even prior to service time, I wasn't accepted. I was a total loner. I think that was one of the reasons I felt so alone when I first got to Vietnam and got off the plane because I never expected to come back. I figured I'd either be killed by the enemy or by my own people—and I really surprised myself when the shit happened, and I didn't run. I guess there was no place to go.

Anyway, when I got ready to go to Da Nang at DEROS the unit was getting ready to go out, and I kept feeling I was abandoning this group of people that finally had accepted me. Something that I hadn't experienced before. And one of the guys, which was Kimbro—one of the guys that had been out on the listening post—he and Murray—Murray faked a toothache, and Kimbro faked something to come into Da Nang for some work—just to come to Da Nang and see me off. That made me feel good.

I was invited to go back to Vietnam about a year ago. One of the things that happened over there was talking to their soldiers and realizing that the Brotherhood—as we had called it—the interunion of warriors, so to speak, was stretched out far beyond the American warrior. We sat down and talked to Vietnamese soldiers, and they sounded just like us. They were talking about the same hurts from the war and the same feelings and how they felt towards us then and how they feel towards us now. There are so many things that just run simultaneous. And we realized that there was a bond that was built up—there was a warriors' bond between us and our enemy. And it was really strange for me, and I brought that back with me, too. There was just something that gave me a real strong urge for peace, so to speak. Even prior to going back to Vietnam, I was going to high schools and stuff talking about Vietnam, telling them what the war was like, what the outcome of the war was, and how it affected your personality and stuff. That just seemed to be really intense.

Shortly after we got back we got the Russian soldiers who were in Afghanistan here now. And we sat down and talked with these Russians face to face, but they've been shot at with our weapons, and we've been shot at with theirs. Talking with Yuri and some of the other Russians, we found out that these guys felt just like us, too, and they were tired of fighting, and they want peace.

The fact is, to the point where myself and a couple of vet friends had sat down and talked about an International Club of Warriors for Peace. Nothing has happened with it too much, because most of us that were talking about it were PTSD people. Three out of the four of us had just gotten jobs recently, so all of our energy has went towards rebuilding our lives right now. So not too much has happened right now. They are good ideas that we can let simmer for a while.

DARREN GATES

It's kind of weird since we got back from Panama. Everybody is so—they don't really let anything show, so you don't know how it's affected them . . . how it affected the other guys. I think everybody's a little closer together. You know, you go out and train, and you always hear

The Brotherhood

how it's important for you to work together, but you don't really know what they're talking about until you really do have to work together—when your life depends upon it.

I've talked with the guy I took back to the aid station a couple of times. He's doing a lot better. Sometimes when I get down on myself thinking about all the bad things that happened, I try to concentrate on the good things I did down there. It helps. I killed two people, but I might have saved a couple of others, so it helps. If I still felt like I had to kill somebody being back here, I'd probably check myself into a hospital—if I started feeling that way. But that's something I really don't want to think about. That's a different situation.

For something as short as Panama, we pretty much worked together. I can see guys in Vietnam for a year, drawing inside themselves into a Brotherhood, wanting to basically fight their own war and to survive and get out of there. That's just human nature—personal survival on a larger scale. You get a whole unit of guys—two to three hundred guys—they're all fighting together, but each and every one of them is wanting to survive.

I've been out to America Lake a couple of times. I see those guys there . . . I just look at them. The war in Vietnam has just really affected them—right down to their roots . . . they lead shattered lives, and all they did was do their job. I feel a lot luckier than a lot of the guys who never came back. I can build on my experiences—try not to let them drag me down, like I see in a lot of these guys down at the VA. A lot of those guys are stuck in that hospital for the rest of their lives—if not for their lives, at least for a lot of years. Trying to get back into society twenty years later . . . it's sad.

CHAPTER 6

Aftermath

> I still cry for the white brother that was staked out.
> I still cry because I'm destined to suffer the knowledge that I have taken someone else's life not in a combat situation.
> I think I suffer just as much as he did. And still do. I think at times that he is the winner, not the loser.
> I still have the same nightmare twelve years later. And I will have the nightmare twelve years from now. Because I don't wanna forget. I don't think I should. I think I made it back here and am able to sit here and talk because he died for me. And I'm livin' for him.
> I still have the nightmare. I still cry.
> I see me in the nightmare. I see me staked out. I see me in circumstances where I have to be man enough too ask someone to end my suffering as he did.
> I can't see the face of the person pointing the gun.
> I ask him to pull the trigger. I ask him over and over.
> He won't pull the trigger.
> I wake up.
> Every time.
>
> Gene Woodley in Wallace Terry, *Bloods*

Aftermath is the dirty little secret of all wars. Especially for those exposed to prolonged combat, wars are open-ended experiences that do not have conclusions. As America revises its social definition of war, it must remember the words of Dr. Ray Scurfield, director of the American Lake program, in the epigraph to Chapter 1:

The history lesson is that for veterans of all wars there is a conspiracy of silence on the consequences of war for veterans. It is a combination of the reluctance of institutions, clinicians, and the public to talk about it and the natural reticence of veterans because of the response from their environment.

Boris Volkov, the Soviet PTSD therapist, said of his visit that he was "struck by the exact identity—the exact parallel—between the experiences of Soviet and American veterans." Against these sobering facts, the notion that citizen soldiers—particularly those with prolonged combat exposure—will return easily to civilian life can no longer be a part of our social definition of war.

Certainly some men returned home successfully, just as some did not. While well over half of the veterans of Vietnam appear to have made this adjustment, nearly 30 percent have been disabled by PTSD—a total of over 850,000 from the Vietnam War alone. For those with severe PTSD, the aftermath of war is an endless, introspective, acutely depressing existence. Some veterans in our acquaintance who do lead perfectly normal lives still experience occasional flashbacks or nightmares. The question is therefore not whether a combat veteran continues to experience war as aftermath, but rather the degree.

Statistical analyses certainly offer important information, but oral histories offer their kind of knowledge, too. Hidden beneath the statistics of the Vietnam, Afghanistan, and Panama wars are aftermath stories—accounts of estrangement, isolation, marginalization, exaggerated startle responses, searching for "the edge," drifting, unemployment, alienation, survival guilt, flashbacks, anger, broken families, substance abuse, nightmares, suicide attempts, and prolonged introspection over having "gone over to the dark side." We quickly learned never to say, "Now that the war is over . . . ," to a veteran. When one man asked his uncle, a World War II vet, how long it would take to get over Vietnam, the uncle replied, "When do you plan on dying?"

Veterans are marginalized in two senses. To many anthropologists, the marginal human is caught between two cultures. The area of overlap between the two cultures is the margin, where these value systems interact and, more often than not, conflict. As we have seen, their continuing allegiance to their old Brotherhood communities is both devout and hermetic. Its values remain inviolate because they continue to believe in values of the Brotherhood. Compared to the honor, dignity, and respect they received from the Brotherhood, civilian life is merely puppy shit (Dave Nelson), static cling (Don Hedges), or thinking commercially (Phil Pearson). The problem is only too obvious. If they are to have purpose and direction in their lives, they must accommodate to the requirements of civilian life. Unfortunately, as Gabe says, many of them know too much.

Michael Foucault and his followers define *marginalized* slightly differently. To them, people such as the veterans in this book are denied an authoritative voice in the public forum. They therefore lack power and are relegated to the outer socioeconomic and political margins of society. Americans assume veterans are empowered by the Department of Veterans' Affairs, but unfortunately "the VA" is a large, centralized, bureaucratic, governmental institution—anathema to men and women who think of their government as the enemy. The most emphatic advice the veterans give in forums and oral histories is that one must *never* trust the government.

At the core of this dirty little secret lie understandings that, as Foucault believes, are only available through empowering marginalized voices, as in this case, in oral history narratives. The aftermath of war has content. Chuck Simms has spent years in VA hospital mental wards. Emmett Finn remains outraged that he was relieved for being too close to his men. Bob Swanson takes regular retreats into the crystalline world of nature. Gabe sat for three days looking at the Vietnam Memorial in New Mexico, wondering why his name is not on it. Nightmares are not phenomena to be quantified, but terrifying visions to be experienced, often night after night. They are so private and terrifying that we do not ask veterans to repeat them. Those which appear ought not to be seen as bizarre spectacles but rather as what can happen to soldiers after the peace treaties are signed. The onset of PTSD is often delayed for years. Veterans who have lived apparently normal lives since leaving the military suddenly "lose it." At a recent Vets' Night forum, a veteran said that he knew he needed help when he put a pistol in his mouth, had two misfires, then put six shots into the wall opposite him.

The wartime service of citizen soldiers must be seen as a covenant. When society sent them to fight its wars, it undertook a reciprocal commitment to reintegrate them and their knowledge back into society when the wars were over. A knowledgeable understanding of the aftermath of wars will therefore break the conspiracy of silence and make possible a more comprehensive, detailed social definition of war.

MIKE MITCHELL

I was really proud when I got out of the service. When I came home from Vietnam, I was out of the service within twenty-four hours. I was really proud, but of course you've probably heard all of the stories about people calling you "baby killer" and protests and all that stuff. I was very proud of what I had *survived,* not necessarily what I had *done* over there. I will always know that if I could survive Vietnam, I could survive anything.

I was immature and very naive when I went over, but I was very, very mature when I got home. One thing that I almost instantly realized was that there was absolutely *no way* I could thoroughly explain all I had experienced over there for one year. People tell me I'm a pretty good storyteller, but I've still felt in all these years that I've never been able to really, truly tell someone what it was like—to really get them to feel it, to taste it, to smell it. I've never been able to sit down and have any patience to read a novel or read a book about Vietnam.

After a few years, all of a sudden a few Vietnam movies started coming out. I believe the first one was *Apocalypse Now.* I saw that one and believe it was a total farce, the most ridiculous representation of Vietnam that I could imagine. Then they came out with *The Deer Hunter*, I think was next, and a great movie, great story, but what it had to do with Vietnam I'll never know—maybe some of the mental problems one may have acquired over there. Then I saw *Coming Home.* That was very touching, very touching, because it was a part of the war I'd never even thought about. It was about the wounded coming home, and how they were going to have to deal with their lives.

Nothing happened for a number of years, but then *Platoon* came out. If you want to really know what I experienced from my year in Vietnam, that's the movie to see. It is so authentic, not only the operations, but the smallest details are very authentic. At that particular time, I was going through some therapy at the Vietnam Vet Center here in Tacoma, and it was a seven-month program for some very emotionally disturbed gentlemen . . . including myself. We were going through this program, trying to open all these closet doors with all these ghosts from the war that had been bothering us. I remember one night they were telling us it probably wouldn't be a good idea for us to go see the movie because it was too emotionally upsetting. Usually when someone tells me, "No!" I instantly want to do just the opposite. I was scared to death when I went to see it, so I took a friend of mine along for support. My hat's off to the director. It was an excellent representation of what I had experienced.

Vietnam stole a year of my life which I'll never get back . . . and has made the last twenty years of my life miserable. There is nothing glorifying about war, no rewards at all, just the loss of young men's and women's lives. I have been working for the last couple of years on getting my mental and emotional life back together, but there is one thing I will never be able to conquer, and that is the fear of fear itself. I am addicted to fear. The next time you see a vet, don't put him down for what he has done over there, but appreciate him for what he has survived.

CHERYL "NIKKI" NICOL

My problem was how to handle the adrenaline when I got home. Nurses tended to take high-stress jobs or work in nursing homes when they got back. Some never walked into a hospital again. I took ICU [Intensive-Care Unit] jobs, OR and ER jobs, night jobs. I got so good at what I did that I took a great deal of pride in it. I worked where I had to be there before the doctor ever got there—I was that good.

The hardest thing about coming home is maintaining your self-respect. For a long time I fought it . . . because very few people enjoy being ill. We're all afraid of getting into victimology—that's the saddest case of all. Vietnam didn't take my youth. I burned that out long before I got there. But Vietnam did take something . . . and I'm scared about just how much I've got left. My army discharge ripped the profession and the life right out of me. Trust is a very big problem for me. In Vietnam, you could take trust, and you could handle anything. You just felt like, "Go for it. Give it your best shot. I can beat you every time." It's very hard to recreate those conditions now.

Linda Van Devanter is a good friend. I read one of her articles on her experience, and I thought, "This woman's been walking around in my brain. Women vets can have problems, too." You can't really tell nurses that they've got a problem because they are caregivers—caregivers *can't* have problems. I have a friend doing a Ph.D. thesis on PTSD. She doesn't see how nurses could *not* have been affected. I wonder about those who say, "Nah—I'm okay." Those are the ones who go off the Golden Gate Bridge. Well—I went to a Vet Center, and over the next four or five years, I saw a lot of other nurses who felt as I did. There has been a lot of suicide. We have lost a lot of women.

Now I'm after simplicity. Simplicity means less stress. I bought an acre and a half in Gig Harbor. I built a home with a big deck. My home is mine . . . where I can get away from everything. I get along with my own company very well. I can sit up there in all that beauty and feel comfortable. Sometimes I answer the telephone, sometimes I put on the answering machine, and sometimes I just unplug it. I've been so involved in the situation of women vets that after finishing the Vietnam Women's Project, I don't want any more of the phenomenal phone bills I've had for the past five years. I'm taking a year furlough—at least a year.

DONALD NEPTUNE

I know maybe in sharing a few of those things, maybe you can understand if one were to be emotional during those times, he couldn't do his job. I was never able to grieve for all those nameless faces . . . and I've lived with anger and bitterness . . . for all these years . . . not being able to get in touch with my emotions. So now I'm trying to do something about that by being in this PTSD program. I'm 100 percent disabled . . . and never wanted to come to the VA because I was more concerned about the wounded getting the benefits. But I'm glad I came, and . . . I'm glad . . . that the war ended, over there . . . but not for me here yet. So I'm trying to work through those things. Probably take my lifetime . . . and . . . I'm glad I shared a bit of my life with you . . . about Vietnam. There weren't many happy times for me over there. And it's hard to be good to myself now. I want to be, but it's really hard to.

BORIS VOLKOV

The American people should be aware that wars like Vietnam and Afghanistan should definitely not be fought. People should protest and make sure that these wars never happen again. We cannot confuse Vietnam and Afghanistan with the second world war because of the facts of how World War II happened. But these little brushfire wars should be stopped—entirely eliminated.

I somewhat agree with the political analysis we heard from one of the other Afghantsis last night at the forum. With political ideology, it's like there are three rings: the leadership, the bureaucrats, and the people. It's the bureaucrats who are the problem. They are the ones responsible for sending troops to Afghanistan. Nobody asked whether the war was just or not—and that was at a time of totalitarian government, much more so than it is now. These people must have had some of their own ideas of what they wanted to do or why they wanted to do it. You know they had their own goals, but there is nobody who really knows why we did it. I do know the commanding generals were against going into Afghanistan militarily. Most of the higher-ups were educated enough to know what this would lead to, eventually.

We live in a world like a big family. Peace is very fragile. That was one reason the top dogs of the Russian army were against going in to do all this stuff. They knew what it would do to the country. Despite their being educated, they were overruled by others—for their own gain or whatever they had in mind. I am totally convinced that the Soviets—all people—should all put up their arms and leave war behind. Technology has advanced to the point that we can annihilate each other. I'm convinced that the strength of both the United States and the Soviet Union is equal—or if not, it makes no difference if we can annihilate each other. Diplomats should solve problems of international conflict. In this day and age, there is no reason to go to war because there is no end to it.

Soviet veterans believe the war ultimately changed them for the better. Before, we were so young that we didn't know what real Brotherhood is—what real friendship means. I'm repeating that because I think it's the meat of the nut, so to speak. Unfortunately, the missions in Afghanistan taught us not to think. We were told what to do, and that was that. After being in Afghanistan, I actually understand that I am an individual, rather than being part of the masses. I started watching my actions . . . the kind I think I may have to pay for. I don't think about what my goals were before the war, but I live in the war every day . . . there's no way I can get rid of it.

My family was really very glad to see me come back . . . but as far as the local populace goes, they just shook my hand and said, "Glad you're back," and that was it. Most people will listen to you kind of casually—sort of politelike—and let it go. They do not associate the two wars—Afghanistan and Vietnam. "You're alive—you're healthy—God bless you." That's their attitude.

I think the government is obligated to take care of Soviet veterans with PTSD, and also to rehabilitate veterans from other wars. They have PTSD, too, even though their war was a long time ago and they are some of them quite old. The conditions in the Soviet Union are kind of rough because of the political and economic change right now. There are shortages of food, and thereby the veterans aren't pressing too hard because of problems with the general population. We are getting some benefits, but they are not what we think they should be.

The war has scarred our country. This last election, we voted in one of the people—he was a hero of the war in Afghanistan, and some people were very up and against his getting any position. They called him a baby killer, you know. So it's about the same thing as here in the United States until just recently. But he did get in, and he's going to work more to see that the veterans get what they should be getting . . . and also preventing any more of these brushfire wars from happening. In his words, "The Afghanistan War was a mistake."

I have been in contact with many Afghanistan veterans since September of 1987. These are my Brothers. I had American veterans stop and visit me in my home near Moscow. We all identify with this stress, and many Soviet veterans just don't know what the problem is. We have a program on TV, which they show at ten thirty at night—which is unheard of in my country—showing this kind of information on television. And the principal person behind it is a lawyer now and also is suffering from post-traumatic stress disorder.

I enjoy America very much. You must keep doing veterans' forums and your book. To repeat something I say many times—I know that one individual is rather small, but if he is allowed to think, by his thoughts he can influence other people into thinking something out of nothing, so to speak. My values really haven't changed since Afghanistan. I intend to do nothing but good in the future and think about my actions before I do anything again—to try to show people how to progress in their lives instead of regress. I feel that I have a responsibility for what happens in my country. Such a great country as ours—such a big country—so much population . . . if the leaders are governing the people like they governed them in the past . . . we can't wait for anything good to come out of that.

RON MITSCHER

I wish there were more I could do to explain the war. The feeling of a lot of us guys who went was, whether what we were doing was right. We questioned that once a day or at a certain stage of the war. We questioned the resolve of the people who sent us to that type of war, only to turn their backs on us halfway through it—the Jane Fondas of the world who actually went to North Vietnam and made statements against the war. I think she did a slick 180 when she apologized to the veterans. She did that because it was convenient. It's people like this who are complete hypocrites, because these people didn't say a word when the Khmer Rouge were slaughtering three million Cambodians. They don't say anything about the thousands of civilians who were slaughtered in the wake of the Tet '68 Offensive. Actually, we didn't lose anything in Tet. We decapitated the Viet Cong, and then there was no more pretense for the North Vietnamese to pretend that there was anything else for them to gain in South Vietnam. In fact, when I was there, I think I was quite lucky, because we fought strictly North Vietnamese units.

Separating the war and the warrior is one of our main objectives in the PTSD program. I think that's part of the difficult process for us, and that is why the Vietnam veteran is having so many problems—whereas the World War II and Korean veteran didn't have quite that problem. There are so many mistakes made with the Vietnam veteran. It's like, "who really cares?" What the World War II generation did was thinned out the population nicely, made rich people a nice profit on the war, and now, with Graham-Rudman, "Gee, guys, thanks a lot. You've done what you could for your country; now we're going to cut your benefits—to ask you to pay for the damn thing."

Unfortunately, it's your generation, our kids, that we couldn't talk to, who are now asking, "What really happened over there? How come you're not writing about it? How come you're not telling it like it is? How come there's all this Rambo shit?" What really happened is that we had a divided generation. The kids who didn't go were the kids who could afford to stay out of the war. The kids who went were the kids who couldn't afford to stay out of the war. That's not always true, but that runs pretty basic for the general population.

Coming back from Vietnam was kind of curious because I came into Fort Lewis in the middle of the night. When I left Fort Lewis, I went through SeaTac. I didn't have any problems at SeaTac, and I really didn't have any problems in Detroit except for a few people who were looking at me and kind of turning their head, and stuff like that. I was very yellow when I got back. I don't think that type of thing would have bothered me. Now, if he would have spit on me, I think that type of person might have ended up with his head handed to him. I wouldn't have put up with that now.

I went to Germany for ten months, but the problem was that I was still out of the country. When I went back to Detroit after I got out, I was unemployed for twenty-six months. A lot of Vietnam vets had trouble hanging onto jobs. I did, too. I changed jobs a lot. But I'd like to say for the record that I'm a twenty-two-year federal employee. There are a lot of us who have actually worked all our lives. I didn't return on a disability. I worked for the government all my life. I spent ten years in the military and twelve years in civil service. I'm not one of the guys who jammed a needle in his arm and never went to work. One of the things that was very hard for us was getting started again. Nobody would have us. After the My Lai thing—the press and the antiwar movement—it took a long time for a guy to find a decent job. A lot of guys just hid the fact that they were Vietnam vets.

I grew up in the early sixties. In fact, I graduated in January of 1964, just after Kennedy was killed. Kennedy could have said, "Troops! March to Mars!" and I would have. When they said to go, we just went. I think my change came before I ever left the war zone. About midway through my tour, in 1969, I knew that the military was not there to try to win the war. It was just a matter of survival. I was disillusioned. I was angry, but I still had to survive, and I had to try to save lives I was responsible for, no matter what I had to do. And I was good at it. I was very good at it. You'll find some people will tell you that they got a certain enjoyment out of it. I did at the time it was happening, but I wasn't the type of person to go at the kill afterwards or take souvenirs.

At this time I'd have to say no to going back to Vietnam, the reason being that I have problems dealing with myself with flashbacks. The uniform would probably set me off. I've been to the Philippines since—and I feel very comfortable in the Orient. I like Asian people. I have nothing against the North Vietnamese per se, or the Vietnamese people. I think I could probably deal pretty well with them and not have a problem, but there is always the chance that I would embarrass myself or try to kill somebody, or get myself killed because of the uniform . . . the flashback to the uniform. I don't know that I could control it. I spent four months in psychiatric hospitals in Reno and Topeka, Kansas, because I flipped out.

The main thing for me is to find a little bit of peace and a little bit of happiness. If I can put that back into my life, I'll be satisfied when it comes my time to die. I feel like I'm on adrenaline all the time—a little like the guy five minutes before a big ball game. My body pumps that much adrenaline all day long. In fact, I'm on enough medication that it would put most people away as far as sleep goes . . . just to keep me under some kind of control . . . and that's not normal. I was able to deal with my pressures for some twenty years. Now I suffer bipolar disorder, along with having PTSD. Bipolar disorder means I have trouble controlling my mood swings. It is aggravated by PTSD.

I believe I am now being initiated into finding my peace. What we are here is like grade school kids. The kid who gets the most is the kid who puts in the most. We have twenty years of really bad habits to break or remedy. We've had a lot of anger and stuff like this. There are a lot of bad habits we used to control our emotions. It's a learning process for us to undo that. The problem is that we go back into these moods automatically—whereas somebody younger could be more flexible. We don't have that flexibility. I think it will take a long time . . .but if I learned to do this one way, I can learn to do it another way.

For me, I was raised in a split family. My father was a Catholic. My mother was a Baptist. I really kind of had a falling out like the lost generation did. I wasn't going to church, and I had no opportunities. What happened to me was that I had so many near misses in Vietnam that I believe it wasn't just chance. I started turning into myself after some of the incidents I've told you about. The hot shell I handed out of the tank and all that. I believed that the only way I could get myself out of Vietnam was to turn to a higher power. We had an Episcopal service in the field in Vietnam—I got closer to religion. A lot of guys didn't, but I did. I'm not the kind of guy who goes to church every Sunday . . . but I'm the kind of guy who has my rosaries on the wall downstairs. I'm the kind of guy who doesn't go down to the chapel, but—every morning and every evening—I say my prayers.

PHILEMON PEARSON

When I came back from the first tour, they told us to change clothes—buy civilian clothes—before we left the base. No way I'd do that. In the Nam, I was just surviving, going along with everybody else, but I went home, and I had the attitude, "You should *know* what I went through. *I'm* not telling you, but *you* should know it. That's my attitude." My aunt said, "I don't *want* to know what you've been through." I sat down with my mother, we cried for seven days . . . and then I just kept on surviving.

When we got back home the last time—coming out of Vietnam with that kind of stress or whatever you want to call it . . . at the time I did not know I was under stress, nor did I care. I was a basket case. I came back to the land of the big PX. I went to my mom's place, and for a week I just kept taking baths, sleeping, and sitting on the porch in my housecoat. I loved that. It took about two months to get that dirt off my skin. It just kept coming out and coming out.

I started dreaming these dreams about things that happened in the Nam, *exactly* the way they happened . . . the troops got killed, and all of that. The same things happened—that was normal—but then the dead bodies started getting up out of the ground. They were coming out of the graves, dust flying. They'd sit up and come out of the grave, and the people sitting up were my relatives—my family. This dream was like a weekly thing. Two Brothers got out of the damned grave . . . one Brother got out of the grave twice. He's retired Air Force now. The other Brother got out of the grave, and he was a minister. I said, "Wait—wait—wait! If I get to my mom coming out of a grave, I've fucking had it!" I decided, if I see Mom come out of the ground, I *am* nuts.

This stuff—what it was was just stress, but nobody knew what it was. In '72, I was assigned down in Fort Hood, Texas, and I would get to where I couldn't hardly breathe, and I'd get nervous . . . my heart would go like a million. I didn't want nobody around me . . . nothing . . . nobody. A car door slamming outside would have me like a basket case. A long time later I was working at the VA—that's where I found out I had stress disorder. This was in 1980, and they didn't know too much about it. One day I told this one medic, "I feel like a stick of dynamite. I'm just going to explode." He says, "What's the matter?" I says, "The goddamned Nam—but I'm going to explode *here—now."* I really felt like I was just going to blow up.

I was headstrong about alcohol. "You got to take my life, man, if you try to mess with my booze. Who the hell are you?" I think the main reason for that is when you're in the service, when we speak to each other, in most cases you can take that information to the White House.

We mean business. When you retire and you try to do this, to get this type of relationship with people, the trust is gone. The honor's just not there. A lot of us don't trust, and I'm one of them. But I trust these guys here at the Vet Center more than I trust anyone in Washington State. They're dumb enough to tell me the truth. If you have a plan and you deviate from the plan, you deviate for a reason, not because you decided to look at the dogs another ten minutes or whatever. I'm the guy that if you tell you're going to meet at seven and you come in at seven twenty, I got the ass with you. I don't understand that. Other people don't think like me—I've got to get out of that.

I'm not used to a lot of things—"thinking commercially," as I call it. Like planning a trip—"Yeah, I want to go with you, but I'll get back to you later." It's like you don't have no respect—like you think commercially. If you don't watch it—me—if I don't watch it, if things start going badly . . . especially between me and my lady . . . I'm vulnerable. I told my doctor about it. When my lady and I aren't getting along too good, it's like I'm in a daze or something. I just let it drift me right into where I say, "Fuck it. I'm comfortable here in this stage, though I know this is a no-no, but sometimes I start thinking negative." That's when the boys here at the Vet Center say, "Hey! Get off your ass!"

I started coming here to the Vets' Center for anger management and everything else that would help me out, but I also was drinking. I went in for alcoholic treatment in November of 1988. I'm still sober. I've got almost two years of being sober. When I gave up the drinking, and I meant it from my heart, that's when I started using Higher Power. I share things that bother me, and I believe in the Higher Power. That is the way I get by from day to day. God is the Higher Power. God . . . not necessarily religion. The reason I say Higher Power is when I went into treatment—I was raised up in a straight church, holy rollers—I defied anybody that said, "You need God." I didn't want that. When they said, "Use your Higher Power. It can be anything you want it to be." I now know I need God. I want God to be my Higher Power.

You'll probably feel better when I tell you, "Why don't you use your Higher Power? You got it." It can be a battery, a chair, a motorcycle—rocks—whatever works, use it. In my case, I'm still wearing my cross . . . this cross I have around my neck. I bought it in 1968 in Duc Hoa, and we've been through some deep shit. Everybody had something. This cross is what I wanted. When I got hit, from then on I held onto my cross.

What happens here at the Vet Center is exactly like that Brotherhood in Vietnam. When our group meets here at the Vet Center, that *is* the Brotherhood . . . same damned thing. We all got involved because we got in similar situations. Now we're here, and that Brotherhood is just as strong. Nonracist, too—it doesn't exist. Everybody belongs in this place . . . those in the rear—women. If you're a Vietnam vet, and stuff is kicking you around, we know what made you wrong. If you need some help, get in here. When I go out to American Lake for medical attention . . . I see these guys that are sent there to the PTSD program because there is something wrong with them similar to us. I say, "Hey, man—come aboard. We been raggedy for a long time, but now we're going to be raggedy together. We're going to keep pushing on this shit until there ain't no more."

Seventy percent of the problems I had, I've still got, but now I know what to do with them. They are not in charge of me this time. Drinking was magnifying the problems. I would get depressed about the Nam, and damn!—here comes the depression along with the booze. I lost time. I really don't know what the hell happened some of the time back then. I was taking my Emempramine, and one day I forgot I took the shit. I drank some vodka I found stashed in my car. I almost bit the dust. If it hadn't been for my girlfriend . . . I don't remember the whole thing to this day. I work at Boeing, and when this garbage hits, you just cry. As it happens, I felt safe getting to my supervisor. She and two other people there I feel good about talking to, but I found that bottle and drank it and ended up in the VA again.

My girlfriend came to see me, and I was asleep. She called to me, and I opened my eyes, and she couldn't see nothing but white. As it kept on coming down, eventually I said, "Fuck it," and I meant that. "The hell with it. So you die, you son of a bitch. Your fucking buddies didn't make it, anyway." If you don't do anything about that kind of thinking, you're thinking about suicide . . . but I just happen to believe in God, my Higher Power. He's got some details on your ass, *if* you throw away this life, and I *know* that. That's why I went in and got my treatment.

I wanted to know, "What is my mission? I've got to have my mission. My whole adult life, I had a mission, so what's my mission now?" This Vet Center, this is my life. When everything gets garbagelike, I can come here. I asked the group, "What is my mission?" I told them, "I have to have a mission." They said, "This drifting around, it's just hell, so set up some goals. One: Pay the bills. Two: You've got a pretty girl to get you off that medication. Keep that if you can. That's your mission." She's got two sons, ten and twelve. I've been with her off and on since those kids were three and five. I quit drinking, and she quit drinking. We don't scare those boys any more. Not only is it good for me, it's fantastic for them, because you can get kids all bent out of shape.

To make a long story short, I found out, "If you want help, asshole, you got to be sober. Period. That's where you start out at." I had always said, "I ain't changing my life for nobody"—*wronng*. That's where you start at. Nobody told me to stop drinking—that's where I started at. I said, "I can't blow this because of the guys." So if I've got a problem, these guys know what I'm talking about.

The problem is, you see, you go to sleep, and you think you're doing pretty good, but your brain says, "Hey! Remember this shit? It's the same shit you did in the Nam!" In this one dream, the Nam comes to me dressed in purple, and it comes from the skies. And it changes . . . and now it's green . . . I'm flying around the place in my dream, and some asshole is sticking me with a javelin or something, and he's hitting me, too. Then I come down on the ground, and we're getting ready to get ambushed—I already know this in the dream. I say, "No sweat, baby—got some shit for you, too!" Then the enemy comes out, and these guys are giants. They're dressed in purple, and they're wiping us out. They get hit—we're blowing the shit out of them . . . and they keep standing up. They take all these hits, and they keep standing there . . . they're blowing us to bits.

I'm hit, but I can't run fast enough. I'm trying to wake up, and the whole world's tying me down. Finally, I jump out of bed, but I'm on the wrong side. I reach down to grab my equipment on the way to the bunker, and I can't find anything. My weapon is missing—I can't find my fatigues, and my jungle boots are missing. "Who the hell got my weapon, and where's the shower room, man?" I wake up, and I'm looking for the shower room, and I still can't find my fatigues and boots, and my weapon.

To be perfectly honest with you, I don't know from day to day how I'll feel inside. Sometimes I'm like a fucking stick of dynamite to myself even, so I just don't know. That's why it's so good to have Dr. Chinn around and Dave and these guys here at the Vet Center. If I get uptight, I can dry out here. They know what's wrong with me. Sometimes I say, "Fuck it," and I mean that with all my heart . . . or sometimes I get angry about something, and I don't know what the hell caused it. When I was in treatment, I learned, "Thoughts create feelings, and feelings create attitudes." So if I can master my thoughts—what the hell was I thinking about when this shit started—I can then unthink it . . . give it to the Higher Power.

I don't think of myself as a failure—no way. What we did in Vietnam was comply to orders. We advanced when instructed, we stopped when instructed. They said to get out of the country, we got out of the country. We'd have been a failure—*if* we'd failed to do what they said. We were just permitted to go so far and stop. If we wanted to stop the war, we should have been up North, making it very uncomfortable for Mister Charles and the NVA, having them hide from us, *but* we wasn't allowed to. We just waited . . . waited for him to come down South and do what he wanted when he was ready. You didn't know who was who, to be honest with you. A lot of people are on both sides . . . it was just difficult.

That's about what I want to say, I guess. I shared it for the students. I tried to simplify to where they know where I'm coming from. What I want them to know is deep at the bottom of my heart, I would do that again if it meant that they stayed free. I would go through all of it again to keep America the way it is, for sure. What do I think about war? It sucks. I *would* like to say that if they have anything to do with voting whether we fight or not, the only thing I say is, *only* fight *if* someone tries to take America from us . . . or tries to make Americans do what they don't want to do in our own country. Nobody's changing anything here. That's a purpose, right there, that I would go to war if I had to crawl to get there—*if* someone tries to change America. If you can avoid a war, by all means do that, but remember—the ones that survive are going to be in a situation like I am. You can deal with it, but there's no way out of that.

CHUCK SIMMS

When I got back from my first tour, I was in the Fire Department and the Military Police. I got promised helicopter school. I got debriefed when I got back from Vietnam by a colonel who told me to keep quiet about certain incidents that happened in Vietnam—that it was classified, and Leavenworth was a possibility for me if I did talk. I felt it was my duty not to. I had to go to Letterman Hospital there, and they had to take a tendon out of my foot to put in my thumb to make it work again. Years later, in a Veterans' Administration hospital, I had to have my whole wrist fixed because there was a bone in there that wouldn't heal. They got a bone out of my foot for that. That was some time later. It's so long ago that I can't get some of those details in order.

One day I was out on a patrol going across the Golden Gate Bridge. I saw a guy climbing up on the north tower cable heading toward the top. I called into the provost marshall's office, and they radioed back and said there was not supposed to be anyone up on the bridge. So I pulled the vehicle over, ran across to that cable on the ocean side, climbed up that cable, and caught up to him. He indicated that he was going to jump when he got to the top, so I grabbed him. He tried to pull us both over. I grabbed ahold of a cable, and I was hanging on and trying to keep both of us from going over. A highway patrolman came running up the cable to help me. He made it just in time. He grabbed him and put handcuffs on him. We assisted him down, and I turned him over to the Highway Patrol and went back on duty. It was no normal patrol.

In the meantime, I volunteered for helicopter school, and they put me through all the paces. I had taken all these tests they wanted me to take—mental and physical—and passed them with flying colors. The night I got off that cable, somebody told me they wanted to see me down at the company. I was thinking, "Wow! They're finally going to give me some credit for something after I helped save this guy's life." The 1st sergeant waltzed me into the company commander, and he said, "You know a man named Robert Cook?" I said, "Yes." He said, "You gave him permission to bring his car on post, and he doesn't have insurance." I said, "Yeah, I gave him permission just to work on it and take it right back off." He said, "You're not authorized to give that kind of permission. We're going to court-martial you." They court-martialed me with a summary court-martial—which is the lowest court-martial you can get—but it's still not good. They restricted me to the post for thirty days. I thought, "What a slap in the face just after I climbed down off that bridge."

When it came time to do the final signing in to get into helicopter school, I walked over there with my black girlfriend. She stayed outside while I went in. The personnel office told me that because of my court-martial, I couldn't go to helicopter school. That was another blow . . . they promised me that . . . I more or less took it for granted that if I keep my mouth shut about what happened in Vietnam, I would get to go to helicopter school. I didn't know until quite recently—when I took the chopper ride the other day . . . it had been bothering me . . . all these years. I couldn't hold it in any longer. I was telling people that I just didn't want to reenlist to go to helicopter school. I couldn't face what the Army . . . did to me. That's one of the reasons I came here to this PTSD program. It has caused me stress all these years, and I didn't know it. When it came out the other day, it relieved a lot of tension.

When I got out of the service, I tried to enlist in another name—to clear off that summary court-martial so they couldn't do that to me again. At the same time, I got a job at the police department. Two police departments, actually, but I didn't like that. I tried to go to school at Oregon State University. I found I was too keyed up to continue school. I joined the Smoke Jumper Team back here, over in Redmond, Oregon, for a while, but I tried to get back to Vietnam. I felt impotent. That's when I enlisted in the merchant marines.

When I finally got out, I wouldn't wear anything that would let them know I had been in Vietnam. I let my hair grow very long. I'd be sitting in a bar, drinking in Vancouver or Seattle, and somebody would say,

"Ah, you hippy fucking draft dodger." They didn't know my history. Then I'd say, "Why, hell, you probably never went there." There would be a big argument. They'd say, "You been there, let me see your ID." I'd show it to them, and they would still want to fight or something. They'd say, "Ah, you baby killer." That was one of their favorites.

I got to where I started isolating. I'd get drunk and take some downers and knock myself out. To put it bluntly, I didn't get a hard-on for seven years. I don't know what to attribute it to—maybe Agent Orange or those other chemicals . . . maybe just stress. I didn't give a shit if the sun came up or went down . . . I tried to kill myself. I ended up in jail. I never did anything bad, like felonies. It was all stupid-ass shit.

I had a nervous breakdown in '74. The cops put me in jail down in Vancouver, Washington. I ended up in a county hospital over at Columbia View. Columbia View transferred me to American Lake. They locked me up for four months. They said I was schizophrenic, psychotic, manic-depressive—some damned thing. From '74 on, I just started going from mental institution to mental institution. Nobody knew anything about PTSD. They'd medicate you, let you smoke your head off and drink all the coffee you wanted, as long as you sat in the corner and didn't bother anyone until chow time.

I got married about five years ago. This is my third wife. We had this baby when I was forty-seven. One of the guys I met in Vietnam and I bought a little ranch out here in the hills about two years ago. He had been in everything from Korea up until the time the *Vincennes* got fired on in the Persian Gulf. He is fifty-nine years old. They marched him off the *Vincennes* at gunpoint—he cracked up. I thank God somebody came up with this PTSD diagnosis to figure out what's wrong with guys like us. We didn't know what the hell was wrong with us. When I found out what was wrong with me, I started shaping up. I could see the light at the end of the tunnel . . . I quit self-medicating . . . I quit drinking at that time. I'm trying to get better.

I could have been dead. I came close to being dead . . . so many times . . . all those people I saw die. I almost died at my own hands that one time. It simply was not knowing what was wrong with me. I know other guys who are dead. My brother is dead. My father is dead . . . they didn't make it. My brother was twenty-seven when he died. My dad was forty-seven, and he died after World War II with PTSD. Looking back on it, I know that was what he had. I didn't get along with him. I feel like, when I finish here, I can go back to school—maybe get back into society. We've got a little boy now. He is three years old. I have a lot of plans.

If there is one thing I could say about war, what would it be? Don't let your son go, that's all I can say. You've lost him once he's gone . . . I don't care what happens. If he doesn't get killed there, your son is going to come back damaged. I wish there were some way for the American people to find an alternative to war. "War . . . , " it's been said so many times before—and I feel it, too . . . "War is hell." It's a hell that nobody should have to go through . . . either side . . . for some lousy, stinking, two-bit government. It tells its sons, "Go fight for me, because you are preserving our way of life. Prevent the war from coming over here." Well . . . the other side feels exactly the same way.

DONALD HEDGES

When I came back from Vietnam, I went to Parris Island for Drill Instructor duty. They wanted me to teach troops. I said, "I can't. I'm sorry. I don't want any part of it." I just wanted out. I went to my screening board, and I took copies of the things I had written—I showed them to this psychologist, and I showed them to this board. I went through a lot of hell, but they let me off drill instructor duty and made me a rifle coach. I got more out of that. I could teach the rifle—I couldn't shoot it, but I could teach it.

I just got by from day to day. I started using pot. I'd smoked once in Vietnam, early in my first tour, but I started using it at Parris Island because most of them there were smoking, and I finally got high on the crap, so I started enjoying it, too. We started an underground newspaper when I was there. We had it all ready to go, but never actually published. We figured our odds of getting out were more important.

I got out May 1, 1970. Except for the days when my children were born, it had to be the happiest day of my life. I just kept singing that song, "Raindrops Keep Falling on My Head." I bought a motorcycle. I was going to tour the U.S., but it was still kind of cold, so I held up in Daytona Beach, Florida—worked at a car wash. I had eleven hundred dollars in my pocket. I toured the southern U.S. and visited one of the guys from my squad in West Virginia. He had been in Vietnam four times. He came to me as a radioman, a private, on his fourth tour. It was one of the greatest teams ever. He knew what to do, and I knew how to get it done.

My parents had been divorced while I was in Vietnam. I went back to Eugene and stayed with my dad until my unemployment came through. I was just going to take it easy for a while. Well—a while turned out to be like three years. I went to school a couple of years at Lane Community College. I just didn't know what I wanted to do, basically. Every summer I'd take off and move back and forth across the country. I had

PTSD then, I suppose. I was stoned and doing what I wanted to do, and I had no responsibilities, so it didn't bother me.

Loud noises really bothered me. I did a lot of things my ex-wife tells me that I did, but I didn't know I had changed like I had. She's told me stories . . . that just blow my mind. I was real passive. I organized a peace demonstration. I didn't fight—I didn't even kill insects. I was a vegetarian . . . I was just totally turned off with death.

I met my ex-wife—my soon-to-be wife, actually. I said, "Look—I'm going to Vermont this fall to experience the fall. Why don't you go with me?" She said, "Sure," and we just took off, but I got her pregnant. I didn't really love her, but I married her, anyway. I had to do the right thing. I'm glad I met her though, because she tells me things about how I was back then . . . things I thought were normal then, but I had PTSD back then, and I didn't even realize it. The surprising thing was we stayed together—that's what's real weird. She tried to love me. I could just never get close to her. I've gotten close to her recently, but while we were married—never.

My kids are beautiful, but they cope with their feelings the same way I have. I didn't physically abuse them, but I terrified them. I was unpredictable and explosive, and they never knew what I was going to do next—*I* never knew what I was going to do next. PTSD is contagious—it ripples—people pick up symptoms. I see it in my kids so much . . . and it just kills me. We're to the point now where they're not afraid of me anymore, which is real nice. As a matter of fact, we're almost friends, but we still need to go a little farther . . . be able to communicate how we feel about one another . . . and that's kind of my mission.

In '76—I actually quit drugs for about two years, after I was first married—I started smoking pot again, and that just led to a lot of acid. Probably in '89, I did hundreds of hits of acid, along with amphetamines . . . started drinking late in '89, and—BOY! That's a beauty drug. You don't dream on booze. Nightmares have been something that have been with me always, so I just figured that was the normal course.

It wasn't until about '76, when I started using pot again, that I got into a violent cycle. I started attacking people on the streets with no provocation—they were looking at me wrong. To me, that was provocation, and my poor wife . . . here I would be jumping on somebody, yelling and screaming in somebody's face, and she's going, "Darling, what was that all about?" I'd say, "Didn't you see the way he was looking at me?" Or somebody would pull up into my crosswalk when I was trying to cross the street, and—"HEY! Buddy! This is *MY* crosswalk." I mean, I was just a maniac. Plus . . . the way I was always mentally abusing my wife at home. She finally had to get out, and I don't blame her. Anyone who gets close to me, I'll find some way to get you away from me. I think that probably goes back to Rudy . . . I really loved him . . . I feel like he took my bullet . . . that's how I feel.

I worked for Weyerhaeuser for sixteen years—that was the last thing I lost. I lost my home first, then my family, and I held the job for about six years after I was divorced, and finally the people I was working with went to the boss and said, "We're afraid of what this guy is going to do to our wives and children." And they had legitimate reasons to feel that way . . . and I thought they were all screwed up—you see?

I was one of the guys who said, "These guys who are collecting money from the VA, saying they're having problems over the war, are just a bunch of crybabies." The war didn't bother me . . . hell, no, it didn't bother me! That's one thing about it. It's like alcoholism—there's that strong denial thing. You honestly don't see it. Then I went down to the Vet Center shortly after I was divorced—sat in on my first group . . . these guys were sitting there telling how their lives were going . . . it was like, "WHOA! That's me!" I was just waiting for somebody to fuck up . . . and I felt justified in screwing somebody up *real* good. The least I could do was feel guilty.

I made some attempts at sobriety through the years, always to relapse again. I've got four months and ten days right now—which is the longest I've ever had. I went through two groups at the Vet Center, and I don't know why I never did anything else. I didn't know anything else I was supposed to do. That's when I really started a lot of acid, and the crisis at work—that was really what did it.

I got hooked up with a psychologist out at Issaquah, Dr. Ellison, and he was hooked up with the VA system, and he could see I was killing myself . . . I sure couldn't. I was setting other people up to kill me, but I never tried to kill myself. I just didn't have the balls. I believe in heaven and hell, so I knew where I was going . . . so I'd find all these subconscious ways to get somebody else to do it for me . . . or, like with drugs and alcohol . . . just self-destructive . . . self-punishment.

This program is excellent. The people care about you. I still don't like this fucking place, though. I'd rather go back to Vietnam and build hospitals, or preach the gospel, or something constructive . . . I don't *need* to be here. I felt bad because we took off and left them. When we first left, I said, "Who's going to stop the NVA if we pull out?" They said, "We're going to Vietnamize." Sure enough, as soon as the Marines pulled out—here come the NVA. I don't begrudge the Vietnamese what they've done here in the States. *We* committed to them, and then *we* up and left them. "Sorry!" Of course, I would like a little bit of compensation myself, too, you know, but I don't begrudge them what they've done.

The only thing I can say about war is, "Don't." I can remember while I was there—the second tour especially—thinking, "There has got to be another way. Here's this little guy fighting that little guy. We don't mean *nothing*. So why kill him? What does it mean?" One man's death does not affect war policy. I don't have—well, I do have some answers. Bring everybody up to the same economic level—that's the first step. Once you have your basic needs met, then you start thinking of other things— like art, and music, and spiritual things . . . your own psyche. As long as there are these little Third World countries—they're still fighting for freedom and territory. That's just the start. I believe the answer is spiritual—it's an individual thing.

When I saved that little guy on the Laotian border, it was like that was the beginning of my spiritual awakening . . . "This is a human being here! We're related. We have a spirit that is common. I care for you, you care for me—we don't destroy each other." I think of God as a categorical imperative. That's why we're here—to search him out—find out who he is . . . and serve him . . . and I believe . . . by serving man, we serve God.

Vietnam was the most important part of my life—the most exciting, fulfilling. I wouldn't trade it for anything, because it's given me a lot of good things. But at the same time, it's given me post-traumatic stress disorder—which is like a broken leg. If I'd known this was going to happen, I might have been able to start taking care of it back in the seventies instead of 1990. So I don't regret Vietnam . . . I wouldn't trade it for anything, but I hope they are telling the people who were in Panama—and Grenada and Beirut—"Get some help now, so you won't have to do it twenty years down the road"—and I think they are. The military is a little resistant to it still, but I think there's some moves being made now.

I did want to mention something about the marines. I expected to be fighting farmers. When I first got there, I said something about "Charlie," and my team leader—we were down in this bunker—and my team leader says, "Up here, he's not Charlie. He's Mister Charles, and you're going to respect that little motherfucker—or he's going to kill you." Let me tell you, the Vietnamese people—especially the NVA—they got heart. A French commander called them the best light infantry in the world. I don't think they're the best—we kicked their ass—but they're good men. I'd really like to meet this guy I captured at the end of my second tour and see how it's going with him, and . . . that's all.

VLADISLAV TAMAROV

I came on the airplane from Kabul to Tashkent, and after that I fly to Leningrad. A friend met me in the airport with a taxi. It was dark, but we went everywhere to see my city, you know? I was drunk, of course, because he had a bottle of cognac with him. We were drinking in the taxi and giving some to the taxi driver. We just look around the city, and after that came to his home. I didn't go home. This was night, and I like to be away from my parents this night.

After that, I called my girlfriend and found out she needed to get married after one and a half months. I did not know this when I was in Afghanistan. In Afghanistan, I have—you remember . . . you defend the dreams of this boy who now sleeps with your girl. This was, of course, not my wife, and this boy is not guilty because this happened to 95 percent of the Afghantsis—this is Soviet veteran of Afghanistan. Some girls sent letters saying, "Sorry, I have a marriage." This was happening *a lot*.

Three days later, I was at the college tavern. Some people just look at you and think Afghanistan, because there is a lot of sun in Afghanistan. Everybody with a white face was tanned not quite like a black man, but close. People can see you're from Afghanistan. Near my home, the place where people drink beer outside, somebody there said, "You were in Afghanistan? Let's go! Let's go!" They left. Some buy me a drink, not to listen to my stories, but just to say, "For you, boy!"

The time just after Afghanistan, I thought this going down there was the right thing to do . . . then maybe so or maybe no, maybe no . . . then I decided this kind of war was wrong. I did not decide all by myself, of course. At first, I didn't say this for me, because I didn't connect my feelings to it, but then I connected feelings with the Vietnam veterans last summer over here, and maybe more this time. This is very interesting and very difficult topic, this kind of war.

My new girlfriend, who I loved, didn't understand anything. When I was in the United States in summer of 1989, I was writing to her. It was a long distance from our country, like Afghanistan. She just came to another boy and left me. She was . . . she didn't feel safe with me. The whole time I am away, she didn't know where I was or what I was doing. She didn't understand why I did it, you know? With him, she felt safer than with me. People cannot understand why sometimes we do what we do.

I can trust for sure, or I can *not* trust for sure, too. In the usual life at home you cannot see this . . . this kind of situation. All parts of people come out in war. One time, some people ask me what I think of difference between those who were in Afghanistan and those who were not. I can tell the difference. I want to say this, because all Afghantsis are different, but those who were good guys, they have special kind of . . . you see, in Afghanistan all parts of man come out and change . . . Afghanistan change these parts, these percentages of the dark side, the bad side, and the light side are changed in war. They change percents of dark and light. In usual peacetime life, you don't notice this changes, but in some kinds of situations, like Afghanistan or Vietnam, you see it—you see this changes of percents, and you know the good guys and the bad guys.

There's a lot of problems, because this is part of Afghan veterans who killed people and came to this line in their percents of light and dark . . . there was another time when making this oral history tape would have been easy . . . you see, I am afraid in Afghanistan, since I don't know how to fight. I know how to kill . . . and if I lose control, I can just kill. I cannot do anything that is me . . . kill, that's all. Sometimes I am now afraid to fight.

What happened when I saw my parents? They became much older because this was such a hard time for my parents . . . maybe more hard for them than for me. I think I have good relationship with my parents. Sometimes you don't like everything, but I think that's okay. But see why I don't want to tell? I don't want people to listen . . . they cannot understand the dark side. I feel . . . and I know they must feel, too, if they hear. They should not have to feel this . . . they cannot understand . . . sometime dark feelings will come for them.

When I came back from Afghanistan, there is a change. Sometimes, I can't stop my anger. I speak loudly . . . I yell . . . I feel the same, but there is a change. I want to talk with people about how I feel, maybe I learn a little bit about myself. Now maybe everything is changing. After Afghanistan, I understand so much more. I think like this. Sometimes I see what people want inside, because I saw people without some kinds of walls around them in Afghanistan . . . how they really look and how they really are inside.

I had some dreams about Afghanistan. I don't know if I still have them—I don't remember my dreams just now. I can tell about a time before this time when I came here, one Afghan veteran's wife told me— and she's right—about her husband. He met Americans, Vietnam veterans. They sit him in front of this American that said, "I have bad dreams after Vietnam, do you?" "Yes." "See! You do, too!" Important to note this—*very* important: "You have, I have, too." Dreams are just one of the ways this war is coming from inside your body to outside. This is another way: I feel so uncomfortable when, for example, I am in the woods alone. I don't like to be alone. Sometimes I am afraid from the dark woods, sometimes from too much light from the moon . . . because I know there's dangers. I'm afraid. I don't know why. When I was in Afghanistan, I was not afraid of these things because my friends were around me, and I had a weapon. Now I don't have a weapon. Maybe I can think why. I try to help myself. I have my best friend, Lenia Ivanov.

He travels with me in the United States now. We can buy a drink, smoke a cigarette, listen to Kitaro, see a couple of girls, you know?

I think I learned a lot in Afghanistan. I understand my place in life and what I need to do . . . this may not be photography, but I know for what reason I want to do that. After army, I didn't go back to this old college. I came to a special kind of cinema institute in Soviet Union. I feel like to be a cameraman, but I decide they try to teach me what I already know. I decide no. I decide to be a photographer, without any kind of this special document. I'm a photographer, which I was also in Afghanistan.

I have some projects. I bring my book of photographs of Afghanistan to the United States to be published. If I publish a book, I would like to bring here some Afghantsis who have no prosthesis. Many veterans have no prosthesis. I would like to bring Americans to Soviet Union to produce this prosthesis. A lot of people can help.

Coming here is a step—so is this book. I want to tell people about war—so you read your book, you read my book . . . you read my book, you will feel how this world looks to me. I don't like this military way, but what can the world do? That's how I feel. I want Iraq out of Kuwait, but what can we do? We'd be great if there's no army, no military, no fighting . . . but maybe this has to be. War will be.

JIM GOLDSTINE

Duty, honor, country. What you have to understand is that I really believe in those words. It's like, "That is truth." Trying to attach a label to those three words—duty, honor, country—is difficult because, like everything else, everybody brings their own baggage and their own filters along about something like that. To me those are very emotionally charged words. The thing that's missing is willingness to accept somebody else's definition—from where they're coming from.

At least we're at the point where each of us allows the other their own space—like the defense of the country against foreign aggressors and all that. Walt Kelly had the best line I have ever read: "We have met the enemy, and he is us." Why don't we get our shit together? All this hullabaloo that recently hit about the desecration of the flag comes to me with the secondary thought that says, "*If* we did something about balancing the budget and dealing responsibly with what's going on in this country, maybe we wouldn't *have* to deal with an amendment to the Constitution about the desecration of the flag." If you take that thought process and transfer it back to where we originally started, I think you start getting a sense of where I am with those words. What it's about is protecting what we have in this country against *all* problems.

Aftermath

I can't even begin to describe what went on in my mind about four years ago when the first crop of Vietnamese kids started coming through the colleges in the United States. In the same year, the honor graduate at CCNY was Vietnamese, and up at the Military Academy, we had somebody graduate second or third who was Vietnamese. Most of the people that got into this country following the fall of Saigon were the whores, politicians, the liars, the cheats, the thieves. Okay? I'm not putting any value judgment on it, because probably the most honorable of the whole bunch were the prostitutes. But the fact that their offspring come here, and essentially by virtue of their own efforts and desire, create their own results—*that* says what this country is all about . . . and that's something worth being protected.

What you've got to understand is that most of the people that came back from the war wanted isolation—up to a point. I became an accountant so I could work alone—and of course I deal with people every day. One of the things I learned from my experience in Life Spring was that I'm responsible for everything that goes on in my life, no matter how peripheral it may look. I at least create the environment in which it happens, and there are levels of causality about what happens. Finally, for me, at least, I want something more than isolation. I've got to tell you that my experience was just about like that . . . and eighteen years after the fact, I stood up in a room of about thirty people or so and said, "I'm Jim Goldstine, and I am a murderer."

The Life Spring Basic Course is a five-day program. One of the commitments I made was to be on time. On Friday night, I was running behind, so I was speeding to be on time. I was out there in the left lane . . . how I really felt showed up in my driving. Wildly aggressive and driving on the edge. That's where I would really show up in terms of what I was carrying around with me. Like I really didn't care whether I lived or died when I was on the road.

So here I am driving seventy-five in the left lane, and some idiot pulls out of the center lane without signaling and parks in front of me. What was just absolutely amazing was, normally I'd go off into a string of expletives—but I didn't. I just backed off about three or four car lengths, and then it hit me what I had just done. Holy Shit! It was the first time I'd had an insight into why I'd been driving like I was driving—without benefit of a seat belt. When my daughter, Kris, came home from school, I had a conversation with her about taking responsibility, and she said, "Yes, I've noticed you're acting more responsibly and starting to use your seat belt." It was true.

Throughout all of this there was this conversation I had with myself: "How can I feel the way I do about what went on when I never was really exposed to the extremes of violence?" All I know is how I feel about some of the violence that went on . . . for me . . . and I just can't imagine what's happening to folks that really had something big happen. It's just impossible for me to get a sense of that except for when I talk to them. Kris gave me a book for Christmas that was taken by a bunch of photographers at The Wall in D.C., and there's one picture in there that just caught me of a guy hugging somebody—another veteran—and the pain on his face . . . I just can't describe . . . but I know what it is. Just looking at that picture, I can feel what I think he must feel. It's there. And you don't have to be a rocket scientist to figure it out. It's just one of those things that grabs you by the throat.

There's part of me that says I'm never going to be different than what I was, because I'm not willing to fight my feelings every day. But there's another part of me that says, "You can beat this any time—just beat it up—you can!" One of the exercises we went through in Life Spring was picking out somebody you were least attracted to—someone who hit your mad button—and sitting down and having a conversation with them. I had one young man, a teenager, pick me out, and one of his buttons was my haircut. His father had been in the military, and all the authority issues that he owned were right there between us. It was amazing to sit down and listen to somebody talk about that symbol. But I embodied everything that hooked him and hit his button. It was amazing to be able to sit down and listen to what he was saying and keep that separation—that he was not talking about you, he was talking with you.

It was out of this sense of romanticism—out of doing something that was important just for the doing, I think—that got me involved a long time ago. My mother cried to give her son as a soldier. I laugh at that still . . . but I guess where I am now . . . I've got five grandkids, and four of them are boys. If some misbegotten son of a bitch tries to send them off to a similar kind of war, he's going to have me in his in-box— and he is *not* going to be happy. At the risk of sounding trite about all this, nothing short of high moral purpose could justify their going to war—and it better be damned high.

EMMETT FINN

I ended up coming home on emergency leave. I didn't know I was coming home. All of a sudden, I was on a chopper, and I came in, and my father was dying they told me. I was flown immediately from there to Pleiku, and I picked up my gear, and they flew me out to Cam Ranh Bay. It was a body plane, bringing back the dead. There was eight of us alive on the plane. There were two hundred–some bodies—something like that. That's how I came home. I came home on a body ship.

I flew into Fort Lewis and got on a civilian plane and flew to Baltimore International Airport. Within thirty hours, I was home . . . from being out on an operation in Vietnam to being in a hospital with my father. He was operated on for lung cancer, so they stationed me close to home. I spent every weekend at home until he died, four months after I got home from Vietnam . . . I spent ten months in Vietnam.

It sometimes bothers me . . . that I even *think* my commander may have been right in relieving me. I really agonized over my men that were still left out in the field. They were very special to me. I'm not bragging that my pain's greater than an enlisted man's, but there's a difference in what I felt at twenty-two. The people I lost . . . I didn't really have the opportunity to really be their buddy and be their close friend . . . but at the same time, I felt very close to them, and they felt very close to me.

I didn't talk about Vietnam . . . I didn't have anybody close to me in my life that was a Vietnam veteran for about sixteen years. Then I started having a lot of emotional problems . . . drug abuse . . . I just thought I was strong enough to carry the pain alone. I didn't want to talk to anybody about it. The memory of my men is very sacred to me. The mental part of the responsibility I felt in making decisions, I have suffered a lot of grief over . . . just the circumstance of sending four men, who I didn't even know their names, into a bunker to have them die instantly . . . that's been a difficult thing for me in my life.

I think the main difference between my distress and that of an enlisted man is that thing about them being my men. I think it was really pointed out to me . . . I went through The Book—the list of the names on The Wall—since I've been in the program here, and found Willy Bridges's and James Harris's names . . . for twenty-two years I thought they were younger than they were. They were about eighteen or nineteen years old. I was only twenty when I took over command. They turned out to be twenty-four when they were killed . . . they were three and a half years older than me.

When I came back from Vietnam, I was very distant and very different. I didn't have anybody in my family—especially my family—because I think they were just glad to have their baby brother back . . . but at the same time, they didn't *get* their baby brother back. There was a lot of anger and resentment and a lot of hatred and a lot of ugly things. I moved back and was taking care of my mom, but I was . . . I'm just getting in touch with this now . . . the nightmares I was having and her coming after Dad died . . .

Mom used to . . . she came in once, and I was standing in the bedroom with a .38 revolver I kept under the pillow. I remember how scared she was. I started drinking a lot and doing a lot of drugs. She'd wait up for me at night, and . . . I was real hard on her. My oldest brother was trying to be my father, and he was all pissed off at me because I was worrying Mom and stuff . . . but it was like . . . I couldn't stand it, you know? I didn't know what to do. I just gave up everything. I just left and hit the road with a backpack and sold my new car and threw away all my clothes and pretty much dropped out. I just bummed around for a lot of years.

I just wanted to be alone. I went to Canada. I've always done things backward in my life—I went to Vietnam, then came back and went to Canada. I lived alone about 250 miles north of Toronto. I'd use snowshoes once a week to go in and get a can of tobacco . . . actually, I went there because I wanted to find out if I wanted to live or if I wanted to die. I decided I wanted to live . . . I did try. I didn't live healthy, but I touched some lives. I'm sure they were glad they knew me.

People in my family, friends of my brothers that saw me grow up as a little kid would stop me in the middle of the street when my hair grew long and I was doing a lot of drugs—they'd stop their trucks and jump out. This one guy, Mack Smith . . . he was just in tears two years after I got back, saying, "What happened to the kid? What happened to that guy who was sitting in my bar, that was going over to stop communism? What the fuck happened to you?" He was crying. I said, "He died, Mack. He never came home." I just walked off . . . I just left him there, you know?

I think the funny, happy-go-lucky, real protected, small-town, Appalachian, coal-mining, Irish-Catholic baby of the family was terrorized. I was a lot older at twenty-four than I am now. I didn't feel close to anyone. I went and saw *The Deer Hunter* once, and people asked me, "What did you find? Was that what Vietnam was really like?" I said, "There was one powerful part in the movie that I had to leave. It was when the guy came back and hid behind the little shack the next morning because they had a homecoming party and all his friends were coming out and playing grab-ass. They were all the same, and he was changed forever."

I really felt that when I had Greg and Gary Cittic, two twins that I grew up with as early as I could remember, threw a homecoming party for me. My friends . . . I thought they looked at me out of the corner of their eye like, "Emmett's really changed." They were curious, and they wanted to know if I killed anybody, and I remember leaving the party when they finally asked me. I just felt . . . I just felt so alone. I guess it wasn't that I died—I lived. There was nobody in my life any more. I couldn't . . . how could I relate to these people? They were worried about whether or not their socks matched their shirt still . . . and who they were going to pick up at the dance Friday night. Nothing seemed important to me any more, nothing had any excitement to it. Everything was like I had just come back from this fantastic, this most incredibly realistic, more than real, technicolor film *into* a 1920s silent picture that was black and white and poorly done. That's what the real world seemed to me. Nothing was like when I grew up. Nobody was left. I just couldn't relate to anybody . . . that's when I started using a lot of drugs and spending a lot of time alone.

God, I'd like to be comfortable in life. I'm going back to Hawaii and see if there's anything I can work on with the relationship with my wife. If there isn't, I'm prepared for that in the sense that I don't think I'll stay in Hawaii. I'll probably move back to the Northwest. I have some options here. Now I feel like . . . I never really felt like I had a right to make choices. On the surface, it looked like I was making choices, but I really wasn't. I would just let things deteriorate to a certain level, and then I would let circumstances dictate what needed to be done.

I was always under the pressure that I could never make good choices . . . healthy choices. Now I'm faced with the fact that the rest of my life is mine to shape. That's pretty scary, you know. I feel like a child. I'm forty-three and got arthritis and shit, and now, all of a sudden, I'm starting life over . . . or just beginning . . . it's like I'm twenty-two and just getting out of the army. I have a lot more wisdom and kindness and caring. I feel like a Rambo Bambi. That's how my wife described this place. I said to her, "I can't accept that I have to be in a hospital, that I need to be locked up and treated for this." She said, "Why don't you look at the positive side—that this is just the Rambo version of the Betty Ford Clinic?"

I laughed when she said that. She's a wonderful woman . . . I never asked anyone else to marry me. It's like destiny or something. She's from Maryland; I'm from Maryland. She moved to Oregon; I moved to Oregon. She lived thirty miles one way; I lived thirty miles the other way. We developed the same mutual best friend, but we never really met. She moved to Hawaii ten years ago; I moved to Hawaii six and a half years ago. After three and a half years, I went home for a vacation. I spent most of my time with Barbara, our friend. Barbara asked me if I'd run into Kevin over there. I said I'd look her up when I got back. I got to the gym two days after I got back, and she walked in the door. I said Barbara said to say, "Hi." She asked me if I was Emmett. I asked her out for brownies and milk, and a month and a half later, I asked her to marry me. We've lived apart for fifteen months of those two years.

Coming to this program has really helped me in the sense of recognizing that all the time you don't get along with people at all personality levels . . . but especially with Vietnam veterans, I've found here that if you scratch the surface and wipe away the dust and wear and tear from living, and get down to the pain, it's all the same. That's where the Brotherhood is today. We've all suffered with the same pain, which makes all the same in that sense. The real heart of people is their suffering, I think. Maybe being Irish, I have a real affinity to suffering being the heart of a man . . . and I'm a Catholic. I've got plenty of excuses for guilt trips. It feels so good to hurt . . . it hurts so good!

I just started dealing with the religion thing a few days ago. In my jewelry box, I have my chain that I took to a jeweler just before I came here. It's thirty years old. I got it when I graduated from the eighth grade from St. Michael's grade school. It has a medal on it that I got for being on the basketball team with "E. Finn/1960" on the back, and it has my dog tag on it. I wore that chain and medal through Vietnam, and that's the only thing I have left of my God and my religion and my basis for morality and everything in my life.

I think people in America should be forced to tour a veterans' facility and hospital and walk through Building 2 over here and see what the real cost of war is . . . broken-spirited people and old people being maintained with no dignity in their life . . . who gave their life and their youth and any hope to protect some principle. There's a lot of suffering that people don't see from war in veterans' facilities. They're like farms that hide the pain from the public . . . and the public wants to wave the flag on Veterans' Day, but they don't want to see the pain. They don't see the missing limbs and broken spirits and broken hearts.

I don't think the public really understands what the real price of war is. This is the first time I've actually ever been in a Veterans' Hospital . . . and it's affected me tremendously . . . just walking around here and seeing people and what the cost of war actually is . . . there is no good war. There may be a "necessary" war some time in our past, but there must be a better way to deal with these situations than to go around trying to always bully the world. We're taking that as our only option.

The destructive "dark side" of me, what goes on inside my own head . . . I really needed to be in this program. I needed to finally get some help, finally find out I'm not alone. I guess the main thing when you're suffering from PTSD, and you're involved with your relationships with your friends and your family and everything, it helps you validate what you're going through. Every time they're upset, they're dealing with—and you're dealing with—your symptoms of PTSD. When you try explaining to them what you're going through, it ends up sounding weird, I guess. I never really, even to this day, grieve for myself.

Now I've been in this hospital for three and a half months—I even extended for two extra weeks. "Okay! Now I'm healed! Let's get on with life!" People who go out of here with that attitude—I've learned this in the extra two weeks—after opening up Pandora's box here . . . they fall flat on their face in a hurry. I came here because I felt I didn't have any more false recoveries left—the cat with nine lives was out of them. By false recovery, I mean just dropping everything—going off to a new place and meeting new friends and everything. I can do that . . . but I want to do it right . . . I just want my life to have a purpose, I guess.

I'd like to find my platoon. I worry about those guys a lot. I wonder how they're doing. I also wonder if there's some of them saying, "Yeah, we had this asshole for a lieutenant" . . . It's pretty easy to paint your own picture when you're sitting here with no evidence of what's really going on. I want to know they're not suffering . . . and not so damaged by what's going on . . . if they're suffering without hope. A couple of people looked me up after the war in my hometown, so I've felt close to them . . . but I don't know where to begin. I've tried some names and places . . . I've hit a lot of dead ends. I guess I've just got to keep my eyes and ears open, put out my feelers . . . hope I run into someone eventually.

I had a real good platoon here, too. That was the greatest gift they gave me . . . was putting me in my place, and it was the first time in my life that I think I've ever been able to accept criticism. It hurt. Oh God, it hurt the foundations of J. Emmett Finn. It shook the cobwebs and made me think, "Hey, this is what happens out there, too, when you think of everybody else and act for everybody else and mind read everybody around you and develop a whole lot of powerful emotions. You're a powerful person." Then you intimidate everybody around you when you get home, and people will start dropping off. That's what I was doing . . . I was shedding people like water. I'm glad it came to an end this way, where I'm learning, rather than out of desperation.

The here and now, I know, is really hard for PTSD patients to hold onto. Here and now issues, stuffing feelings, becomes such a habitual way of dealing with everything. My rage and my anger—that was my battering ram, that's how I kept people at arm's length . . . I'm amazed that anybody even cares about me. That's a real plus, because I do have a lot of real good people in my life. I keep adding more, and that's a real hopeful thing for me . . . and I've made it difficult for those around me. I didn't trust them enough to reveal . . . or burden them with . . . what happened to me there, what really happened to me. I've never really talked about it. It's still hard.

I have these great big holes in my head about my tour in Vietnam, and I thought I had my tour all figured out . . . every minute of every day I thought I knew, until I started processing it here. A few names came back to me. I'm going to The Wall on September 1 again. I went the first time when I wasn't ready . . . it overwhelmed me the first time. It's a very sacred place. There was an awful lot of pain there, but there was a lot of healing when I was there, too. I was so shaken emotionally . . . I couldn't even find Willy Bridges's name in the directory. I found Harris, and that was it. Once I got to that wall of names, I was a goner. I just . . . . that was too much.

When I talk about it, I'm right back there at that minute when I lost them. James Harris was, I guess, my favorite, maybe because he was from Maryland. He was Black . . . he was a funny, funny person . . . and it just ripped my heart out when he died. I tried to get him . . . . When I look at The Wall, I just go to pieces. I can't find all their names on it . . . I don't know a lot of names. It's a real lonely, empty feeling . . . something that's so powerful in my life. I've locked every bit of it out. That's what's really bringing me down to earth, for myself, hammering the point home of what a traumatic experience it was . . . and validating the suffering I've endured—the pain I've suffered.

A lot of this is still up in my head and not really in my heart. I think you can create a lot of that by just opening yourself up, you know? I'm not looking for a bunch of gurus. I'm not looking to be one, either. It's just opening your heart up. I've seen it here. When you open your heart up, a lot of people come into your heart. They open up, too. It's a beautiful feeling . . . you see guys here, tough guys, and they're hugging men and telling them how much they love them. That's a real powerful thing to have seen . . . and to have been a part of . . . I feel real blessed with that.

At this point, just living one minute, one day at a time, and not really giving a shit about the future, not really feeling like I was doing anything with my life that meant anything . . . I want to make an impact on somebody's life. If I can put a smile on somebody's face, that would mean a lot. I could help children . . . let them know that war is *definitely* not where it's at . . . and let a lot of people in. I can say that intellectually and verbally, but I really mean to have people get close to me. I can shut down in a real hurry if I feel any ambivalence, or I'm going to be hurt. I just have a lot of habits that way.

I've got to be very careful when I leave here. I don't know what I'm going to do. I've been a carpenter for twenty years, and I've got arthritis in my right hand pretty bad now. I've been clean and sober for about eighteen months. I think that's a big step toward recovery. It's going to take a while for me to get comfortable in life . . . I feel kind of naked right now. I don't have my drugs, I don't have my alcohol, and I don't have my anger. I feel pretty vulnerable. When I leave here for a weekend, I think I'm really feeling good about myself . . . and two days out of here, I'm really feeling traumatized by the real world. It's like I've got to get back here . . . and now I'm flying to Hawaii tomorrow. I'm pretty scared, I guess . . . I guess I could say that. I don't feel too bad about being forty-three and afraid to go home . . . but it's kind of a strange feeling.

As for what I'd say to the public about war, people need to know that what seems to be such a good and righteous idea that somebody's telling you, that there's bad guys over there that we need to kill—that those bad guys over there are being told the same thing about you . . . that they have hopes and ambitions and dreams and families just like you. War just doesn't make sense. I guess it had a place in history. Somehow, I can't accept what's going on without trying to establish some kind of dialogue with people and telling them how important it is not to hide behind patriotic, nationalist slogans and realize the Soviet Union and other nations are filled with people just like us. They bleed just like us. We're all part of a family, and we have to get along.

HENRY MINCEY

Every time I went anywhere when I came home, it was crowded, so I became a loner. In fact, I became very pissed when somebody wanted to go with me. I learned how to survive by myself. I found it very rewarding . . . but colored people saved my ass and stopped me from getting kicked around. I was definitely on the way to a dishonorable discharge. I had enough problems without creating more. That last year, I really started to turn around. I think it was the whole seriousness of the situation began to sink in. I realized I better not get one of those general discharges . . . that's like going home and saying, "I failed." I couldn't do that. I was close to getting kicked out for racial stuff and just being rebellious. "He looked at me the wrong way, so I smacked him"—that kind of stuff.

You know, I look back on that, and I think of all the hell that I went through . . . 90 percent of it I brought on myself. I realized that the older I got, but when you're back there—nineteen to twenty years old—it's hard to understand that kind of thing, especially when you see people doing the same thing and all that shit happening to you. You come out with a lot of mixed feelings and screwed-up thoughts, then you start hitting the booze, and you know . . . I did booze in the service, but I was scared of that other stuff. I wasn't going to stick no needle in my arm, and I ain't going to take that hit off a joint behind the lifeboats. But getting drunk? I could drink about two thimbles full, but I'd still do it.

I guess the biggest letdown is you finally get out, and you come back home, and they give you this orientation shit. "We introduce you to civilian life. We take your military skills, improve upon them, and you get an occupation." They've got these representatives from business saying this—this—this. I didn't know what I wanted to be. I wanted to be a mechanic, but I didn't learn shit. I learned how to do a rivet or two. I learned how to cut a machine part or two. But I didn't know how to *do* anything. I'm dumb—I'm definitely where I left off, just four years older.

I can relate to guys in a penitentiary when they come out. They're lost. I went down to the employment office. When you go down there, they say, "You are overqualified." "Overqualified for what?" "Okay, then—why don't you collect unemployment?" "Fine. If that's what you want me to do, I'll draw unemployment." They jacked me around, said I'm overqualified for this and underqualified for that. Finally, they said, "Why don't you go back to school? Use your GI Bill."

I joined school and loved it. I partied the first year—nothing but party. I went to San Bernardino Valley College, about sixty miles from L.A. I got good grades. All of my classmates were kids. It was one big party for us—we didn't know what was happening. Vets would think we was back overseas, tearing up shit. I just went to class when I needed something to do. The second year, the shit's starting to ripen—things are just getting crazy. I still didn't know what I wanted to do in life, and I'm starting to listen to shit about the war. I found out the worst thing you'd ever want to do is let anyone know you're a veteran. Some people just turned on you. I found that hard to understand.

You come back, and you remember your father and your uncles talking about World War II and Korea and how people were glad to see you because you're home. I'm back from Vietnam, and what do I say? "Hi. I didn't kill nobody. I ain't no hero. I was there. Nothing happened." Most people looked at you like you were on dope, anyway . . . you're a boozehead—who knows, you're probably some kind of weirdo, probably got some kind of psychological problem. They don't just come right out and say it up front, but it's an underlying thought.

Fortunately, I hit it at the right time because Braniff Airlines was recruiting minorities. I just happened to be there one day to pick up my unemployment check, and the guy said, "You were in the Navy, right?" "Yeah." "Aviation, right?" "Yeah." "You want to go to work for an airline?" "Sure, doing what?" "I don't know. Let's see." He talked to a representative who told me to come out to the airport. He had me taking tickets and checking baggage and shit. I said, "What's the purpose of this?" "Each one of these tags represents a city, a city of destination. You've got to make sure these get on the right planes." I remember my mom saying, "You got to start somewhere. If you got to start at the bottom and work up, so be it." We were out there loading bags on planes, which was a menial job, but I also saw it was like working on the flight deck.

So right there, even though I was a newcomer, you start building relationships, and you get respect going. I had a lot of good friends. A lot of those guys had been in the Nam themselves. We just had one big party. We never got serious. That was the Brotherhood when I got back here. It was just—for some reason—the supervisor could be Mister Redneck Charlie, but for some reason, he'd treat you different than he would someone else that he knew was not a vet. We had our fights and stuff. We'd say things. Somebody would throw punches. Fighting is a part of being in the service, you know, and you don't take it personally . . . otherwise somebody would get a gun. You'd fight, but that was it. I guess it's something you develop in the service. A funny thing, though. When I got out of the service, I completely stopped drinking— just stopped for a while.

It helped when I moved back to the Midwest. After all the bullshit I went through, I turned out to be a cop, believe it or not. I was a cop for eighteen years in Kansas City—Jackson County Sheriff's Department, actually. I turned out to be a good cop—enjoyed it, loved it, got along well. I did it all. I started off as a corrections officer and ended up as a supervisor. I would tell them, "I was prepared by the best racists in the world to deal with any organization on racial stuff. If I perceive something wrong, I don't get crazy, but I do know how to deal with you. You are not going to intimidate me. The navy didn't beat me, and I'll be damned if a police department will."

They thought I was going to come in and take out my anger on civilians. It was just the opposite. I would bend over backwards to keep a person out of jail. I didn't see race, personally . . . that's the thing I still have a problem with. I see racism in others, and I wonder how they can do it. If you really get off into what you're doing, you don't even see that. I look at people just like with clothes on. I'm wearing gray and blue—so what? He's wearing blue and gray—so what? That's the way I look at people. Some are just a different shade, that's all. I've got to admit a lot of the stuff I learned in the navy helped me when I was a cop, too, especially dealing with people. I think that really helped me the most.

To my knowledge, I killed no one in Vietnam, but I killed a man here in the States as a cop. I said, "I really fucked that one up. I hopped into a war, and I had no gun in my hand—but I'm still in a war when I come back . . . that's really crazy." I was at home, minding my own business, watching the news, and a guy went off and started shooting up the complex. I called the police. I knew the procedure. Then I saw him . . . that's when I had to go out and see what courage is all about. I found out something . . . I could see why guys would be curiously made to go on a battlefield and do what they had to do. I was scared to death. Training helps to overcome that. I knew what I had to do, knew how I had to do it . . . all this stuff was being regurgitated in my head. Even though it's only a matter of seconds, that goes to show you how fast your brain can process stuff.

I didn't get an adrenaline rush . . . it made me sick. It did do something, though. It did make me a little tougher, mentally. I prepared myself to deal with it if it ever happened that fast again. I would probably take a few shortcuts, but shooting somebody? Never. I still get sick about it. You just go against everything you ever thought would happen. Can you imagine how long I would have lasted in 1964 in the Marines? They have trees now as tall as this building that I would have fertilized.

The sad thing about the incident was that the department didn't focus in on it like they should have. The other officers saw the same thing, but the supervisors were in denial and just didn't give a shit. I was the one in on it, you know? The drinking started up again. I was real moody . . . had a real give-a-shit attitude. Fortunately, through self-healing and talking to friends, a lot of very good friends, friends that were there for you . . . to this day, I couldn't tell you what his face looks like . . . even though when he died he was *that* close.

When I came back from Vietnam, I could very easily have been one of those vets in jail, but I chose to be a cop. I had the same destructive activity—boozing it up and hanging out with the rough set doing crazy shit. I guess it was to try and keep some kind of edge. That's just something you had to maintain. From the point of view of a cop, the vets were just out doing crazy shit on the streets. I'll tell you one thing that's very important. Vets are very careful with weapons. Some gang member kid who has no experience with weapons cay spray a lot of rounds around, but they don't know what they're doing. Does it strike you as weird that with all the fire they can put out they hit very little? But from my point of view, the vets were far less dangerous because they knew what they were doing, and they were just getting crazy—maintaining that edge the only way they knew how.

I came here to Tacoma a couple of years ago. My mother became very, very ill and was going into surgery. It just so happened that a month prior, I had resigned. It just froze my retirement. I came out here, tending her and watching her, and she made a miraculous turnaround. I started thinking I better start looking for a job, so I went to the Urban League. They are throughout the country, and they can find you employment. They asked me if I was an ex-cop, and I said I didn't want to be a cop again.

I got a job here at Safe Streets, which is a citizens' antidrug, antigang organizing program helping neighborhoods so they can play a role in maintaining safe streets. When I walked in, I knew what I was facing. I came here and talked to Lyle Quazim for about an hour. By coincidence, he was looking for a director to run his new outreach program, and he asked me if I wanted to fill the part. I said sure. I'm dealing with the negative side of a problem more positively, whereas as a cop, you might think positively, but you still have to come up with a negative reaction, a negative result. This side here, "Here are the alternatives. Here is another alternative you may not have looked at. Here is what your neighbors are saying about you, and here is how you can change your ways." That's positive. Nobody's getting hurt. I walk away from a situation, and I feel good. The person doesn't mind coming back to me later on. They say one week they don't want to talk to me, and they come back a week later and say they're ready—they want to deal with it. Regardless, it's a positive act.

The gangs here in Tacoma were organized by the gangs from Los Angeles, mainly. They took Tacoma–Pierce County by complete surprise. They were hardened criminals. You put people in these human warehouses we call jails, and they've already got enough hate, rage, and confusion in their minds and hearts. You put them all in the same place, and all you've got is share hate for hate, rage for rage, and confusion for confusion. When they come back out, they're going to be hating more than when they went in—a multiplier effect. At least now they think they have a focus, something to focus that hate on. Gangs don't just pop up. They're there for a reason—there's a sense of belonging. Since the old gang members have left, we get a lot of this real crazy criminal activity. It doesn't fit our norm, but I can understand where they're coming from. I can understand that this is their group, and they will do whatever they have to, to protect it. They don't care what society says. They don't care if society wonders how somebody can do something like that. It's real easy to go crazy. It's tough to stay sane under those conditions.

Now the gangs from outside places seem to have left Tacoma, and what we're left with is a bunch of amateurs who are very dangerous because they don't have a focus. These kids running around here now with Uzis—fortunately, there's not too many of them—but everybody looks at the kid like he's the one that created the gun, supplied the ammunition, supplied the cocaine. These kids don't even have shoes, let alone transportation or anything like that to bring drugs into the country. Drugs are coming through the same ports everything else comes through. It seems we focus on the "downtrodden" group. It's easy to kick them in the ass . . . there's a lot of resources being used in the inner cities to bust a very small population. I could never understand that. I mean, the money we spend on street prostitutes is a joke. Prostitution is a street bust—a lady supporting a habit. The way they're treated is totally different from girls in nice New York hotels who don't even need to worry about the law.

I've been talking to one gang member for about four months. I want to see what he's all about. He wants to talk. He's not Black or Hispanic—that's why I say race isn't that big of a deal, because the hate and anger are already there. One of the things that really pisses him off is the way the government screwed over white people. I told him to give me examples. He said, "You look like you're old enough to have been in Vietnam. How do you feel about the Vietnamese and Cambodians coming over here?" I said, "Personally, it doesn't bother me at all." He said, "Listen, you send a guy to war and the very enemy he's fighting comes here and gets a better deal than he does. Look at you, for instance. You're a black guy. There's parts of the county that if you go to, you're liable to get arrested by the police . . . and that's right here in the city of Tacoma. I wouldn't even be allowed to buy a house in the neighborhoods I'd like to live in."

Then he said, "The first day I met you, I knew you were cool. You're not pretentious. You're cool in your own way, even though you're older than I am. You say what's on your mind. I see a lot of cop habits in you, but so be it. You gave me justice and tried to help me out. I look at you as an individual. In fact, I tell my friends, this guy's for real. He's not going to lie to you, and he's got an understanding of what the system can do to you. I have parents that were screwed up, beating me up and making me mean and tough and stuff, but the reason was that it was always the other person's fault. It was either the blacks, the Mexicans, or somebody else. They're the ones beating me up—my own parents! I'm confused, but I know I've got to stay alive. The element I'm in now is keeping me alive. You forget about normal things. You're there to survive."

This thing with Iraq—you would think after Vietnam this country would say, "Now wait a minute. This is stupid. There's no clear reason for us to be there." Here we are in 1990 . . . the same thing. It's stupid. I even look at Colin Powell, a black general, Chairman of the Joint Chiefs of Staff, and I wonder if he is really, really looking at what is going on and what position he is going to play when it all comes down. What about all these young people that go into the service for a better way of life . . . which I believe in. They know that wearing that uniform means you are trained to kill, with a possibility of that really happening. But you don't look for this stupid shit when you sign on the line. I can imagine what's going through a lot of minds over there. Even if nothing happens, those people coming back are going to have some serious thoughts about what we have come to.

So I guess the key to me is to find something positive to do for a positive result and to stay out of bureaucratic organizations.

YURI KIRICHENKO

I would like the American people to remember this: War can never be noble. It's a very ugly business. Man is such a strange being that in strange conditions . . . strange situations . . . strange things happen. How did this affect me and my comrades after we got home? Toward the end of my tour I had this eagerness my friend spoke of as being—to him, in that situation—like a wild animal. What do we do with all those feelings and anxieties . . . these strange things in each day of our lives? It's very strange, and I still don't understand why it happens like this . . . but all sorts of psychological things that happen after one returns, I can explain most those things to people . . . but this period toward the end of the tour . . . I can't explain it.

As I think I said earlier, a certain horror sets in during the last six months. You worry constantly that you can get killed, yet there is not much time to go before you're going to return home. We had to struggle with this fear for half a year, knowing what we had seen and learned in the first year and a half, too. It seems we had to throw ourselves into combat—we had an eagerness for combat—because we were extremely desperate people.

I know that your veterans of Vietnam have been going through the same thing for twenty years, and I think of them as elder brothers. I learn about their homecoming. My parents pitied me. And the first month was awful for my wife. I had the experience of being with my wife in a thunderstorm . . . when the lightning hit quite near us, and I thought it was a grenade, so I hit the ground. My wife said, "If it's so hard for you to deal with this, maybe it doesn't make any sense for us to stay married, and we shouldn't live together." I have to work this out in my mind . . . I have a long way to go.

One good thing about the war being so unpopular, many veterans because of this when they returned, couldn't find a wife. And now we have the opposite problem. After 1983, the government gave certain benefits, so that a different situation arose where women are very eager to marry the Afghantsis because we are heroes and because of the financial benefits. They didn't understand that this was a big mistake, because in his own way, every Afghantsi is a little bit crazy. Right now there is a very high divorce rate among Afghantsis.

I am not divorced, but there is the situation where there is a lot of—a lack of—understanding. I see myself now, standing at the edge. If I'm not able to—if I continue where I am now and am not able to return—to become more aware of how I was—and return to my former self, I can see it leading to a divorce. I have already attempted to start the process a couple of times, but I have stopped because of my child. In general, for all of us, the problem is that—psychologically—I do not think things are in order. I know from my American veteran friends that I will have a long time to work on it, and I must be patient while still feeling a sense of urgency.

HENRY TALMADGE

When I got to San Francisco, I went to visit my sister and a girl I used to go with in 1946. She never married. She used to be a hot tomato at one time. They sent me on a jet to Portland. When I got on the airplane, nobody spoke to me. Nobody said shit. When I got to Portland, they put me on one of those twin-engine jobs, a small one, with about eight people on it. I got to Yakima. This guy was going in a limo to some hotel, and he said he would give me a ride to wherever I was going. I said, "You don't have to do that." He said, "No, I want to do this for you. You're a decent person. I want to do this. Besides, I want to see this big homecoming you're going to receive." It was early in the evening. I got home and knocked on the door, and I could hear the kids in there, then they're running to me, and pretty soon the neighbors were coming over, and this guy has tears in his eyes. That was pretty cool—a big homecoming in a limo.

After I visited my family in Yakima, I got stationed in North Carolina. I got word that they were going to promote me—*and* I got word that I was going back to Vietnam for my next tour. They were going to send me back to Vietnam. I didn't give it much thought. If that's what I've got to do, then I'll do it, but then I was talking to my dad about it, and he said, "I don't think you better do it. I don't think the time's right for you to go. I don't think you're prepared." My wife said the same thing. I told her when we got married, "This is my job. This is my mission. This is what I do for a living. If you can accept that, fine." I hadn't even *seen* my wife and kids for two years. My head was still up my ass. I felt they had catered to these "New Marines," so-called, and they were on my ass. I was really disappointed, really hurt a lot by that, so I said, "I'm going to put my letter in and get the hell out of the Corps."

Aftermath

We had a 1960s blue Chevy with a dog and a cat, three kids, and matching luggage—one seabag apiece. We went across the country. It got late in the evening, and we were coming up through the South, and I was really dark, like I was back in Vietnam. My hair was really short. We stopped by places trying to get a motel. Everyone had vacancies—the sign said they would have vacancies—but the manager would say, "Oh! There's a convention in town. We didn't turn off the sign, but we're full." The first night, we tried three places and ended up sleeping out in a wheat field. The next day, the same thing. My lady is Caucasian. She said, "I know why they won't let you in. They think you're a nigger. Next time, you send me in there." Sure enough, the next place we went to, she went in and came out with the keys. At that time all that racial shit was going on. In the Marine Corps, it didn't matter what color you were. You were a Marine.

So I retired. It was like divorcing my family. I went to work for the Postal Service a year later. They gave me a job walking route. I had my pack and shit, and I was getting the job done. I was still operating like I was back in Vietnam. One day I was breaking in a brand new pair of jungle boots. These people were sorting out those plastic wrappers that go around magazines. I stepped on one of those plastic things. It popped just like the fuse of a grenade. My fuckin' head went some place. I took a dive—I went under this table. Everyone was saying, "What the fuck?" I said, "WOW! Did it go off yet?" When I went to work there, I told this guy, "One of the things I'm going to ask you is that you not touch me. I don't want you to come up behind me, and I want the people here to know that if you touch me, I'm going to hurt you, and I don't mean to." He said, "What do you mean?" I said, "I get spooked."

It seems like people need some kind of skirmish to prove themselves. I think the American people are some of the cruelest people in time of war. People off the streets or a reservation—or in the ghetto—make the best fighters. They are angry to begin with, so that's a pretty good start. The educated didn't fit in too well. I've got a kid thirty years old who wants the challenge of going to war. It's like he needs it. I say, "How can you? You'll end up dead."

You can't win a war unless you've got that little buck ass private—scuzzy and dirty and illiterate as he may be—to kick the son-of-bitches out of the goddamn foxholes. You can have all the rockets and whatever, but in order to occupy land, you have to have that guy kicking ass and taking them out of the foxholes—but that type of person is getting to be fewer and farther between.

Right now, if we have a war it's not going to be with a warrior. It's going to be a war of minds. The Japanese and other countries are coming in here and buying things and in essence taking over the country. I read in the paper that all of the people in the Peace Corps in the Philippines were called back to Manila because the communists made threats that they are going to kill all Americans. How short their memory. I almost died for them. How many Americans lost their lives there? They don't want the bases there. What's wrong with these people? I can't understand it. It irritates me. Okinawa is the same way . . . same thing with Korea—the South Koreans don't even want us there. That's part of the things of war that bothers me. I think that where the services were short was on teaching us more about the history of the countries. In Korea we had little books on language. I don't even know a word of Vietnamese. Thirteen months, and I never learned a word of Vietnamese. Isn't that weird?

I went over to see my brother in Colorado a while back. He made the landing on Iwo. He was on his belly going up Mount Surabachi, which tells you the casualties they had. Before that, he had been in Guadalcanal and New Caledonia. I told him about my going to this PTSD program at American Lake. I said I wanted to see some spiritual leaders. He said, "You're not going to find any here any more. They all went to Utah. They're disappearing. All that's left are the markings on the rocks in caves. All the ranchers took over, and they're gone." There used to be hundreds of those leaders out there, but the markings are still on the rocks in the mountains.

When I got out of this PTSD program, they said, "You're going to have to keep coming back twice a week for group sessions and once a week with Cathy Olson. There's no immediate cure for it." The biggest thing to me was to know that something psychologically went wrong with me, and that it was natural—that it wasn't unnatural for me—because I didn't know what was wrong with me. You come back here and hear the same bullshit coming from others. There were twelve of us. It's different when you read it or hear it on tape. In group sessions, you see guys squirming and churning and crying and getting emotionally upset. They would shut down for three or four days.

It is really hard for me to believe it's good for me—that you have to relive the trauma to get well. I don't feel anything redeeming in telling you these things. I can't wholly believe what they teach—that it was a part of war . . . "That's how it is, and it wasn't your fault." We don't have to have anyone forgive us for what we have done, because there is nothing to forgive. The only thing we have to do is forgive ourselves within ourselves. I did it because it was my job to do, so I feel quite content with that, but you're so caught up with doing what you're doing that you let the spirit handle it. Maybe that's a way of saying, "It was the spirit I listened to. The spirit led me to do that. I don't take responsibility for that. Maybe it's the spirit that has to have responsibility for doing that."

I don't see the value of saying, "I killed this girl," and going through all the bullshit of how she flew against the wall. I really can't wholly believe that this is going to make a better person of me. I find no relief in it . . . I find no joy in doing it. I think that somewhere within my mind I need to relive that within myself, but down deep inside I don't want to do that. I was having nightmares every day of my life for years, even when I was over there. We were sweeping this village, and this girl was there in this hooch. She was screaming. The people who set the trap for us were in there, too. I had seen them going in there. When I went in, suddenly she went up against the wall, and I shot her about two times. At the time that I did that, she was kind of like in a little altar, and she flew up against the wall.

There was a picture hanging on the wall. It fell down, and I stepped back and put my foot on it and broke the glass. I went out, and we swept the village, and when we came back, I went back in there again to check the area. I got the picture and put it in my pack. I fixed it so it made the pack frame fit better—it kind of padded it. It was like a woman standing there—the Virgin Mary or something—and a little kid sitting on a toadstool-type thing. I think it was some Catholic or Buddhist type of painting. That was in the middle of my tour, and it was with me everywhere I went from then on. When I got back to the States, I had that thing redone all nice with a nice frame. It used to hang over there above the china closet. I should have gotten rid of the picture, but no . . . I had to bring it back. It seemed like I had to punish myself. Finally, I decided I was going to send it back. There was a guy from California who was going to Vietnam, and he promised me he would take it . . . he took it back. Part of the therapy helped me with that nightmare. They have a dream therapy they can give you a printout on. I went into my nightmare and negotiated with that girl in my dreams, so now when I dream she doesn't blame me—she understands why I did it.

Now they tell me I've turned this place into a compound with a perimeter around it and all that bullshit. In a way it's true . . . my mother-in-law lives back to the side of our house here. My son is on two and a half acres I own over there across the road, and my daughter lives on the two and a half acres next to him. I take care of the two and half acres behind my mother-in-law's place, so I guess maybe it is like a defensive perimeter. I always make it a point to have a two month's supply of food on hand. I get my grandsons over here to clean up for me, and I feed 'em good food. My lady and I are going to have marinated chuck steak tonight. It's quiet out here, and I can sit here alone while she's at work.

If it was up to me after a war, I'd shut down. I'd shut down everything . . . the communications with other countries . . . everything. I'd start growing the stuff we need and attending to our needs, getting our shit together, for quite a period of time.

There is one thing that still scares the shit out of me. I woke up one day, and I couldn't talk. I tried, but I couldn't talk . . . no words would come out, and it scared the shit out of me. I didn't know what to do, so I got in my car and drove over to American Lake. I still don't know how the hell I got there, but I did. They fixed me up after a while. I mean, here I am gesticulating about how I can't talk, and they're all yelling at me, asking me why I can't talk. The thing that scares the shit out of me now is, it might happen again.

GABE GARCIA

When we came back, we was supposed to land at Travis Air Force Base in California. The plane had to circle the airport two or three times . . . because the fuckin' hippies wouldn't get off the runway. How could the hippies get on an Air Force runway . . . unless the fuckin' government let them on? After waiting a long time to come home, you get off the plane . . . and you're rejected by your own country. That's why I isolate myself a lot. I don't want nothing to do . . . with nobody. I don't need to learn, because I know too much already. The three or four times I died in Vietnam . . . it wasn't fun. There were incidents that took place over there . . . that today . . . I don't know how I made it. I never killed children . . . I tried to explain that to them at the airport in Travis. Everyone I shot had a weapon.

I wrote my relatives back in Texas in 1969 and told them . . . "Please consider me a permanent POW . . . MIA me for life." That's the last time I wrote to them. I lived in the mountains in Oregon . . . California . . . but I have to keep moving when too many people . . . know where I live. I had this friend who would visit me once a week. One time . . . she brought a friend with her. That really fucked my whole day . . . I had to move . . . to find another place to hide. The reason I have to keep hiding for the rest of my life . . . is because after your government has tried to murder you . . . who can you trust? On a dollar bill it says, In God We Trust. That's a bunch of bullshit . . . the fuckin' government is the worst enemy anyone can have in this country. For the rest of my life, I'll try to get even with the fuckin' government. I'll never salute the flag . . . I'll piss on it, but I won't salute it.

I was going to college. I was going to St. Mary's University in Texas . . . but they had a pub on the grounds, and I got kicked out . . . for drinking too much. I had seven months in. "I don't need to know anything," I told my professor . . . "I know too much already." I came back like this . . . with gray hair . . . when I was nineteen. I'm forty years old now . . . but I'm in the body of an eighty-year-old man. When I drink, I turn into an animal. I've been stabbed twice . . . I'm immune to pain. I quit drinking a while back . . . but it's worse, because it's harder to deal with the nightmares.

I was living with this girl in California until she said the word "love" . . . then I said, "You know, bitch . . . color me gone. I'm taking off." She didn't know why I left. She had a nice place . . . and she bought me a new Volkswagen in 1983. She bought me beer every day . . . and I would just stay home while she worked. Everything was cool. She just said she loved me one day . . . and I just got out . . . packed my shit and left. Her names was Bianca. She was a knockout.

I wish somehow . . . some way . . . this country could hear what I can't say . . . about the fuckin' government. As long as you pay income tax . . . they're happy with you. They'll pat you on the back. I'm not going to work . . . I don't need to work . . . I know too much already. Here they tell us when we leave this program in three weeks I'll be able to hold my head up . . . and I told them I was sorry to disappoint them. I haven't found any reason why I should hold my fuckin' head up. I came back as a nineteen-year-old killer-alcoholic. I label them as murders . . . what goes around comes around. I have tons and tons of anger inside me, and . . . I don't know how else to express it. I haven't been taught. They brainwashed me . . . they pounded it into me . . . "Kill, Kill, Kill."

When I used to drink, women would appeal to me. I've had the opportunity to get married three or four times. As soon as a girl says the word "love" . . . she can color me gone. I've never abused a woman before in my life . . . or a kid. I have a daughter and a son . . . I don't know what that means. I have a nineteen-year-old daughter and a fifteen-year-old son. I haven't seen my daughter since she was three months old . . . until she flew down to Idaho to see me. She's now in her second year of college taking psychology. She flew down to Idaho at Christmas . . . and spent two weeks with me and some of my friends. I didn't hug her . . . I didn't kiss her . . . I didn't talk to her. She doesn't deserve to know me . . . until she feels the same way I do. Then she deserves to know—when she's been beat up and abused a few times . . . I'll talk to her then.

I got a bunch of kids down there . . . I got Cathy and Leo . . . and they've kept me alive. They are good Mormon people. They—when I first got to Idaho, I was freakin' out bad—fightin' . . . never got to jail . . . but I got stabbed here and back here . . . got shot a couple of times . . . and they've kept me alive. They never hurt me. They accepted me when I was sick and drunk. They accepted me when I was violent . . . vulgar . . . now I realize how much I really need them. They're good people . . . they have never lied to me. They are the best thing that's happened to me since 1968. When I was freaking . . . Cathy would go drag my ass out of the bar.

The only reason I didn't knock the shit out of her . . . is because I've never hit a woman . . . and I never will. She drug me out of a lot of bars . . . she slapped the shit out of me . . . I don't know how many times. Her husband laughs because she went through the same trouble with him. He's a Vietnam vet my age . . . and he's been clean for eight years. I've been clean for seven months . . . but they say, "Once you sober up . . . everything will be alright." That's a bunch of bullshit. Once you sober up . . . it's harder to deal with things when you're sober. You get up, perspiring and sweaty from a nightmare. You know, back home when I was drinking . . . I'd go to the icebox and take two or three beers . . . just so I could go back to sleep. When you're not drinking . . . you just stay awake the rest of the night.

I've never been to jail. That's what disappoints the fuckin' government. I've had restraining orders in California . . . Oklahoma . . . Texas. I haven't had a flashback since June of last year. I've been in and out of VAs since 1977. I was locked up in the Long Beach VA for two years and seven months in the psychiatric ward. I was locked up in Brentwood, California, for eleven months. I was locked up in another VA for nine months . . . in Topeka for eight months . . . Sheridan, Wyoming, for eleven months. Thank God I'm still healthy.

I got a lot of good out of the program this week . . . going on the helicopter ride. The first thing I looked for on Monday was the blood . . . on the helicopter floor. There was no blood. My hands didn't have . . . no blood on them. My clothes didn't have no blood, and we didn't have to load any bodies . . . or take any bodies off.

I think I could have been a good missionary . . . if I still had the belief I had back then. I had everything going for me . . . yet today . . . I'd still be a missionary . . . I know that. I work with abused kids back home . . . I love kids . . . because they can't hurt me. They are beautiful kids back home . . . that I really love. I spend most of my time with them. They call me "Uncle Gabe" . . . but I'm not allowed to go to the child abuse center on Sundays . . . because that's when the parents show up. I don't want to meet or see . . . the ones that are abusing their kids.

I haven't gone home to see my parents and my two brothers and my two sisters . . . because they don't deserve to know me. When they fix me up . . . one of these centuries . . . I might go back. I don't have a home right now . . . I just live in the mountains by myself . . . I've been that way for twenty-one years. You know, we've been asking for years . . . they keep telling us there's a reason why . . . we made it back, you know? When is the pain going to go away? It's been hell . . . but I'm surviving. That's one thing I did get trained good in . . . is how to take care of myself.

BOB SWANSON

I came back, and I had a really bad attitude. It was carried over from killing people who had nothing against me and that I had nothing against. And then, coming back here to the States, it was hard for me not to react the way I wanted to when people here were fucking with me and doing it because they want to. And I had trouble getting it straight in my mind that I couldn't kill these people when they deserved it ten times more than the people I had been killing. And that's what really started the conflict inside.

A little later, I started upon a Christian Crusade, looking for some type of healing—and I got saved. Quit smoking pot, quit smoking cigarettes, quit drinking. I was going to church to study the Bible for almost a three-year period. There was a time when I was actually preaching at nursing homes and stuff like that. I used Christianity, I later realized. I was using Christianity as a way of punishing myself. The thought of being the sinner, the dark person, the one that needs saving . . . and I just never accepted forgiveness for myself. I took more of the . . . I guess what you'd say . . . the abuse of it. I used it to punish myself. If I was screwing up, then there was something more to fret about.

Then it just seemed like the bottom fell out. I thought I was gaining ground. I was being able to do things I couldn't do before, then all of a sudden I couldn't do anything. I was angry all the time. I was violent most of the time. I had actually turned a lot of anger and violence toward Carol—which I couldn't believe I was doing. I had trouble understanding how—if I felt bad about hurting people in Vietnam, how was I trying to hurt this person that I loved? There was a certain time period I hit down there—I said a prayer that was, "Promise me, O Lord, to get me where I need to be to get this shit taken care of." I didn't even realize what was going on. I knew something was . . . I just thought I was nuts.

Anyway, at the State Mental Health Center there was this guy that was really supposed to help me. He was a Vietnam veteran, and they just figured that was the person I ought to see. And I wanted to see him—and the first thing out of his mouth was money. And he refused to treat me 'cause I couldn't pay the fee. I remember calling him a REMF and told him I was going to show him what PTSD was all about. I chased him around the building until the police came and escorted me out.

They didn't file any charges, so I was only held for a couple of hours in the police station.

So finally I came to the PTSD unit—well, came to American Lake. I spent six months in the psych ward pre-evaluation, and I was held out for thirty days—then I went into the PTSD unit. One of the things I remember was coming into Tacoma and telling them that I wanted to go to the PTSD unit. Their first question was, "How in the hell did you hear about that?" It wasn't even supposed to be publicized yet. The pilot group was just going through, and so I ended up in Group 2. I think 38 and 39 are in there right now. I relocated in the Tacoma area to stay around the active care. And the rest is kinda history. I set up a good support group for myself and ended up going to Tacoma Community College.

For the first year that I was going through recovery, I didn't see much happening. I was going through the motions of doing what they said would help, but nothing seemed to be happening. And I remember going to one of the groups and voicing that—that I was getting really tired. Just prior to that, one of the guys that had been in the group right after me . . . that I was really close to . . . committed suicide. He had given himself six months to get better, and he offed himself. I remember the last time I talked to him, he was talking about how tired he was. And that's just the way I felt. It seemed as if there was just no energy at all. And I kept going because I knew the old way of handling things didn't work—so I knew that I was a loser. So I just kept on, and finally things started happening—and the payback started coming.

I had a Cambodian girl . . . my first day at school . . . oh, this is a trip! I'd just been out of PTSD treatment for about six months, and I walked into my first day of class at TCC. There was only one oriental person in the whole room, which was a Cambodian girl. Where did she sit? Right beside me! What was our first assignment? Interview the person beside you, and introduce them to the class! I remember looking up and saying, "God, this is a test. You want to see how serious I really am about this, right?" And so I turned around, and I was honest with her. I told her I was a Vietnam veteran and stuff. And she told me something, and I actually had to get up and leave class for a bit. She said, "You know, it's really sad that the American soldiers suffered so much from Vietnam. If it wasn't for you, I wouldn't be able to be here." And it was just WHOOSH! I got up and walked out of class, and she thought she had insulted me somehow. And the teacher didn't know what the hell was going on.

I regained my composure, came back into the class, and introduced her to the class. She's probably twenty-two now—she was nineteen then. She lived with her folks and had quite a bit of trouble with her parents—because they are old standard and she was trying to adopt her Americanism and fit in. She wanted to get her education, and she didn't want to get into any relationships with anybody. She was just trying to get through school. She was a REAL girl, and the guys just chased her all over the place—especially oriental guys. These two oriental guys were talking with her once, and she said something, and I saw her motion over to me. And these two guys got this really weird look on their faces and turned around and walked off. She walked over and sat down. I said, "I see you got boys chasing after you again." She said, "Yeah, they asked me if I had a boyfriend, and I told them, 'Yes. Him.'" I said, "Thanks a lot! I really needed that!"

I don't think I could ever have gone back to Vietnam without that break in school. I talked to one kid, and he's my Vietnamese friend. He sat right next to me in accounting class. One day we had our graduation out at the PTSD unit, so I was wearing a suit and had my ribbons on. He looked at me, and he goes, "What are those ribbons?" So I told him, and I could see he was shocked—I caught him off guard. So the next day he ambushed me, and he says, "So you were a soldier in Vietnam?" I says, "Yeah." He said, "Me, too." And he pulled up his pants leg, and he's got this scar on his leg from a bullet hole.

The big thing, of course, over this last year was that I got asked by Dr. Ray Scurfield and Jim Carioso if I wanted to go on the Vietnam trip. It took me about a half a second to say yes. I called Rachel—she's my wife now—and I was really excited, and I said, "Guess what? I'm going to Vietnam the first of the year for three weeks." She was kinda stunned, and she says, "Can we talk about this when you get home?" I said, "Of course we can, but I'm going to Vietnam! Sure we can talk about it . . . but I *am* going."

I had come a long way through PTSD treatment, and I'd learned to deal with it very effectively. And all of a sudden, Vietnam was back in my face again. The only memories I had of Vietnam were twenty-year-old memories. So all the scenarios that ran through my head for that three or four months before we left—of what might happen while we were there—were all related to twenty years ago. I even had to go on an anxiety vacation, which had been the first time for a quite a while, because I'd been on my recovery without any medication at all. I was taking light doses of a manic-depressant, which they found out that most small doses help relieve panic attacks and stuff.

We left in January, and we got over there . . . and it was all different. All the things that we expected to happen, didn't happen. All the things we expected to see, we didn't see. My personal experience was a lot of fear. I remember flying between Bangkok and Vietnam, I cried for half the trip. I think what finally dawned on me was I had finally accepted that we were in the air heading for Vietnam. Up to that point, it had just been a dream. As much as I loved the country, I hated it. April Gerlach came and was sitting next to me—one of the counselors who went along—and all of a sudden she started crying, and she later said that she realized that what she was crying about wasn't her pain, but the pain of all the vets that she'd had to deal with over the last three years.

We landed in Hanoi, and the first thing I saw was MIGs on the runway. The second thing I saw were these uniforms. My experience was in I-Corps. Everything I saw was in NVA uniforms, and we landed, and here were all these NVA uniforms. "Oh, no!" Then things just started escalating. We went in Hanoi Airport, and I was kinda weak from the emotional stress on the flight. We went in, and I was overcautious. My hypervigilance was way up. I kept watching all these soldiers and officers in NVA uniforms, and I couldn't even concentrate. One of the cameramen came up and had a camera on me and says, "How do you feel?" And I just looked at him and said, "I'm not. I'm too busy . . . get away from me! I'm protecting myself here!"

Wherever we went, Gabe Roberts and another guy passed out these little American flags on toothpicks. And everybody went for them. Some of the guys passed out flag pins. We figured communist soldiers probably had come through and confiscated them all after we left, but we were in downtown Hanoi, and all of a sudden we heard this guy screaming and yelling and following the bus—this was three days later—and it was one of the guys from the airport. He was pointing at his hat! He had a flag on there. So that made us feel a little better. Steve Smith got blown away when a man—I'd probably better say in his late forties or early fifties—came up and grabbed Smith's hand, and kissed his hand. Steve had been stationed in Chu Lai. He was just stunned. He just stood there looking at his hand, and we went up and asked what happened. It was a while before he could gather himself to tell us that he had kissed his hand.

As we were leaving Hanoi and we went to the airport . . . I still had some fear in me, and as we got off the bus and went into the terminal, here was this little girl. She was probably about three or four years old and had on a little tan fur coat. And she just kept staring at me. And I knelt down and said, "Hi! How are you doing?" Of course, she didn't understand me. She just kept standing there watching me, so I knelt down and stuck an American flag pin on her shirt, and she grabbed hold of my pants leg and went running across the terminal. She took me over to meet her mom. I went back to being with the crowd, and I felt this weight on my pants leg again, and I looked down, and here's this little girl. She's got ahold of my pants leg again, and she stayed right with me

Aftermath

the whole hour and a half we waited for the plane. That really broke the ice for me.

We flew down to Da Nang, familiar territory. It was a little warmer than Hanoi, but it was only about forty-two degrees. That was our first broken expectation. In what was South Vietnam—we expected we were going to step off and feel that blast of heat. We got off, and it was just like Tacoma! So that was our first expectation blown. The second expectation blown was the reception of the people. I think the most moving thing of the whole trip was that we got a better welcome back from the enemy than we got at home when we came back home. In our group that first night, that is what it dealt around—the whole group was in tears. And Mr. Minh, the cameraman for ABC who had been a South Vietnamese soldier and had escaped to Thailand—he's trying to film us, and he's in tears. Everybody was reacting with us.

One of the things I require is a lot of alone time . . . I remember in Da Nang, we had been around so many people by this time, and I was really tense. Some of the guys went out on tours, but I had to stay in and gather my thoughts together. Back here in good old Tacoma, I need one or two days a week where I can take off for two or three hours and just be totally by myself. Fact is, once a year, I need to take off for about three or four days up in the hills and sit naked on a rock in the sunshine by myself.

The farther south we went, the better our reception got. In Da Nang we had ex-NVA and ex–Viet Cong soldiers come up to us, telling us the war was over . . . and it was time to be friends and stuff . . . and that whole thing that I remembered from back in 1968, that feeling that if the government was out of the way, we could sit down, have a beer, and be friends—that's exactly what we did. One of the NVA soldiers that was talking to us just mimicked my exact words. He said, "Our government told us what to do, and your government told you what to do. Nobody is telling us what to do right now."

There was an ex-VC captain who was missing his leg all the way up to his hip. He walked up to me one night in Da Nang, and he told me had lost his leg due to an American artillery shell, and he said he'd been bitter for several years. But then he learned that the bitterness was destroying him and that it was time to put it behind him and make friends. And he came up and shook my hand. I was dumbstruck. I didn't even know what to say to this guy . . . WOW! It was just too powerful, and I was overwhelmed by it. This little guy could speak enough English that we sat down and talked for about an hour, once I got my voice back. I remember bits and pieces of the conversation. We were talking more about what we were doing. He's a carpenter. I guess you would call it a wood-carver. He had lost his leg in 1970, and he had a disability payment from the government equal to about fifty cents a month. That's his disability payment.

Every place we went for the whole trip south, we'd come into a village, and they'd be throwing these strings of firecrackers around the bus—because of Tet. They weren't trying to intimidate us. They were trying to bring us into their celebration. The fireworks is like two hundred M-80s . . . and that's when some of the memories from the old '68 Tet came back.

Billy Ray and I were standing up on the hotel balcony and were watching some of the stuff that was going on. He and I had both been in Tet, and we started reminiscing. And Billy Ray turned around and said to me, "You know, the only thing that's missing right now is the AK-47 fire." And I swear to God he must have cued somebody, because off in the distance, two soldiers in their celebration cut loose with their AKs. It wasn't as loud as the fireworks, but that pattern stood out like bold print. He and I just looked at each, both with chills.

There were so many things that happened in Nha Trang—like when we first got there, they were throwing things at us, telling us to go home. They thought we were Russians. When they found out we were Americans, they started running up to us—coming up to try out their English, because they have an English language school there at Nha Trang. And then they found out that we were all ex-soldiers, all Vietnam veterans. Then they started inviting us into their homes for Tet celebrations and for dinner and stuff. That night at the hotel they had a Tet celebration and had several tables set up. There were Czechoslovakians, our American group—there were ex-VC and ex-NVA soldiers there. There were a couple of ARVNs who had already been in and out of reeducation camps, and there were some people there who have kids in the States.

And we were all sitting there . . . it wasn't the Americans sitting here, the Vietnamese sitting there. There were nine people at my table, and there was just myself and one other American person, and there were some Czechs and Vietnamese. When I got home, I told Rachel, "That Tet celebration is the best New Years I've had in years." It was that everything I had said earlier, in that first tour of Vietnam, was happening—was really happening. That night we were really sitting down, partying together, sharing together, and it just all came together in a nutshell. It seemed like all the fear that I had had suddenly dissipated there.

Shortly after we got back, these Russians came. And we sat down and talked with these Russian soldiers. We've never fought the Russians face to face, but they've been shot at with our weapons, and we've been shot at with theirs. So we've been kind of surrogate enemies, so to speak.

Talking with Yuri and some of the other guys, we found out that these guys felt just like us, too. They were tired of fighting and wanted peace. So my motivation was enhanced . . . just from that alone.

Out of the whole thing, I've learned to use a really bad experience—I've learned to turn it around and use it to help people. Not just Vietnam veterans . . . I find myself even at school having rape and violence victims feel comfortable talking to me. One of the things I've learned about, by talking with even the Vietnamese back here . . . you hear a lot of vets say, "I got a lot of unanswered questions." The Vietnamese have some of the answers we're looking for. I remember one of the Vietnamese I talked to—one of the first ones I talked to, he says, "I've got a question for you. Why did you leave?" Not why were you there, but why did you leave? That answered one of my questions. We were wanted there by some of the people.

DARREN GATES

When we took off, it had been under blackout conditions in the whole inside of the aircraft. You couldn't see your hands in front of your face, and I'm laying on my side when they turn the lights on so the medics can see what's going on. I look over, and the first thing I see is this lady about thirty years old and a little kid—Panamanians. She was shot, and the little kid got burned or something—I don't know what it was. He was pretty screwed up, and I remember he asked his mother why the soldiers came and blew up their house . . . I'm glad the kid asked his mother that and not me. What the hell do you tell a little six- or seven-year-old kid—having to justify it . . . and I think that's the worst part about it.

You know, grown men fighting in a war is one thing, but it's too bad that the kids and the civilians are usually the ones who end up getting hurt the most—emotionally *and* physically. I'm sure that the guys I killed—I'm sure they had families . . . I don't hate the Panamanians . . . and I don't hate the guys I killed. I can't hate them. They were doing a job, and I was doing my job. Sometimes I hate them . . . I don't really hate them, but I blame them for me feeling the way I do sometimes. It isn't fair, but I do.

All this time when I got back, I kept seeing them in my dreams . . . it was so realistic, I could feel the recoil of my rifle in my dream . . . the blood. I've never seen—growing up in the United States, you don't see things like that. You don't see people bleeding to death, unless they're in a car accident or something. I think—looking back on it—that if you kill somebody, take somebody's life, you kill a part of yourself too in the process. I think you lose some of your morality . . . no matter how much you try and get it back, it's gone. I'll never be the same. I don't think anybody else who's ever been through a war would ever be the same. You can't be.

For the guys who went through it, signing a peace treaty doesn't make it go away—it will never go away. I remember when I was in the hospital when I came back, at Fort Lewis. It was like the first night I was back. I was lying there in bed, and it was like going through the whole thing over again. I could smell the smells—that's something I'll never forget, the smell of Panama. It sounds kind of weird to say a country has a smell like that, but there was a smell in Panama . . . and there was another smell, too, and that was the smell of death. You could smell it. I swear to God you could feel it, too, when there were people dying around you. It's one of the weirdest things I've ever had happen to me . . . that feeling.

It's sad, but that's a lot of what war is—people getting killed needlessly—and basically getting blown out of their houses for something the leaders argue over. I think the government is doing a better job of giving a reason. I think that's something they learned from Vietnam—giving the public reasons. No matter how believable they are to the public, it gives the public something, some sort of justification for the costs, the expenses, the lives—more than they did in Vietnam. From what I read or talked about with other people, nobody really knew why they were fighting in Vietnam. There were standard answers, but they didn't really hold up to close scrutiny.

But it was exciting, too. As bad as it was, it was exciting. I think fighting for your life is just a basic instinct. It was pretty much cutting it down to the bare bones . . . that's all you have. If it would have been a fragmentation grenade, I wouldn't be here. I was real lucky—I had a lot of friends who were real lucky. A good friend of mine got hit in the chest with a rocket-propelled grenade. They're supposed to explode on impact, but it hit him in the chest and bounced off. It blew up about five, ten feet away from him. He came out with a small chunk of shrapnel in his arm.

Then again, I had friends who weren't so lucky. I lost one of my two best friends in the Ranger battalion . . . he was killed . . . that was kind of hard. Sitting in a hospital in Texas—sitting there watching TV—they start flashing the soldiers' names who had been killed on the TV screen . . . and it was like, "Holy shit! I just talked to him twelve hours ago . . . and now he's dead."

Somebody said something a couple of months back that really made me pretty mad, saying that Panama—because it was so short of a time span—they called it a "police action." I just don't see where people get off saying something was a police action when you've got your friends dying . . . friends lying there crying for help because their guts were falling out. That's a war. I don't see where people even—I mean, who are these people that dream up different names for war? That's what I'd like to know—maybe they think war is an ugly word, and they try to clean it up a little bit. "Police action" sounds better . . . but it doesn't make anybody feel any better—at least not the soldiers. It makes them angry. I can imagine what guys in Vietnam must have felt like . . . for ten or twelve years it was a "police action"? What the hell is that?

When I first got back, before I saw my wife, Marley, I was waiting in the house for her to come in . . . and I thought, "What's she going to think?" The week before, I was normal old Darren, and now—I was scared she was going to think I was some kind of psychotic killer—that I just went on a rampage—and I was afraid. I didn't want her to feel bad for what I had gone through. I don't think anybody else does—for the people close to them, they don't want them to feel the pain that you're going through. Physical pain—I was busted up pretty bad. I was in the hospital for a couple of weeks, a cast for a few weeks more. Emotional pain is something that's in your head. It's hard to get that out of your system.

I decided to go on my own to get some help with the emotional pain. For some reason, I have a hard time remembering what brought it up, but I went on my own. I realized I was having some problems, and I didn't want it to—just from past experiences, I know I'm a terrible person at keeping things in. I knew it was just going to eat me up if I didn't do something about it. So I went in to talk to a PTSD therapist and started talking to him. I'm glad I did. I feel like it helped me.

It's weird when you get in a situation like that because your level of awareness goes up. You see everything—hear everything. If they could bottle it, put a new drug on the market, you'd have a monopoly. I'd read all these horror stories about guys being in combat and just holding it in, and I'd seen guys on the street that you just knew were fucked up for the rest of their lives. I didn't want that to happen to me. I knew if it did, Marley would be gone in a couple of years, and I'd have nothing.

Recently it's been getting a lot better. I've been getting back into working—concentrating on work. I've got two more years' enlistment. I think I'll enlist again. I like it. It gives you a certain feeling of accomplishment. I want to say, "No, I won't go again," but deep down, I know I would do it again . . . no matter what I'd put my family through. Knowing now what I know about combat, knowing that I have a fairly good chance of getting hurt or killed, I'd do it again. I don't know where my deep sense of patriotism came from, but it's there. The way I see it is that this country gives you a hell of a lot for what it asks from you. I don't know—I don't think it's all that much to serve for your country for all your country gives back in return. I probably will stay in until I retire. After that, I'll probably finish my degree and teach or something. I'd like that.

I don't see a major war starting. I see low-intensity conflicts in Third World countries. I think that's the way it's going to be for a while. When I say "low intensity," I mean just short, sweet, bang-bang-bang, get it over with—in and out—get it over with, but I don't see any long, drawn-out war. I don't think it will happen. I don't think the American public will stand for it, unless it was a foreigner invading the shores of Los Angeles.

If the American public would somehow bear the weight and feel the way these kids' parents felt when they found out their kids were dead, the U.S. would never be involved in a war again. It's easy to pick up a newspaper and say, "Oh, well! The U.S. soldiers are in Panama," then throw the paper and go on with daily life . . . not even give it a second thought. I went out and talked at a school, and these kids were asking me, "When your friend died, how many times was he shot?" I sat there and thought about it and said, "It's not really important. The important thing is that he's dead and gone. Just hope that never happens to your friends."

CHAPTER 7

Steve Tice: Healing

> In general, it's been a good experience, a positive one. I learned in the war that there wasn't a right and there wasn't a wrong. I saw very quickly from the kid who had the grenade in Nha Trang that we were not necessarily right for being there. . . . I've come full circle at this point and have discovered that there is no black or white. It's all a matter of perspective and of which side you stand on when viewing life's events. For every negative there's a positive; for every bad there is something good that will develop from the experience. Those bits of information are not always easy to see nor are they always easy to accept. Regardless, you just keep going. . . . If you never try to work through something that's tough, it really isn't a valuable lesson. Vietnam absolutely heightened my awareness level by giving me the experiences so few women have the opportunity to have. . . . It's as if my head got screwed back on with greater perception and understanding. . . . It's like I have a special extra or reserve self that I can use when the going gets tough.
> Jeanne "Sam" Bokina Christie in Keith Walker, *A Piece of my Heart*

When we finished recording Steve Tice's oral history, he said, "I hope you put in a section on healing—for us now, it's the most important part." Steve is correct, and we happily oblige. While their nations' political and social institutions start and end wars, individual soldiers fight them. From the larger perspective of aftermath, they discover that the experience of war is lifelong. What therapists call healing is the problematic, often prolonged, highly individual process through which veterans return home from war. In return for the soldiers' trust, society has the reciprocal obligations of providing a political cause to justify war, honoring their sacrifices, and respecting their knowledge of warfare. Our collective interests thus encompass far more than official histories of events and arguments over the merits of particular wars. Our interests are also in the psychological, moral, and spiritual dimensions of war that are not included in declarations of war and peace treaties. They are embodied in war stories and in the painful anxieties of Post–Traumatic Stress Disorder.

Therapists such as Dr. Ray Scurfield and Steve Tice have identified a healing process—a heuristic or "way" through healing—which they have abstracted from the veterans' collective experience. Trauma sets in motion the process that ideally eventuates in healing. Trauma is followed by an outcry response, which appears to take many forms, depending upon the individual's experience. Without timely counseling, there may follow a prolonged period in which the traumatized veteran seeks to maintain emotional equilibrium under extremely trying circumstances. PTSD results from trying to maintain control over the often tenuous balance between intrusive recollections of the trauma and emotional "numbing" mechanisms.

Traumatic events are beyond the usual human range of experience, and most people would find them profoundly stressful. Wars, earthquakes, rape, and murder are beyond the normal human experience, and they often cause post–traumatic stress. The situation is complicated in war, because soldiers are trained to deal with traumatic stress by automatically sublimating it into the rage of killing frenzy. Under certain circumstances, post–traumatic stress can drive soldiers "over to the dark side" in order to survive.

As we have seen repeatedly in these narratives, trauma is followed by an outcry. This outcry is a highly individual response, and manifests itself in very individual ways, times, and places. Dave Nelson recognized instantly that he had sacrificed his morality to the pilot's need to be released from unbearable agony. Gabe Garcia wondered what an enemy soldier was thinking as he died. Tice lay in Letterman Hospital wanting to bring civilians in to see the consequences of war, hoping that perhaps the sight would end war. When Mark Lomax visited a class recently, he said outcry from him was asking "Where do I belong?" when he returned to civilian life.

These responses evolve into a sometimes prolonged period of conflict in which intrusive recollections of the events alternate with efforts to deny the trauma through various numbing mechanisms. By distancing themselves from others, "self-medicating," and refusing to be tied down to domestic and employment routines, veterans who experience stress can block the memories well enough to get through the days. Without a safe place to confront what they call their pain—their quite legitimate stresses, anxieties, and fears—they may get stuck in a vicious, self-perpetuating cycle of dysfunctional behaviors. By finding a secure place and understanding counsel, they can begin working through the traumas and the disorders they entailed. Becoming less concerned with safety and self-preservation, the veteran begins to face the experience instead of numbing it.

The process reaches completion when the veteran integrates the trauma into an evolving whole-life perspective. The narratives in this book dramatize many moments of rejoicing at this sudden and profound countertraumatic illumination. Jim Goldstine had tears in his eyes as he described talking to the long-haired adolescent in an awareness seminar. Bob Swanson's face broke into a delighted smile as he described meeting Southeast Asians in his college classes and during his trip back to Vietnam. Tice's encounter with a Russian amputee was shown on national television and has now achieved the status of legend among American and Russian veterans. According to Tice, another highly respected PTSD therapist, Shad Meshad, believes that the healing process is not complete until the veterans tell their stories publically and have a political impact upon society. Societies have a mixed record of honoring their part of the covenant, often confusing the warrior with the war, or the messenger with the message, or becoming distracted by self-congratulation or guilt, or rejecting the message outright.

The last stage is particularly crucial, because it requires a response from society. Here our World War II–based social definition of war provides both an answer and an insight into the fickleness of society's response. Although men such as Henry Talmadge returned from World War II changed, the response from society assisted in their reintegration. Jobs, educational opportunities, and mortgages provided the security they needed to heal. Many raised themselves and their families far beyond the expectations they had prior to military service. The rightness of their war is reinforced still. The political rhetoric of World War II still permeates our foreign policy, and its dynamics are the very stuff of our social definition of war. Unfortunately, the return from World War II also authorizes the pervasive notion that all veterans return to civilian life easily after all wars. In the aftermath of Vietnam and Afghanistan, civilians are ignorant of their responsibilities and have not fulfilled their part of the social contract under which the soldiers went to war.

Tice and others find that the sense of mission, the sense of an achievable purpose, which so many veterans find lacking in their lives, provides a final measure of healing. Dave Nelson is considering going back to school to learn to counsel abused children. Mike Mitchell is the premier housepainter in Tacoma. Nikki Nicol finds beauty in her home in the woods. Phil Simms looks forward to living on a ranch with his wife and young son. Vlad Tamarov tries to publish a book of his photographs to pay for prostheses for Afghantsis. Henry Mincey works with street gangs. Henry Talmadge looks after his children and grandchildren. Bob Swanson is deeply conscious of being a success story for the American Lake PTSD program. These are missions—"costing" (as the poet Eliot once put it) "not less than everything,"—to which they can commit themselves unreservedly. These missions are simple because they are achievable, but they are no less morally profound than the most intellectually complex theories and calculations.

The message they bring back to society is equally simple and equally profound. Having killed, they understand the terrible consequences of breaking one of the Ten Commandments. They know that the lingering effects of having a broken moral taboo are not worth it. As Gabe Garcia says, soldiers return from the war zone knowing too much. They know why killing is taboo and why war no longer can be considered an alternative to foreign policy negotiations. The veterans in this book, each in his or her own way, affirm Yuri Kirichenko's message to society: "Wars like this should definitely not be fought."

STEVE TICE

I was born in Santa Barbara, California. I have seven siblings. My father was a surgeon in World War II, in the Medical Corps, and he was captured by the Japanese early in 1942. He was on the Bataan Death March and was interned in the Philippines, in a prisoner of war camp, for three and a half years. He returned home in 1945. He was then sent to Santa Barbara. He and my mother and my oldest brother decided to stay in Santa Barbara. Then my father then went back into the military when I was young. My first day of school was in Germany. My parents got divorced, so I grew up going back and forth between my parents' homes, my father's home being in Santa Barbara and my mother's in Nevada. From the time I was seven years old, I had two families, and my siblings were kind of split between the two. I ended up going back and forth. I liked sports a lot. I played basketball and baseball primarily, and surfed. My father was a manager of a store in Santa Barbara after he got out of the military, which he did right after the divorce. He was really active in the community. He had PTSD symptoms and did not know it. My family was very middle-class. In Santa Barbara it was really hard to tell, because there were a lot of rich people and a lot of poor people, but not a lot of middle-class. I thought we were poor because we had only one boat, which was a kind of weird view of the world. The part of the community I lived in was very white and very affluent, as were the schools I went to. I had an unusual view of the world, a fairly elitist view.

People in my family served in the military. My father was very patriotic when I was a teenager. That's what I remember mostly. My older brother went to Vietnam. He volunteered to go to Vietnam when I was in high school. He was injured in Vietnam. He was burned badly in combat action. He healed and stayed in Vietnam to finish his tour, and then came home. I got out of high school and went to college. I decided to go to the University of Nevada. I wanted to play basketball. I was also getting pretty flaky. I was struggling between being a jock and an underground guy. I played guitar and grew my hair long, which a lot of people did in those days. I was falling in love a lot. I wasn't keeping up with my studies. My family was wondering when I was going to get responsible, so when I dropped out of school and went to work, that was okay because I was being responsible. I had a job, and I was living with this woman, and then I got drafted.

I decided I didn't want to go. My brother told me I shouldn't go because I'd probably end up in Vietnam. I started some petty ways of avoiding the draft, like not showing up. I went to my physical. I lost a lot of weight thinking I would get out. It didn't work. Then I just didn't answer the letters. I got worried about that, so I started sending changes of address. I got some really stern letters. I finally decided to go into the service when I was watching television with my girlfriend and watched Bobby Kennedy be murdered. I had hoped he would be elected because the kind of leadership we had in the country didn't seem to take into account human life, and it seemed like he valued human life to me. Right after that, I showed up.

I went into the service in San Francisco. There were a lot of protesters outside. I looked more like them than I did the soldiers. I tried to flunk basic training, but didn't. I got sentenced to the infantry. I realized that I needed to get in shape. I was in pretty good shape because I played sports—ran cross-country and played basketball and surfed. I went to training here at Fort Lewis. I decided to get in shape and learn how to use all the weapons. I had never hunted or anything. My father wasn't interested in those things. I worked very hard in advanced infantry training. I learned how to use the weapons and was in very good shape.

I really couldn't see myself killing other human beings. I essentially made the decision to go out of despair and depression. The alternatives didn't work for me. Going to jail or to Canada or feigning gayness just weren't part of who I was. Even though I was protesting against the war and even though my brother told me not to go, a real strong part of me said, "This is unfair, this is not right. America is making a huge error, but for me personally it would be a huge error to leave my family and go er country and/or jail." It was part of what I was to be in the even though I was really clear about the political ramifications of what was going on in Vietnam. I didn't go to stop communism. I went to Vietnam so I wouldn't have to go to jail or Canada and so I could live freely in the United States and so I get some help going back to college—which I planned to do. I was going to go to junior college and play junior college basketball and try to get into a major university and play ball. I needed to build up my upper body strength. When I was younger, I was really skinny and didn't have good upper body strength. The military did that. I knew I was going to be a mean rebounding guard when I got out.

I took a two and a half week leave, which is kind of a blur to me. My family had Thanksgiving dinner early for me because I was going to be gone by Thanksgiving 1968. My girlfriend had broken up with me. I tried to develop some really quick relationships with old girlfriends, which was somewhat successful. I flew out of Oakland, through Alaska and Japan, to Vietnam. I thought I would come back okay. They put us through a training exercise in Vietnam. I got deployed to the 101st Airborne Division. I had heard about them. Everybody said, "Watch out. Don't get into the 101st Airborne." I could type. I had a fairly high IQ. I was pretty articulate. I thought I'd get a job in the rear. That was my fantasy. None of that ever happened.

We got sent to Camp Evans in I-Corps, which was up in the northern part of South Vietnam, where the marines and the 101st were. I remember walking out by the bunkers and seeing these guys out there. When I got there, there were guys who had been there eleven months, guys who had been there five months, and guys who had been there a couple of weeks. The guys who had been there a couple of weeks were very friendly towards me and helped me get settled in. The guys who had been there five months were kind of standoffish. I only spoke to one of the guys who had been there eleven months once or twice. They didn't have anything to do with me. Quite frankly, they looked like really old guys, though I was actually older than some of them. I was twenty. I became really close friends with the platoon sergeant. His name was John Nicholas. He in particular was really friendly to me. He had been there just a few weeks. I also met a couple of guys who had been there about five months. One guy was from California. He was really helpful to me. He had been one of those guys who had hunted as a kid, so I thought he could get me through firefights. There was this other guy who had been there for five months who was from North Carolina. He had been shot before he ever went to Vietnam by a farmer with buckshot. He was great. The four of us ended up being really close friends.

As I was getting acclimated to the platoon—having come from a guy who fought against the war and didn't like it—I really became acclimated and never really came in from the field. I'd get banged up or hurt and just stay out there. I broke my nose once. Another time my knee got hit with a bunch of crap and was swollen, but I stayed out there anyway. I was part of these guys. I felt really close to them. I was an RTO, and I felt part of the team. It was not that I thought we were doing anything worthwhile as far as the war goes. It was about how close and about how much I cared for them and loved them. That really started with combat, knowing people cared about me and would try to protect me—and I would do my best to do my job well and protect them. There were two RTOs in each platoon, one with the platoon sergeant and one with the platoon leader. In my job, I would be the person who called in medivacs, and I felt I did my job well. They gave me a lot of compliments, and the company commander treated me well.

I remember once I fell face down in some mud. I had all this stuff on my back, all this equipment. I fell face first down this hill and smashed into this cactuslike plant. I broke my nose. My nose was twisted and cut up. The medic came over. It was raining, and he said, "I don't know if we can get you a medivac or not." I said, "Oh, no. I'm okay. Just put my nose back." He put it back and bandaged it, and I stayed in the field. The company commander really appreciated that, particularly because I was this flaky California guy who had a reputation of not being a real warmonger. That's part of why I became an RTO, because I didn't have to be part of the firepower all the time. I didn't want to shoot anybody, but I wanted to make sure we were okay. I remember when we came back, the company commander threw me a cold beer and said thanks. From this guy, that was a major compliment. If I had the chance to leave permanently, I would have done it, but to leave the guys in the field for a few days wasn't something I was going to do.

My friend Cliff was from Sacramento. I remember one time we went on this forced night march where we went across some pretty tough terrain—at night—and Cliff was point man for the company, and we were the point platoon. We were in front of the whole company. We were moving at night, and we sounded like a herd of elephants in the jungle. We were supposed to be sneaking up on somebody someplace. Cliff went right off a cliff right into a river. It was only a five-foot drop, but he didn't know it was there. The guys who cared about him jumped in and pulled him out, but the suction of the mud pulled one of his boots off. We had guys looking for his boot under water at night. He had to stay out in the middle of this jungle with one boot. I mention this because I just remembered how people reacted to him in the water out there at night in an unsafe place.

I would describe myself as cautiously brave. Cliff and I had a reunion about a year ago. He saw me that way, too. He couldn't imagine why I was in Vietnam, but he looked at me, and he said, "When we got in trouble, you were just like a hellcat." I saw myself as cautiously brave. In other words, if somebody was injured, I would try to help them, but I wouldn't endanger myself as some people would. Well . . . I endangered myself, but I didn't go first. I tried to see what happened when somebody else went out there. If it looked okay, I would go. Some people would just hide.

I want to talk about one of my most difficult experiences. I was in the battle for Hamburger Hill. We got sent back for this R&R thing, where I actually tried to surf. We were in the China Beach area. I was having a good time, drinking some beer, but I knew where we were going because I was with the headquarters people because I was their RTO. I was in a weird position. I started telling the guys where we were going. The belief was that we were going to the A Shau Valley. When anyone said we were going to the A Shau, everybody just started writing letters home, saying good-bye. I tried not to do that, but the tone in my letters really changed. The tone is really a good-bye letter. I don't remember perceiving of it as that. We were at this beach fatting the calf, and one of the guys got drowned. It was like God was saying, "I don't like this. This is not good."

We flew in by chopper in a combat assault. I was a lieutenant's RTO at that time. His name was Jim Stavik. He was from Texas. The medics were black. I got to know some more about their culture and who they were, and I really liked those guys. I got to learn more about other cultures, which I had really been separated from growing up. I liked the people I was with. I really cared about them. Within a couple of days, it was really clear that this was not what they thought it was going to be. We were going to be the headquarters unit, and we were going to plant ourselves on a hill, and we were also going to be part of the blocking forces. This other unit was going to go up this hill—which became Hamburger Hill—and drive the North Vietnamese off it. They were going to drive them right into us, and we were going to kill them.

That company immediately ran into all this intense fire they weren't expecting. The North Vietnamese were heavily armed. It was a regiment. They had underground tunnels and hospitals. They had artillery. They had rocket-propelled grenades. They had automatic weapons. They were all shaved, with boots, well-trained, well-uniformed. They were coming over from Laos, right on the Laotian border. Immediately, the unit that made contact with them started doing this thing in the movie—assaulting up and retreating back down this hill—and losing a lot of people. Immediately the strategy changes. Our unit was supposed to go to their rescue and come out on the other side of the hill, but we were being shot at at every step. Our point man got shot in the head really early on by an NVA trail watcher—a North Vietnamese. I had just been speaking to him. He was a guy from Pennsylvania. Several guys took off after and shot the Vietnamese. We kept on going through the jungle after that and getting shot at.

We came to this incredible village right in the middle of the jungle. I couldn't believe it. It was just like Santa Barbara! You know how lush Santa Barbara is. The A Shau Valley is very lush. It had a *huge* garden complex. I remember thinking of home and wondering if I was going to see my home again. Nobody was in the village. It was a base camp. There was food cooking. We couldn't find anybody, and couldn't find their tunnels. Some of the guys sat down and started eating their food. They had been in-country for a while. I had been in-country for six months at this point. Some of these guys had gotten pretty flaky at this point. They sat down and ate. It looked like bamboo stew to me. We called in defoliants to take out the garden.

It was really hard to move in the jungle. We got on the ridge line and dug in and got hit with this incredible storm. It was like a typhoon. I remember taking my rifle and putting it between two trees and hanging on. My body was straight out. The wind and the rain was so *hard*. The war stopped. There were huge bolts of lightning. Two guys on the perimeter got hit with lightning. I was thinking, "God doesn't like this." I was raised in a fairly religious family, and I used to go to all the church services in Vietnam. I would wear a rosary although I wasn't a Catholic. I was really superstitious about spirituality. I used to attend all-denominations services because I didn't want to offend anyone's God. I knew God did not like us to kill people. I knew that because I was raised that way, so I was trying to make amends along the way for what I was participating in. I remember when we medivacked a couple of my black friends who were hit by lightning. We had to wait out this storm. They were like bowls of jelly. They were alive, but their bodies were just like Jello. It was really scary to see them like that. We were all wiped out by it.

We got to the top of the ridge line where we were supposed to be. The next day—on the seventeenth of May 1969—our platoon got wiped out as we tried to go down the hill. The Vietnamese were in bunkers along the side of the hill with machine guns, and we didn't know it. We thought they were on the other side of the hill where our other guys were fighting. The point men were my friends, Cliff and Paul, the guy from Sacramento and the guy from South Carolina. They had been in-country for a little over eleven months, and they were asked to be point men for this operation. I didn't like that because you didn't ask guys to walk point in the A Shau—especially not if they were so short. They went down this complete hill on their bellies. They looked around, and they couldn't see anything, so they said, "Come ahead, but be cautious." We got in three columns and started going down. I was behind Lieutenant Stavik. I remember this so well because it's my nightmare of Vietnam.

We were coming down this hill . . . and the North Vietnamese waited till we got all spread out. Cliff and Paul were all by themselves down at the bottom. They opened up with machine-gun fire from their bunkers. They hit Joe Mants—who was right next to me . . . they blew his whole chest up. Lieutenant Stavik got really excited and started running right towards the fire . . . and my job was to follow him. I didn't do it. I stepped behind a tree. That's what I did when people shot at me. People were screaming, and some guys went back up over the hill. The Lieutenant was running towards the fire, and Brooks looked at me and said, "You're an asshole if you follow him." I followed him. That was my job. I remember running down this hill, and this tree came apart next to me—it was completely blown apart. My lieutenant got all the way down to where Paul and Cliff were—and so did I—neither of us got shot. There were several guys wounded, and they were trying to get them back up the top of the hill. A lot of the guys were making excuses to help the dead and wounded so they could get out of there.

There ended up being the four of us at the bottom of the hill. We got behind this huge tree with all these roots, and we spent part of the day and part of the evening there. I remember that tree like it was in my backyard. It had these big roots which were up above the ground. Another guy got down, Paul Burgmeyer, a new guy. He had only been in-country a month. He was a gung ho type of guy. He was eighteen and had volunteered for Vietnam. I thought he was dangerous. I didn't like him, and I didn't want to be around him. We sent Burgmeyer away from where we were . . . and he was immediately shot in the chest. There just wasn't enough room there behind the tree. I was in the back part, and the ground around me was constantly being kicked up by machine-gun fire . . . there was no room for him. Lieutenant Stavik . . . we sent him away . . . I felt badly for years about that—still do. About that time, Sergeant Nicholas got shot in the foot. He had been on R&R in Hawaii with his wife, who was pregnant. Then Page got hit in the chest . . . both Page and Nicholas were crying and moaning. Nicholas went out to try to get Page . . . and got hit . . . he was killed.

We got pissed. We were really cut off. Now there was nobody but us. We were down there all alone with the North Vietnamese all around us. Powell, the other RTO, moved back when those guys got killed. He moved back to a safe place. There was nothing else he could do. He had been in-country eleven and a half months, and we didn't want him to get shot. So the four of us were there, and we fought the North Vietnamese all day. We ran out of ammunition, and some crazy guy brought us more. The company commander said he wanted us to be down there—he wanted us to direct fire right on top of the North Vietnamese—so he couldn't let us move . . . and quite frankly I don't know how we could have. We had to call in artillery rounds right on top of us. The shrapnel was flying right by us from our own shells.

It didn't work. We started to move . . . they opened up on us again. Then we called in Cobra gunships. We started to move again, but we couldn't. The helicopter stuff wounded Cliff. He was hit in the chest and was bleeding. That's when I hurt my knee. The debris from the next explosion—all the tree limbs—hit me right in the leg. I thought I was wounded and, quite frankly, I wanted to be medivacked. I had had enough. I pulled up my pant leg, and all it was was this big bruise on my knee. I wanted to be medivacked, and I wanted more blood inside me.

Then we called in napalm on the enemy . . . these human beings . . . incredible . . . it burned them up really bad. I was trying to take care of Cliff. We didn't have any medics any more. I was bandaging him. Then we called in the napalm, and it hit so close it singed off our faces. The North Vietnamese came out of their bunker and charged us. They were all wobbly and really hurt—but they opened up and charged us. The most frightening thing was the way they looked—the way the whole thing happened. We went crazy. We got enraged. Cliff was screaming things at them like, "YOU KILLED NICHOLAS!" Then it was over. The company commander lined all the rest of the company along the side of the hill. They threw smoke grenades down and enveloped us all in smoke . . . and we ran back up the hill . . . and picked up bodies. I don't remember doing that. We medivacked Cliff. He had to go out with the dead bodies. I was so sad. I couldn't believe the stuff I had lived through. I was really sad. I hid and cried. That was the only time I cried in Vietnam. I knew I was in trouble . . . because my system of numbing wasn't working any more. I was really sad. I still believed I wasn't going to get wounded.

The next day I got wounded. There weren't enough guys in our platoon to do anything, so they put us in the safest spot they could and had us direct fire. We accidentally gased ourselves. We were trying to gas the North Vietnamese. I was sitting in a foxhole eating some food. This gas canister rolled into my foxhole. I picked it up and threw it. It burned my hand. The Lieutenant was yelling at me to come up there and get on the radio and find out what the hell we did wrong. I came over, and he was lying behind this big tree. A firefight was going on, and there was all sorts of shit flying. I was nauseous. I crawled over but didn't use the gas mask, because I knew I had to be on the radio. I was lying on my stomach and leaned out to pick up the radio, and I got hit with an RPG directly in the hand. It blew off my hand and hit the tree we were behind. The Lieutenant didn't even get hit. He got knocked up in the air by the concussion. The RPG blew off my hand and hit really bad in my shoulder . . . and it took off the side of my face and put a hole in my chest and put a bunch of holes in my stomach. I remember feeling surprised that I got wounded. I couldn't *believe* I got wounded.

I knew my hand was gone. I was really awake and lucid—and I knew I was in trouble. I was asking for Paul because he was the only one of my friends who was left, but he was fighting the enemy. He was now Platoon Sergeant. He was the guy who didn't want anything to do with leadership. Lieutenant Stavik a little while later got shot in the head, and Paul ended up being Platoon Leader. Paul said that Stavik was so distraught about my being wounded that he was not the same the rest of the day . . . he ended up putting himself in danger and was shot and killed. To medivac me was really hard because they couldn't move me. I was just wiped out. A neat guy from another platoon came over and spent time with me. He talked to me about my family. He stayed with me and lay next to me and talked to me. To me . . . it was like having Jesus next to me. There were big trees everywhere, so they dropped a basket down and put me in it. They put me in the basket, and I was flying out . . . I remember this peaceful feeling even though they were shooting at me . . . it was like total peace. When they got me aboard the medivac, I got really scared. There was all this crying, and there was blood all over.

They got me to a hospital, and I felt really good and really safe. I think I survived triage because I talked so much and was so lucid that they gave me *so* much attention. The records show me telling these guys where I was, what I was doing, what was going on when I got hit—in the first person. With most guys who got wounded as bad, they just had to guess. I woke up later, and I was having my last rites. I didn't know it at the time. This guy was praying over me. I ended up doing some prayer. I went to a hospital in Japan from there and went into a coma and had all kinds of problems there . . . I'm not too clear on that period. I had a sucking chest wound, some organs gone, some real problems. I had a heart attack and a coma there. I ended up in Letterman Hospital in San Francisco. The first person I saw when I woke up was my mother. My father came. I kept ending up making it through all this stuff. I was really supportive of the other guys on the unit. I looked at my mother and said, "I understand my hand isn't there, but I got out of there. I couldn't take Vietnam anymore, so I'll just deal with what I got, and I'll be okay." I didn't know I had all this other physical and psychological stuff to deal with. I knew there were all these machines hooked to me.

I used to have people get me up, and I would walk. I was insistent on walking. I'd walk, and they'd trail me with IVs and machines. I wouldn't let certain people come near me who had hurt me—I called them Dummies. I told my mother, "Don't let the Dummies get me." I got really good care by most of the staff. I ended up doing about the first year straight on in the hospital and over a year and a half in and out. Since then, I've had only one surgery. I take really good care of myself, although I didn't at first. I had a lot of problems. I was married in 1970. Earlier, I was so sick I got down to ninety pounds. That's when they had to amputate the arm because of gangrene.

I had a lot of trouble with nightmares. One nightmare that kept recurring all the time was that I was in Vietnam and we were being charged by the enemy, and I was on this bunker line and had only one arm. I had an M-16, but I couldn't get it to work. We were being charged by the Red Chinese army. It was always the Chinese who were charging us. It wasn't the Vietnamese. I was terrified. I'm telling Stavik, who is still alive in my dream, that it is not fair that I'm still there, that I should be medivacked out. I had this nightmare for years, and it was really terrifying.

I was married in 1970 to a friend of mine from before Vietnam, and we had a child in 1972. I tried to tell people what had happened to me in Vietnam, but many people were really cruel to me. They'd say I should have gone to Canada or ask if I was on drugs when I was wounded. We just didn't do that in my unit. It was really a disciplined unit, and that just wasn't done. I was really hurt by all that. They would ask me about Vietnam, and then they would tell me about Vietnam. I was in so much emotional pain that I just pulled back. I thought I had not been thinking about it, but Lisa and I got into some old stuff and found some of the poetry I wrote during that time which was really powerful. I was thinking about it and writing about it, but I wasn't talking about it. I didn't tell her what had happened to me for a long time. I went to school and got a bachelor's degree, and then I went to graduate school.

I was having a lot of trouble interpersonally with my wife in the midseventies. I was pushing her away a lot. One of my brothers was killed in the early seventies, and I didn't deal with it. I just kind of took care of the family and all that. So by 1977 my wife left and took my child, and I went to graduate school. I was getting straight As because that was where I was putting my energy. I had a graduate teaching fellowship. I did fine with all that intellectual stuff. I didn't want to be a counselor. I was in this really intellectual program; I wasn't in the clinical. I went to see this doctor because I was having these heavy-duty headaches and neck aches. I figured the shrapnel was moving around there and hurting me, that it was some kind of war wound, that it wasn't emotional. The doctor somehow convinced me to talk to a social worker who talked to Vietnam vets. They called it Post-Vietnam Syndrome then. It wasn't PTSD. Most of the therapists didn't understand why we were so angry all the time.

I went and talked to this guy. I was really pissed off and was pretty resistant to him. He started to talk to me about grief. He started telling me this story about his own life and about having lost someone close to him. He wasn't a Vietnam vet. He tells me this story, and pretty soon I'm in tears and he's in tears. I said, "Well, you think you've got grief—hear this." I started telling him about my friends in Vietnam, and we were both just sitting there in tears. I felt the relief of the ages. Then he started to talk to me about my brother's dying, and here we go again. I hadn't cried in years, and here I am sobbing. I kept going back, and pretty soon we got through that part, we got through the part where I started trying to deal with my feelings of injustice about losing my arm and trying to live disabled in America, the prejudice I was running into . . . because I grew up privileged and never ran into prejudice where people would prejudge you because of the way you looked. I had been a really athletic guy, and now the side of my face doesn't look the same, and I have my arm gone and other injuries.

I started treating Lisa a lot better, and she came back. We had another child. I did therapy for a year—really intensive stuff. I felt really good about it. I got a job teaching at the university. The Ph.D.s didn't want to teach the extension courses in prisons, so I was the one who did those. I had a really close friend who was a Vietnam vet, and he came to me and told me he was having all these problems. I was sitting in his driveway with him in tears talking about his issues and problems. I told him to go to the VA. He didn't want any part of it. I told him I actually got through the embarrassment of asking for help, and it really helped me. He was clutching me and crying and saying he was going to die and all this stuff. It was still so fresh for me that I didn't have the wherewithal to stick with him and go through it with him. It was taking me back to some pain that was just too fresh for me. I didn't want to do that . . . I couldn't. He ran into all sorts of bureaucracy and ended up killing himself. I had a lot of trouble forgiving myself and had to work on that one a long time.

The way I decided to do it was to try to change the system. They started the Vet Center program shortly thereafter, and I applied for it. I didn't think they'd hire me because I didn't have a clinical degree, but they hired me and put me through all this counseling training. At first I was there to solve the problems of the world—to change the VA forever. As it turned out, I stopped trying to do that as I wised up. I realized that that would happen on its own as long as I stayed pure in the heart and didn't keep the conflict alive. I kept doing the counseling with Vietnam vets. I thought I'd do it for two years, and then I'd have repaid my debts. I feel strongly that when you get something, you give something back, and if you give back, then you'll always get something. If you don't give back, then you don't get anything. You just get old and sour. I went back and taught while I was working at the Vet Center.

I started getting involved in all these other things. I got on the Presidential Committee on the Handicapped and the Committee on Disabled Vets, and I started doing work nationally, and I started writing some things and doing some TV, and I ended up not going back to teaching. Now what I do here is I am Assistant Director of this program. I see my job to be to keep us as pure as I can keep us on the mission of helping vets and dealing with the system. I can deal with the system, and they have trouble dealing with me. The system has difficulty dealing with me negatively. It's hard for them. I'm talking about people who are bureaucratically inclined in the system. I don't want to give this system a life of its own. There are wonderful people in the system who are people-oriented, who don't let that get emphasized in their lives—and I try to do that. I try to keep us on the objective of helping vets. That's what I do.

About a year ago, the twentieth anniversary of my being wounded came up. I was coming up on forty-one, and I was coming up on twenty-one when I was wounded. As I approached that year, I started thinking of the different things I could do for me that would help me deal with that time. When I hit that point, I wanted to do something for myself that was really positive. I'm real affected by my anniversary dates . . . of my wounding . . . and that whole week at Hamburger Hill—I recognize that. That anniversary would mean that I had lived more of my life as a disabled person than previous.

I was going to treat myself and go to a workshop with Scott Peck. His work is about healing and taking personal responsibility for your own self. There's a spiritual part to what he does. He combines what mental health professionals have learned with a spiritual process—which is real rare. Many mental health professionals have it, but they don't acknowledge it. I'm attracted to his work. When *The Road Less Traveled* came out—which I think was 1981—it was helpful to me in two ways. One, it helped me with my own healing process, and also that was a period of time when I was trying to develop a framework for my own approach to treatment. I think that there are three parts to us—mind, body, and spirit. What most mental health professionals focus on is the mind, and most medical professionals focus on the body. We miss the spiritual part, and that—I think—is the critical part in the healing process.

Anyway . . . I was thinking about the Scott Peck workshop, and I got a phone call from this person who said, "We've heard about you, and we want you to go to the Soviet Union and help us." And I said, "Okay." Then I thought, "What? I don't want to go anywhere!" I had always told Lisa, "I won't go anywhere." She's traveled all over the world—to India, and I didn't want to go anywhere. Then I thought, "This is right. I need to know if I can truly forgive these folks. It was a Russian weapon I was wounded with, and if I can truly forgive them and help them, then it will help me, and this is what I need to do. This is my mission." I went.

"20/20" TV followed us around. We went over to Moscow and worked with the Afghantsis. We went to hospitals, where there were guys with their legs blown off, and I worked with them. It was really powerful. There was a big party, and this guy kept tugging at me. He said, "I've heard about you, and I need to talk to you." Finally I got over to him and said, "I've never met you." I got the ABC interpreter to come over and help me. The Russian vet told me about how he had been wounded by the American equivalent of a bazooka. It had blown off his leg. I told him that I had my arm blown off by a Soviet weapon. He said, "I know that about you." He looked at me, and these big tears started rolling down his face. He said, "Do you have children?" I said, "Yes, do you?" He said, "I've got children, too. We've got to do something about this. We can't let what happened to you and I, our countries do this through other countries or to each other." I said, "You're really right." He said, "We really need to do something for world peace." I noticed the camera was on us, and I looked right back at him and said, "I think we are." That was part of what they put on the ABC Special. That piece with him and me was how they closed that thing out—he and I hugging each other. That was really powerful.

I'll tell you who's influenced me most—that's Joseph Campbell. I was watching television one night—it was the series he did with Bill Moyers, I think—in 1987. There was one piece he did called "The Journey of the Hero" or "The Adventure of the Hero." I thought, "This guy's been reading my mail." Essentially what they were talking about was something that people have been talking about for centuries—since people could talk to each other about their experiences—they talk about people dealing with trauma. That is the journey of the hero—the hero being the person who takes on the risk of growth—I'm not talking about John Wayne stuff. I'm talking about the person who takes on the risk of growth. Campbell talks about *The Hero with a Thousand Faces*—that's his most famous book—which I've gotten into after watching these programs. Human beings all over the world from all different cultures go on a journey, and there's an adventure, and this particular motif is the adventure of the hero. A person can be drafted into an adventure, a person can choose to go on an adventure, or a person can just fall into it.

Steve Tice: Healing

They just happen to be walking along the street, and they encounter this remarkable thing that is affecting us, and we are drawn into it. Well, I was drafted into the big adventure in Vietnam.

The second piece is that the person goes on the adventure, and it can be adventure of transformation or the transformation can come later. In the adventure, we are faced with our dark side. George Lucas, the guy who did the *Star Wars* trilogy, was influenced by Campbell. We're faced by our dark side, and we also get in touch with our goodness. Campbell talks about Vietnam vets in the sense that Vietnam vets show this most incredible form of enlightenment that people can have—in Vietnam! That is the dropping of one's own ego to help another. He shows a scene of some GIs, during combat, getting somebody to get him onto a medi-vac. He says that when people do that it doesn't matter what the issue is, why they were there. What they did personally was they risked themselves—their own lives—to save another. They bonded as one with this person . . . and that's the highest form of enlightenment. I've worked real hard in my work with Vietnam vets and with myself to get in touch with what I learned in Vietnam that was some type of goodness. There were guys that helped birth babies and do a lot of wonderful things. I didn't personally get involved in that. I went through some rather incredible events with other people, and in that—that camaraderie and that care for each other and our willingness to risk our lives for each other—I think by being there. Vietnam vets by going to Vietnam, where the other people did not go, took a risk at some level.

Throw out that political stuff—people get caught in that. Moyers did in that interview, and Campbell said, "That's not what I'm talking about. I'm talking about the act of self-sacrifice leading to a moment of enlightenment." During the adventure, one is faced with one's dark side, and I certainly was. I was a part of killing human beings, and also the goodness—I was a part of trying to save human beings, too. That's what war brings—a kind of technicolor magnifying glass on what human beings go through every day in this world. We had the opportunity to deal with it at eighteen, nineteen, twenty years old. From that point, one can go through some transformations, during the adventure or after the return. Some people did go through some transformation in Vietnam, some after their return.

What Campbell says is that often society refuses the return, and oftentimes the adventurer will refuse to return. I think the key for Vietnam veterans is the return. Many vets refused to return—they were here physically, but really weren't here. Then society rejected the messenger, which is a real typical thing. When the messenger is bringing back a message that society doesn't want to hear, society has a way of rejecting messengers. Historically, they crucified Christ, they shot Ghandi, and they shot Martin Luther King. Society has a way of not wanting to hear the message. Obviously, the average Vietnam vet is not that threatening. Rejection is a lot different than assassination. It's more like an assassination of character. "The messenger is tainted. There's nothing wrong with us." The messenger is only trying to tell society about their dark side . . . and about the healing process.

I think we as Vietnam veterans, and I include myself, have trouble saying that because at first we weren't very sophisticated in our message giving. We reacted both to our own pain from our experience, our own lack of clarity, and society's rejection by all going underground. Now what you see, including this book and including Oliver Stone's movies and Kovic's book, was a few people started telling their stories in the seventies and got rejected. Kovic's book is being accepted fifteen years after he wrote it. The message is finally starting to filter through, and some people are starting to hear, and the message is essentially about war.

As I see it, the message is that society may want to take a look at other ways of problem-solving—that war is very painful and hurtful to people. People who live in the countries where the war goes on. The Vietnamese people were hurt badly by this war. The veterans who fought the war were hurt—physically and emotionally—and their families were hurt. It's been passed on to other generations—post–traumatic stress disorder. War is a very painful and hurtful way to problem-solve. I thought about that as I was laying in the bed in the hospital. I was laying in bed, and I was thinking, "I wish the *San Francisco Chronicle* would come in here and interview me. I could tell them about the pain I am going through." I was wounded at the end of the battle at Hamburger Hill, so I wanted to tell them about all of the pain I was experiencing. But I realized at the time, I wouldn't have been a real articulate messenger.

Verbalizing is the key piece in the healing process for anybody that goes through trauma—coming back as witness. Campbell talks about bringing a boon back to society—bringing a gift. In the case of the warrior, the gift in many cultures has been the warrior as wise man who is bringing back information. The warrior is not Rambo. I think of American Indian culture. The warrior comes back with wisdom and leadership. He also comes back as witness who tells the people about war. The survivor's mission gives some meaning to the pain of war. The survivor takes the pain of war and brings some goodness and meaning to the sacrifice and carnage of war.

I believe that I lived in Vietnam to do this work. I believe that God had this place for me, because he had given me the ability to speak well, and the intellectual capacity to learn and to speak the language of therapists, and to speak the language of the system, and also the language of

Steve Tice: Healing

people who are not educated, and also the language of people in pain, and also to be open to hearing what anyone else's story is. It does not matter what culture they come from or if they have been disabled or not. That was the way I was raised. That was emphasized to me in Vietnam, and I believe that was my journey—to go through what people learn from war, and it's my mission to bring that message back. I've appeared on a number of network television shows and panels. I've taught classes all over the United States, and I've been on presidential commissions—and I've done all that—that's not for ego. I'm not telling you this for ego reasons. I do it because that's what I'm supposed to do. When I go through the pain of working in a program that's so hard to do, with these guys' anger and pain, it's that I'm here to help them express all that and to find personal peace. I believe that as human beings find personal peace, they can find it in their communities. As they find it in their communities, they can find it in their states. I believe if we start treating every human being with respect, we'll have world peace.

I have a lot of sadness about Vietnam. You saw it. I continue to have sadness about it. I take that sadness of war and my participation in it, and the things I did to other human beings there, and I've asked their forgiveness, and I've asked my own forgiveness . . . and I look forward to helping other people healing. In your work, that book, there needs to be a section on healing, about the healing process. What that looks like to me is that we forgive, and we come back as witness, and we tell our stories as warriors, and when people learn what happens to people in war, they'll make their choices not to hurt other human beings. If we could have gotten . . . on the orthopedic ward I was in in Letterman Hospital—if we could have gotten the American people to walk through there—the war would have ended. People just need to know.

CHAPTER 8

The Soldiers' Knowledge: A Summing Up

> The warrior's knowledge as expressed in memoirs, poems and plays by the soldiers, together with reports by oral historians and essay journalists, posits a literature about the war that contradicts the war-managers at virtually every level. Yet these narratives have failed to influence the conventional assessments by both the "error in judgment" and "self-imposed restraint" schools [of military analysis of Vietnam]. How can a major war like Vietnam be absorbed into the historical record without listening to those who fought the war, especially since over 200 books have been written by soldiers and their close observers?
>
> James William Gibson, *The Perfect War*

What should we add by way of analysis of these truly compelling narratives? Our first obligation is to the veterans. We owe it to them not to debase their experience by analyzing it from an alien and therefore absurd perspective. We are particularly concerned that readers not get the impression that these oral histories are part of the media-centered spectacle of post-1960 warfare. From the perspective of soldiers in combat, in the chapter entitled "How to Tell a True War Story" in his book, *The Things They Carried,* Tim O'Brien says, "War is hell, but that is only half of it, because war is also mystery and terror and adventure and courage and discovery and holiness and pity and despair and longing and love" (pp. 86–87). Wars are contradictory and ambiguous. They are a great deal more than news clips, sound bites, expert testimony, and appeals to patriotism. From the truths of their daily lives, these veterans know the significance of the basic therapeutic principle at the American Lake PTST program. Surviving combat in contemporary war is a whole-life experience for men and women whose lives have been thrown out of kilter by the traumas of war.

THE SOCIAL DEFINITION OF WAR

We asserted at the outset our belief that the soldiers' knowledge deserves authoritative standing in public discussion of contemporary warfare. These oral histories provide ample, varied, often horrific insights into exactly why the soldiers' knowledge is deeply significant to all of us. We are belatedly realizing that sacrifice—a surrender of something of value for the sake of something of greater value—is the soldiers' half of the covenant in our social definition of war. These veterans believe they made honorable sacrifices for their countries. Society carries reciprocal obligations. The political cause for which its soldiers fight must motivate them and justify the very real possibility that they will kill and die. They must believe their deaths will not be in vain. The nation is also obligated to show its gratitude by publicly honoring the soldiers, ensuring their healing and return to civilian society, and listening to their war stories with interest, sympathy, and understanding. The sacrifice is not in vain as long as the covenant is maintained in good faith.

Many veterans have spent much of their lives since their return trying to figure out what went wrong. Unfortunately, because contemporary wars are fought far from their homelands, civilian life goes on more or less unaffected. Veterans return home unalterably changed and into a world that civilians believe is unchanged. One man told a Vets' Night forum that he felt like a piece that had been removed from a jigsaw puzzle, and when he tried to put himself back in, the puzzle had changed. In this, civilians are not so much culpable as ignorant. The delayed onset of post–traumatic stress complicates this situation, but that does not absolve society of its responsibilities to men and women whose lives have been blighted. Further, understanding soldiers' knowledge is central to society's responsibility to update its definition of war by bringing it into congruence with existential facts such as those in this volume. Finally, when soldiers kill, the events surrounding death entail profound moral consequences. It follows that men and women who have broken a commandment have a very significant message for their society when they return from the war zone.

THEORETICAL PERSPECTIVE

Since we have contracted to empower these veterans by supplying a cognitive framework for their stories, we have given very careful consideration to the theoretical perspectives from which we view these texts. They are studded, or perhaps infused, with theoretical riches. They illustrate, quite unconsciously, insights as diverse as Foucault's theory of power/knowledge relationships, Julia Kristeva's concept of abjection, and the regeneration through violence thesis of Richard Slotkin.

One of the stronger subtexts of the 1985 Asia Society conference, "The Vietnam Experience in American Literature," was the question of whether any theoretical framework can bring coherence to the experience of contemporary warfare. Few theoretical distinctions apply to this literature. William Broyles pointed out that in order to tell the whole truth of Vietnam, authors were "reinventing the form of the experience." As one consequence, autobiography sometimes becomes indistinguishable from fiction and fiction from autobiography. Only through that process can a storyteller invent "images and metaphors that will stand as an unforgettable memory of the war" (Lomperis, p. 47). We chose these veterans because they are respected by their peers, not because they proved the truth of their stories by showing us their discharge papers or because they told the most spectacular stories. One of the reasons they are respected is that they tell war stories properly. It follows that their stories conform to the conventions within a mode of discourse peculiar to the experience of contemporary warfare.

As we edited the texts, our approach became increasingly multidisciplinary. It eventually involved rhetorical and military theory, political and military history, psychology, gender and narrative theory, linguistics, and cultural and social criticism. Throughout, we were aware of the novelist John del Vecchio's range-finding metaphor for understanding Vietnam, which he believes can be understood at least more coherently if viewed from a series of perspectives (Lomperis, p. 45). The critical and theoretical perspectives that have most influenced our editorial practice are listed in the bibliography.

James William Gibson provides an insight into the exact nature of the theoretical problem. He suggests that the experience of contemporary warfare evades theoretical formulation because of the exponentially multiplied killing power of technological weapons and, therefore, the sheer scale of the killing and dying. Even with Foucault's highly sympathetic theories, he concludes, "The analytical appropriation of the warrior's knowledge has its limits. In this corpus men and women live and die; the stories of their lives and their deaths have their truths beyond incorporation in any theoretical arguments" (p. 476). Under these circumstances, we conclude that our best option is to describe the most encompassing, most significant pattern of experience in these narratives.

GOING OVER TO THE DARK SIDE

One theme can be abstracted from the texts and does provide a comprehensive framework for understanding the impact of combat on soldiers. The lifelong process whereby young men and women enter a profoundly moral rite of passage naively, encounter death, descend into the dark side, and return home provides that framework. Jim Goldstine summarized it after reading the manuscript: "We all got there by our own paths, but it appears to me the central thing we have in common was that we were brought up with a set of values and put in a situation which blew the devil out of those values. Don't teach young men it's wrong to kill and then expect them to kill in war and not be affected."

The veterans agree that this formulation explains many of the existential patterns, paradoxes, and discontinuities in their lives, then and now. As with any analytical scheme, however, this approach is reductive. It distorts the experience of contemporary warfare by making it appear more amenable to order than it actually is. On the other hand, the narrative sequence of a tour of duty closely parallels the chronology of going over to the dark side. This minimizes the problem of reductiveness, but we underline our skepticism about such schemes by choosing the epigraph to this book from Ralph Ellison's *Invisible Man*: "the mind that has conceived a plan of living must never lose sight of the chaos against which that pattern was conceived. That goes for societies as well as individuals" (p. 567).

NAIVETE

Since they were raised in the insular environment of post–World War II nuclear families and their values had not been tested by the time they were inducted, these men and women were, more than anything else, ignorant about war when they entered military service. Tim O'Brien's description of them in *Going After Cacciato* is perfectly accurate. These soldiers went to war because they did not know and because they trusted their country (p. 313). It is a melancholy experience to hear veteran after veteran add that his or her decision to join was impulsive at worst, a priori at best, and in either case hopelessly innocent. Phil Pearson was dazzled by a uniform, Don Neptune idolized his older brother, Mike Mitchell got tired of trying to avoid the draft, Dave Nelson wanted to follow in his father's footsteps, and the Soviet soldiers took for granted their country's universal service system. They had never felt it necessary to question the social definition that underlay their expectations. They expected to make sacrifices, and they expected society to support them

The Soldier's Knowledge: A Summing Up   235

in war, welcome them home as heroes, meld them back into civilian life, and learn from their experience.

If basic training did nothing else, it disabused them of the notion that military life was as they had expected. Bob Swanson got his ears boxed when he smiled, Vlad Tamarov carried balls and rolled cubes, and they were all aware that their individuality was being eliminated. Henry Talmadge, who trained Marine Drill Instructors, leaves no doubt that the basic training was deliberately designed to reduce recruits to desensitized killers. While their training had little in common with the tactics they learned to use in combat, it did teach them the skills that got them through the first weeks in-country.

Basic and advanced training were the first in a series of jarring dislocations for these men and women. The traumatic experience of going from adolescent civilian life into the military anticipates the shocks that follow, as does their instinct to draw together for self-protection. No one seems to have investigated the culture shock of going from Soviet and American homelands into the Third World cultures of Afghanistan and Vietnam. J. T. Hansen, who was a Fulbright lecturer in Iran in 1976–77, identifies two forms of culture shock in these narratives. The most immediate is the sensory overload caused by sudden exposure to the bewildering, often exotic details of a much less advanced and alien society. Combat has the effect of overriding sensory dissonance, because in order to survive, our soldiers had to learn very quickly to identify threats to their survival. The cognitive dissonance side of culture shock is much more subtle and ultimately more threatening to psychological survival. It manifests itself in the condescending, even racist attitudes of many soldiers toward Vietnamese and Afghans. They were shocked by the native populations' poverty and filth, impassiveness, the apparent cowardice of friendly forces, and the pit bull tenacity of the enemy. In the course of time, cognitive dissonance dissipated, and the soldiers came to realize that the enemy were human beings just like themselves. Many of those who came to this realization also knew that their days as effective soldiers were over.

COMBAT TRAUMA

Combat trauma results from disparities between what these soldiers expected and what they encountered, and the presence of death precipitated their descent into the dark side. They went into combat unprepared for what they were getting into, yet trusting that their government had a genuine need for their sacrifices. Their expectations were an imaginative projection, based on their nations' lingering memories of

World War II, especially those in the popular media. Vietnam veterans still feel humiliated by their naive belief in John Wayne movies. John Wayne gestures are shallow and dangerous in the heat of an ambush. As Philip Caputo says in the "prologue" to *A Rumor of War*, "We kept the packs and rifles; the convictions, we lost." (p. xiv).

Their repertoires of field-expedient techniques gradually developed into a code for surviving the exigencies of combat. They soon realized they were required to do things that they genuinely did not want to do, often because they were ordered to do things they found morally repulsive. Many of their most traumatic memories involve killing civilians, a fact of all wars which their media-based expectations had not prepared them for. No matter how hard they tried to numb their emotions, they were morally outraged by the pointlessness of the carnage. In order to survive, they mastered the rules of war, and they sometimes found they had to go over to the dark side to maintain a grip on functional sanity.

These problems were compounded by the strategic planning of the chain of command. Both American and Soviet military leaders chose strategies of attrition, in which victory and defeat are measured by the damage—casualties, materiel, communications, and so forth—inflicted upon the enemy. In a war of attrition, a soldier's sole purpose is to kill and destroy, but in the events of war in Vietnam and Afghanistan, killing and destroying proved inadequate justifications for being put in harm's way. Lacking a compelling, explicit moral purpose, the attrition strategy was impossible to distinguish from murder or genocide.

The policy of rotating men in and out of the combat zone combined with these factors to create an environment that was unpredictable, ephemeral, and claustrophobic. As James Fallows demonstrates, war is by definition unpredictable, largely because it is dominated by friction—the unexpected, accidents, mistakes, good and bad luck, and so forth. Casualties heightened the soldiers' sense of the ephemerality of events even more. Concern for their own survival developed into an instinctual obsession, an aspect of the dark side, which gave them the edge in combat. With no sense of the grand design, the experience of war became claustrophobic, and the soldiers were driven even further within themselves. The unreliability of military intelligence and exaggerated official claims of victory combined with these factors to make the experience of combat hermetic—heat-sealed, compressed, and inviolable.

The Vietnamese and Afghans deliberately developed strategies and tactics to heighten the Soviet and American soldiers' anxiety levels. The biggest problem both armies had was finding their enemies in order to engage them. Simply by declining to fight, the Vietnamese and Afghans frustrated the attrition strategy. They gained an incalculable tactical advantage by setting the time and place of engagement against the Ameri-

The Soldier's Knowledge: A Summing Up

can and Soviet forces. With less well-equipped troops, they launched surprise attacks when the odds were in their favor. Mitchell says it perfectly: "Then Charlie would hit us—always when we least expected it. Always." Hours of boredom, of "humping the boonies" or "waiting for something to happen" at a firebase, interrupted by moments of stark terror and the presence of death in brief and bloody firefights, precipitated their descent into the dark side.

THE BROTHERHOOD

In order to surmount abjection, the soldiers bonded spontaneously into Brotherhood communities. Since it was based upon their immediate needs, the survival code of the Brotherhood was purely existential. Things that promoted survival were moral, and those which threatened it were evil. As they became acclimated to combat, they came to understand the full potential of the survival code and Brotherhood. Mike Mitchell says the Blue Bandanas were like a high school social club, and Phil Pearson recalls that the Brotherhood would allow you to be everything the army would not. If an identity, feelings, trust, and filial love were not "General Issue," then the Brotherhood provided them. If the chain of command put them at risk, then the Brotherhood enabled them to reduce the risk. Customs, rituals, totems, and taboos developed as ways to affirm each person's identity, to express trust and mutuality, and to maintain their humanity in the presence of evil and death.

The profound importance of the Brotherhood is evident throughout this book, but we have not described it as a social organization. There is a tradition of such organizations in our culture. In times of need, Americans spontaneously pull together, even in the absurdist world of Joseph Heller's *Catch-22*. The Brotherhood has no formal organization or rank structure and relatively little specialization. Racism and sexism are irrelevant to the members' survival. It is a pure democracy in which competence and trustworthiness establish each person's rank within a fluid yet utterly functional pecking order.

The great strength of the Brotherhood is that it is a single-issue organization. Its only objective is the troops' survival. From that highly moral standard of judgment, all other values derive. The organization is fueled by the extreme emergency of being together in mortal danger. Others are valued to the extent that they may be trusted to carry their share of responsibility and to cover for each other in a firefight. Admission requirements are stringent. Men whose foolhardiness puts others at risk, themselves risk being ostracized.

The Brotherhood provides for psychological survival as well. Veterans from all wars have a lasting commitment to the male bonding that combat engenders. The terrifying welcome Don Neptune endured testifies to the cohesive force with which the bonding took place in Vietnam. As Stephen Crane has observed, the psychology of Brotherhood communities is difficult to retrieve because it is subject to a silence taboo. In a war zone over a period of months, the psychological dimension of war is so powerful, so complicated by the implications of manly love, and so delicately balanced, that talking about the Brotherhood destroys its most precious qualities. The resources of language are inadequate, and understatement rules. When Mitchell said he was "very close" to the men in his unit, we asked him to be more precise. He replied that he was "very, very, very close to them." The loss of close friends was so devastating for many veterans that they still cannot talk about it to others, but Pearson is surely correct about the reemergence of the Brotherhood—this time to counter psychological threats—in postwar Vet Center support groups and counselling programs.

DEATH

When Yossarian unzipped Snowden's flak jacket in *Catch-22*, he learned the fundamental truth of war—man is made of meat and bone and entrails (pp. 429–430). To the men and women who do the fighting and the mopping up, death is not a statistic to be calibrated into measures of victory or defeat. Real people die. Steve Tice had just talked to a friend who died when we took the point on Hamburger Hill. Dave Nelson, Henry Talmadge, Don Hedges, and Chuck Simms were nauseated by the "stench" of human remains. Pearson's nightmare brings death successively closer to him as the enemy is transformed through death into his own family. Contrary to the Brotherhood's cautionary "Don't take it personal," death is utterly personal—immediate, brutal, and final.

Using the word *death* is the Brotherhood's strongest taboo, a practice that enabled these men and women to numb their emotions and avoid too conscious a confrontation with the horrifying facts. Euphemisms for death show how they frame death in their own minds. To Mitchell, "He's history." To others, the dead are "wasted" or "blown away" or "taken out." Boris Volkov's "pretty bad" war story draws unusually explicit distinctions between kinds of death. In a section of his oral history that three translators agree is accurate, he says:

> We got up for breakfast one day, and we were alerted to go and rescue an outfit that was under fire. We took off in our helicopters, which carried fourteen men on board. We got there and fought with mortars, grenades,

The Soldier's Knowledge: A Summing Up 239

and our automatic weapons for over three hours. Many people were annihilated on both sides . . . including some women and children. When the action was deemed to be all over with, we flew back. Our helicopter had fourteen people on it. The other helicopter thought that four of their men, who should have been on their helicopter, were on ours.

When we found out they left those four men out there, we turned around immediately and went back. Naturally, we found that they had been annihilated. They were murdered. One of those men . . . rather than being taken prisoner . . . killed himself by falling on a hand grenade . . . there wasn't much of him left for us to pick up. We lost four men for no reason.

This is similar to Gibson's intimate knowledge of death. The first—including women and children—are recorded in the passive voice. They "were annihilated," so they just died by the cruel logic of war; yet the pauses in Volkov's narration indicate a deep emotional subtext. Although his unit immediately mounted a second rescue mission, "naturally, they were annihilated," according to the same abstract logic of war. Then he corrects himself, "They were murdered." Killing under those circumstances violates Volkov's moral code, and he assigns guilt. In the survival code of the Brotherhood, the fourth Soviet soldier did not commit suicide. He killed himself because dying was preferable to being taken prisoner. Volkov returns to the bitter language of the Brotherhood by saying, "We lost four men for no reason." They died in vain.

Madden shows that death constitutes a foundational claim to moral knowledge. In these narratives, some dead are simply KIA, some die because they followed orders, and some die heroically defending the Brotherhood. In either case there is an implicit moral judgment. Emmett Finn goes on to say, "The memory of my men is sacred to me." The power of sacralization is undoubtedly the greatest force in fusing the soldiers' knowledge of war into a hermetic value system. All things gain or lose moral stature to the extent that they measure up to the deaths of individual men performing individual heroics and dying to ensure their brothers' survival. These deaths linger in the minds of the veterans as the "something of greater value" for which they sacrificed. The dead brothers are something of undoubted meaning, sacred and inviolable, and even today a cause worthy of their commitments.

THE DARK SIDE

In a culture wherein the dark side is taboo, it is enormously difficult to define just what it is. The problem is inherent to our language, because too often we can only define the dark side negatively—as the *sub-*

conscious, *un*conscious, *ir*rational, or *pre*verbal. Perhaps the best way to discuss it is in terms of its effects. There is no more terrifying symbol of the dark side than a war for survival in tropical jungles and swamps—or in mountain valleys for Vlad Tamarov and the Soviets. In war, the dark side is the psychological dimension of what the Brotherhood signifies by the cliché, "There it is." Robert Stone and Julene Fischer write,

> "There it is," they used to say in Vietnam. It was as if an evil spirit were loose, one of the demons known to the Vietnamese as *ma,* weaving in and out of visible reality, a dancing ghost. It would appear suddenly out of [the] whirl, shimmer for an instant, and be lost. . . . Recognizing it, they would say without excitement, "There it is," with emphasis on the last word to let their friends know that they had seen it and to be sure their friends had seen it too. . . . It was at the heart of every irony, however, innocuous, however hideously cruel. It might appear as a droll incongruity along some nameless road or as guilty laughter over things that weren't funny. It was as palpable as a tumbling bullet. . . . It had no life of its own because it used human lives with a brave prodigality. . . . Nobody and nothing was innocent, free, or neutral. (pp. 8–9)

Soldiers with prolonged combat experience soon became what D. H. Lawrence identified as the essential American character: hard, isolate, stoic, and killers. They had to be in order to survive. In a world in which control means survival, events can accelerate out of control in a flash. Bone weary from humping through the jungle or impatiently following Soviet minesweepers, they could suddenly be in an ambush in which twenty people died in the first ten seconds.

By their understanding of what we intend by "the dark side," these men and women demonstrate the extent to which the psychological theories of Sigmund Freud and Carl Jung have permeated Soviet and American culture. In Jung's version of the theory, two aspects of human nature are identifiable by means of the light and dark symbolism of cultural discourse. In *Regeneration Through Violence,* a monumental study of the implications of Jung's theory in American culture, Richard Slotkin analyzes the abstract characteristics of this symbolism. Qualities associated with light include the ego, consciousness, reason, order, discipline, and moral purpose. The dark side is counter to the light and is repressed. It represents the id, the subconscious, animal instinct, chaos, passion, violence, and evil. For these soldiers, the experience of the dark side is most immanent in stories about killing other human beings. They have, Gibson reminds us, personal knowledge of killing and the terrible consequences of breaking cultural taboos and a religious commandment. A descent into the dark side is therefore an exploration of the repressed and taboo dimensions of human nature.

The Soldier's Knowledge: A Summing Up

Within its broader outlines, going over to the dark side involves passing through several identifiable phases. No matter how well they are prepared, soldiers enter the experiences of war utterly naive about the realities they will encounter. In the technologically intensified and culturally estranging environment of a Third World combat zone, they are violently disabused of their naïveté. Alone in a world gone out of control, they bond spontaneously into Brotherhood communities in order to survive and maintain some vestige of their humanity. The inexorable logic of death leads them through a series of rapid transitions to abjection and, ultimately, to the realization that the enemy they are killing are also human beings, not the demonized abstractions they were taught to hate in basic training. Unable to find a purpose for their sacrifices, soldiers spiral down into the dark, instinctual, and (by their culture's standards) depraved side of human nature. The vortex of a firefight symbolizes the entropy at the dark center of mortal combat. While they may experience the adrenaline rush and effortless competence of the "combat high," they may also find it necessary to go over to the dark side in order to survive. In either case, in the aftermath of war they must confront the experience of the dark side and find a way to cope with the implications of what they have done. They realize in retrospect that "unwinding" the conflicts between civilian, military, and Brotherhood values holds the key to healing and completing their return.

They have roughly three choices. They can try to avoid situations in which the dark side emerges, but avoidance would mean risking a court martial or, worse, dishonoring the Brotherhood. On the other hand, the dark side includes two of the most effective survival mechanisms. On rare occasions, when the action heats up, they find themselves in control, experiencing the giddy high of adrenaline and performing acts of unimaginable competence and bravery. On even rarer but ultimately even more traumatizing occasions, they can surrender to the laws of war and go over to the dark side.

Achieving the combat high and going over to the dark side have a great deal in common. Both arise from becoming habituated to the combat zone, and since they are situational, experience teaches the soldiers to anticipate them. Indiscriminate, technologically intensified warfare has a logic of its own. Soldiers learn how to respond to signs of imminent danger and to rely upon the adrenaline rush. Moral values are suspended on entering the dark side. It has only the primal logic of kill or be killed. As a consequence, experiencing the dark side engenders cynicism about lofty war aims or the inherent decency of human beings. Slotkin believes that experiencing the dark side, particularly its violence, can have a cathartic, regenerating effect. All the repressed frustrations, the desire to revenge dead friends, and just plain animal aggression can be released in the killing frenzy of a firefight. Soldiers can learn to control this response and achieve "the edge," which Nelson describes as the essence of the warrior's code.

The difference between achieving the combat high and going over to the dark side is one of control: Nelson "out there" performing superbly as a sniper or Talmadge leading his men on patrol felt in control of the situation. However, when Nelson's unit was overrun and Talmadge's men died because the new M-16s jammed, they could no longer maintain control. Neither can remember more than an occasional incident during the last weeks of his tour. Then, too, as Tamarov points out, the "percents" of light and dark varied according to the situation. Later, perhaps many years later, they suddenly realized that going entirely over to the dark side, willfully participating in evil, entails moral consequences. It is one thing to try to control the forces of evil, but it is quite another to succumb to them.

AFTERMATH AND POST–TRAUMATIC STRESS

In the aftermath of war, combat veterans exhibit a full range of reactions to their wartime experiences—from pride and fulfillment, to realizing that they have been forever changed, to struggling with the debilitating aftereffects of trauma. Many veterans were honored on their return, and many have led successful postwar lives. Even the most traumatized veterans in this volume have pleasurable and productive postwar memories to look back upon. In the final analysis, however, we agree with Michael Norman's assertion in *These Good Men:* "Nowhere was it written that perhaps the real disorder, the true sickness, might be found in the man who, after surviving a year of bloody campaigns, returns home and acts as if nothing at all has happened" (p. 113).

According to Dr. Ray Scurfield, post–traumatic stress is a response to events outside the range of normal human experience. Traumatizing events appear out of control, morally depraved, and horrifying in the finality of their destructiveness. Normal people would be traumatized by the sudden loss of close friends, participation in death and maiming, and the loss of ethical and moral values. Post–traumatic stress is therefore a normal response to abnormal events. It manifests itself as fluctuations in behavior between the poles of deliberately numbing emotions associated with the trauma, on the one hand, and experiencing intrusive images and thoughts related to the trauma, on the other. Individuals seek relief by denying or numbing emotions of rage, grief, and blame in order to maintain an effective psychological balance. Their penchant for inventing survival techniques reasserts itself, but for many postwar survival becomes an entropic combination of fact and phantasmagoria.

When their lives become dysfunctional, they have Post–Traumatic Stress Disorder. Scurfield believes that veterans with PTSD are profound experts on how to survive over long periods of time, isolated and believing they are uniquely crazy. Current Veterans' Administration diagnostic criteria for PTSD include survivor guilt, moral and ethical conflicts, self-denigration, impulse control problems, phobias related to the trauma, and excessive "type A" behaviors. Over 25 percent of the Americans who served in Vietnam currently exhibit PTSD symptoms. A total of more than 850,000 Americans have PTSD as a result of their service in that one war.

Therapists at the American Lake PTSD program have learned that revisiting the trauma with others who have been through similar traumas offers several advantages. Most of all, one learns that "I was not uniquely crazy." Others have "self-medicated" with drugs and alcohol in order to numb their feelings, or drifted from job to job, or experienced marital difficulties, or "bunkered up" when their issues threaten to get "out of control." Scurfield and his staff have been particularly adept at creating peer groups through which veterans rediscover the bonding they once experienced in the Brotherhood. They have discovered that forcibly rebonding veterans—by sending them rafting down a hazardous river or learning to communicate with the college generation they have long detested—significantly enhances their willingness to confront their issues and thereby to form trust relationships after years of isolation.

HEALING AND THE RETURN FROM THE DARK SIDE

Until recently, healing experiences have been rare for these veterans. Few have been as fortunate as Bob Swanson, whose encounters with Vietnamese since the war have provided answers to some of his questions. Steve Tice found himself in Russia, healing his psychological wounds on the twentieth anniversary of being physically disabled. Jim Goldstine heaved a sigh of relief as he recalled telling a Life Star group he felt like a murderer. The Soviets who visited the American Lake program joined American Indian veterans in a purifying sweat bath. Most of their attention, however, has been consumed by long, solitary periods of fear, rage, introspection, and recrimination. Given a secure, trustworthy environment, they can begin to heal. As these narratives have demonstrated, healing is a series of epiphanies, each of which offers insights into higher levels of understanding.

The most traumatizing and most persistent lessons of war result from conflicts between types of knowledge, value systems in particular. Healing can be seen as the resolution of conflict between values they have been taught by their culture, the military services, and their own experience. They are taught the first two value systems by social institutions and learn the third by surviving. This is a surprising conclusion, because nonveterans are not accustomed to thinking that war veterans are intellectually capable of grasping complex abstractions. As a consequence of the conspiracy of silence, the veterans have been stereotyped as sociopathically self-destructive in both the United States and the Soviet Union. These men and women are remarkably articulate, and their ability to analyze contemporary warfare as an infinitely complex, lifelong experience is prima facie evidence of intellectual sophistication. They have spent years trying to figure out what happened to them, and they have succeeded to an admirable and often inspiring degree.

By about halfway through their tours, most of them questioned the moral rightness of what they were doing. Their doubts grew when they suddenly realized that the enemy were human beings, too. From then on through the aftermath, conflicts between value systems gradually and inexorably have occupied their time. Dave Nelson goes out in the woods to be alone with his ghosts. Chuck Simms sits in a succession of mental wards smoking cigarettes, drinking coffee, and trying to "get a handle" on his past. Phil Pearson converses with his Higher Power. Nikki Nicol retreats to her home in the woods on a hill overlooking Puget Sound. At forum after forum, the veterans urge students, often tearfully, to learn about warfare, to examine their values, and to question any authority which uses value-laden language to justify itself or expects unquestioning loyalty from those subordinate to it.

Their surest hope of healing is to unwind the intractable but altogether real moral issues entailed by their descent into the vortex of the dark side. As untested young adults, they had unconsciously absorbed what they call civilian values. These are the white, Anglo-American, Protestant, middle-class values that pervade American society. These values have been inculcated in them by their parents, their schools and churches, the media, and their national leaders. For soldiers, they are extremely powerful, ironically because they are unexamined and unconsciously held. Even so, the evidence of these narratives shows that soldiers ultimately judge the morality of their actions from this moral perspective.

The primary purposes of basic and advanced training are to override the recruits' civilian values and to condition them into obeying a higher

The Soldier's Knowledge: A Summing Up

duty to the chain of command. Talmadge, an expert on basic training, says that the purpose of every training activity is to instill blind obedience into recruits. Training is designed to replace the Protestant, middle-class, civilian values with the killing code of the warrior. It is a closed value system with an answer for every military contingency. Recruits do not have the luxury of quitting—they violate "the book," the Uniform Code of Military Justice, and the Rules of Engagement at the peril of a court-martial or a dishonorable discharge.

When they enter the combat zone, they are sucked inexorably into the horror and abjection of killing and death. Most military values prove easy to discard because they either do not work or put soldiers at greater risk. The chain of command has the enforcement power to make them continue to serve in the combat zone.

As they developed into battle-hardened combat veterans, they began to understand and adapt to the survival code of the Brotherhood. Since the survival code works and is honorable, it displaced military values. Simultaneously, however, it came into direct conflict with their submerged, unexamined, but deeply held civilian values. Events inevitably forced them to make choices between civilian values and those of the Brotherhood, creating situations of excruciating moral complexity.

This is the crucial juncture, because in retrospect they made decisions, no matter how instinctual they might have seemed at the time, which resulted in the worst traumas they suffered. It was bad enough to break moral codes as a result of following direct orders from the chain of command, but too often they did something, which seemed honorable at the time, only to discover later that it was evil. While digging a grave for enemy dead is a perfunctory task in the Brotherhood, Swanson was shocked to realize he was sitting on the body as he ate. Nelson and Talmadge reacted instantaneously to threatening situations, only to realize they had killed young civilians. In retrospect, they know that killing civilians is not forgiven merely because they did not intend to kill them. Good intentions do not resolve the anguish in their nightmares.

To return from the dark side healed, even many years later, soldiers must learn to think backward, from consequence to original cause. Their traumatic encounters were often motivated by allegiance to the Brotherhood. They acted on the values of the Brotherhood, but later—sometimes many years later—they realized that they had thereby violated the civilian values they also believe in. The choice is not between values that work and those which do not. Soldiers find themselves caught between values they believe in more or less equally, but that eventually prove to be mutually exclusive. The lesson of aftermath is that it is the consequences of decisions and actions that ultimately determine the morality of fighting and surviving contemporary warfare.

Without reorientation after their tours of combat duty, they can remain mired in post-traumatic stress until events force them to confront the moral consequences of things they did. Lacking a compelling cause, such as defending their homelands, they have no social sanction for what they did. They are left to their own devices to understand what happened to them that changed them so profoundly. Society, however, can assist in the process of understanding and healing. Understanding the descent into the dark side does not mean condoning things for which soldiers feel moral culpability. Understanding does make possible forgiveness, however, and the healing lies in forgiveness.

Graduations at the American Lake program are inspiring healing ceremonies. The graduates acknowledge that although they have a long way to go, they have started the healing process. At the graduation of Group 49, Jim Fraser summed it up beautifully:

> Anything worth having is worth working for.
> And that we have done. Together, we have worked through a gauntlet of emotions. We have laughed and cried and shared with each other our most intimate feelings and secrets.
> Now we have reached a new beginning.
> That's pretty damn good for a group of guys that have gone over twenty years without showing or sharing the emotions so long hid inside each and every one of us.
> Don't think that the anger, guilt, sense of loss, and all of those emotions that consume each and every one of us aren't still there, because they are. We have just learned that these emotions can be shared—most amazingly enough, we have learned to listen, not only to ourselves but to the voices of others.
> We came here from nowhere to end up somewhere, with a feeling of being no one yet wanting to be someone—all of us with a past, but none with a future.
> All of us one way or another have carried a label—alcoholics and dopers and just plain crazy. We have shied away from our families, as well as our families from us.
> Our lives have been shattered, not shared, but we have all survived at least to this point in time. It is now time for us to go on, for this journey of newfound feeling for us has just begun.
> But because we are someone, starting from somewhere, we now know we have a future. Our feelings of hopelessness and helplessness have been replaced by a good feeling—one of hope, one of caring.
> We'll never get over this disorder called PTSD. But at least we have a start, a new beginning. What we do with it is now up to each and every one of us.

With a more complete understanding of the soldiers' experience, society can fulfill all of the provisions of its social contract with the veterans. It is through this understanding and forgiveness that society will supply the final measure of healing. In learning from their experience and fulfilling our obligations to them, we will have brought our social definition of war into congruence with the soldiers' knowledge of contemporary warfare.

OPERATIONS JUST CAUSE AND DESERT STORM

Thus far, we have spoken of all post–World War II military conflicts as contemporary warfare. There remain the issues of "Operation Just Cause" in Panama and the "Desert Shield/Storm" war in Kuwait and Iraq. Darren Gates calls them "short, sweet, bang-bang-bang" wars, which are over so fast that no one would appear likely to be as traumatized as the soldiers in Vietnam and Afghanistan. Gates was actually on the ground in Panama for fewer than twelve hours, only two of which were spent in combat. Still, he reflects, "I think—looking back on it—that if you kill somebody, take somebody's life, you kill part of your morality . . . no matter how much you try and get it back, it's gone. I'll never be the same. I don't think anybody else who's ever been through a war would ever be the same. You can't be."

Fortunately, relatively few soldiers actually engaged in combat in Kuwait and Iraq or endured rocket attacks in Saudi Arabia, but the ominous signs of post–traumatic stress have already appeared. A West Pointer who was with the armored unit that stopped the Iraqi retreat from Kuwait City is reported to have said, "They just kept coming, and we kept killing. After a few hours of that, part of your brain dies. It's very hard to do, but it's your job."

We do not take these fragments as proof of our thesis so much as signs that, although post–traumatic stress will affect fewer veterans, all of them have been affected. Veterans' centers in the Tacoma area, adjacent to Fort Lewis and McCord Air Force Base, report increasing numbers of calls from men and women just back from Operation Desert Shield/Storm, who are bothered that their sacrifices appear not to have contributed much to world peace, human rights, or stability in the Middle East. For veterans, no war is over just because cease-fire agreements are signed or they are honored with a parade when they get home. Society owes them a debt of understanding. We must provide for their healing and integrate them back into society, and the process of revising our social definition of war must include a full and generous understanding of their knowledge of contemporary warfare.

Select Bibliography

Beidler, Philip D. *American Literature and the Experience of Vietnam.* Athens, Georgia: University of Georgia Press, 1982.

Bernstein, Richard J. *Beyond Objectivism and Relativism: Science, Hermeneutics and Praxis.* Philadelphia: University of Pennsylvania Press, 1983.

Bleicher, Josef. *Contemporary Hermeneutics: Hermeneutics as Method, Philosophy and Critique.* Boston: Routledge and Kegan Paul, 1980.

Broyles, William, Jr. *Brothers in Arms: A Journey from War to Peace.* New York: Avon, 1987.

Caputo, Philip. *A Rumor of War.* New York: Ballantine, 1987.

Crane, Stephen. "The Open Boat," in *The Red Badge of Courage and Selected Stories.* New York: New American Library, Signet, 1960.

Del Vecchio, John M. *The Thirteenth Valley.* New York: Bantam, 1984.

Ellison, Ralph. *Invisible Man.* New York: Random House, Modern Library, 1963.

Fall, Bernard B. *Street Without Joy.* New York: Schocken, 1961.

Fischer, Julene, and Robert Stone. *Images of War.* Boston: Boston Publishing Company, 1986.

Fisher, Walter R. "The Narrative Paradigm: In the Beginning." *Journal of Communication* 35 (1985): 74–89.

Foucault, Michel. *Power-Knowledge: Selected Interviews and Other Writings,* ed. Colin Gordon. New York: Pantheon, 1980.

Fussell, Paul. *The Great War and Modern Memory.* New York: Oxford University Press, 1975.

———. *Wartime: Understanding and Behavior in the Second World War.* New York: Oxford University Press, 1989.

Gibson, James W. *The Perfect War: Technowar in Vietnam.* New York: Atlantic Monthly Press, 1986.

Giddens, Anthony. *Central Problems in Social Theory: Action, Structure and Contradiction in Social Analysis.* Berkeley and Los Angeles: University of California Press, 1979.

Hackworth, David H., and Julie Sherman. *About Face: The Odyssey of an American Warrior.* New York: Simon and Schuster, 1989.

Haines, Harry W. "'What Kind of War?': An Analysis of the Vietnam Veteran's Memorial." *Critical Studies in Mass Communication* 3 (1986): 1–20.

Heller, Joseph. *Catch-22.* New York: Random House, Modern Library, 1961.

Herr, Michael. *Dispatches.* New York: Avon, 1978.

Kristeva, Julia. *Powers of Horror: An Essay on Abjection,* trans. Leon S. Roudiez. New York: Columbia University Press, 1984.

Lomperis, Timothy J. *Reading the Wind: The Literature of the Vietnam War.* Durham, N.C.: Duke University Press, 1986.

Madden, Michael Patrick. "A 'Covenant with Death': The President's Epideictic Message of Legitimation and National Sacrifice." Ph.D. diss., University of Iowa, 1988.

Medhurst, Martin J., Robert L. Ivie, Philip Wander, and Robert L. Scott. *Cold War Rhetoric: Strategy, Metaphor and Ideology.* Westport, Conn.: Greenwood Press, 1990.

Norman, Michael. *These Good Men: Friendships Forged from War.* New York: Crown Publishers, 1990.

O'Brien, Tim. *Going After Cacciato.* New York: Doubleday, 1989.

———. *The Things They Carried.* Boston: Houghton Mifflin, Seymour Lawrence, 1990.

Rorty, Richard. *Philosophy and the Mirror of Nature.* Princeton: Princeton University Press, 1979.

Schrag, Calvin O. *Radical Reflection and the Origin of the Human Sciences.* West Lafayette, Ind.: Purdue University Press, 1980.

Sheehan, Neil. *A Bright Shining Lie: John Paul Vann and America in Vietnam.* New York: Random House, 1988.

Sheridan, Alan. *Michel Foucault: The Will to Truth.* London: Tavistock Publications, 1980.

Slotkin, Richard. *Regeneration Through Violence: The Mythology of the American Frontier, 1600–1860.* Middletown, Conn.: Wesleyan University Press, 1973.

Terry, Wallace. *Bloods: An Oral History of the Vietnam War by Black Veterans.* New York: Ballantine, 1985.

Van Devanter, Lynda, and Christopher Morgan. *Home Before Morning.* New York: Warner, 1984.

Walker, Keith. *A Piece of My Heart.* New York: Ballantine, 1987.

Wander, Philip. "The Rhetoric of American Foreign Policy." *Quarterly Journal of Speech* 70 (1984): 337–353.

White, Hayden. *Metahistory: The Historical Imagination in Nineteenth-Century Europe.* Baltimore: Johns Hopkins University Press, 1973.

MICHAEL PATRICK MADDEN
(1948-1989)